COINS,
CULTURE, AND HISTORY
IN THE ANCIENT WORLD

COINS,
CULTURE, AND HISTORY IN THE ANCIENT WORLD

NUMISMATIC AND OTHER STUDIES IN HONOR OF BLUMA L. TRELL

Edited by Lionel Casson, New York University
and Martin Price, British Museum

Wayne State University Press, Detroit, 1981

Coins, culture and history in the ancient world.

Includes bibliographical references and index.
1. Numismatics, Ancient—Addresses, essays, lectures.
2. Classical antiquities—Addresses, essays, lectures.
3. Trell, Bluma L., 1903-   . I. Trell, Bluma L., 1903-   . II. Casson, Lionel,
1914-   . III. Price, Martin, 1939-
CJ208.C64   930   81-10491
ISBN 0-8143-1684-0   AACR2

The publication of this volume was in good part made possible by a special grant from New York University and by contributions from Dorothy Applebaum; Blanche and Milton Brown; Julia and Lionel Casson; Elsbeth and John Dusenbery; Marie Figarsky; Isabel and Ralph Gordon; Marjorie Hyman; Annalina Levi; Joy and Philip Mayerson; Grace and Herbert Mayes; Helen and I. I. Rabi; Louis Sackin; Theresa Shirer; and Dory and Marvin Small.

CONTENTS

Contributors   9

Foreword by Blanche R. Brown   11

Abbreviations   13

NUMISMATICS

1. Styles in the Alexander Portraits on the
Coins of Lysimachus
Blanche R. Brown   17

2. A New Coin of Vima Kadphises, King of the Kushans
Joe Cribb   29

3. A Hoard Dating the Destruction of a Temple at Palmyra
Aleksandra Krzyzanowska   39

4. Une drachme d'Alexandre de Phères surfrappée en Crète
Georges Le Rider   43

5. Architectural Designs on Papal Coins
David M. Metcalf   47

6. Une monnaie de bronze frappée à Pella (Décapole)
sous Commode
Hélène Nicolet   51

7. Numismatic Evidence for the Southeast (Forum)
Facade of the Basilica Ulpia
James Packer   57

8. Paintings as a Source of Inspiration for
Ancient Die Engravers
Martin Price   69

9. A Rare Greek Imperial Coin of Gangra in Paphlagonia
Anne S. Robertson   77

10. The Basis from Puteoli: Cities of Asia Minor in
Julio-Claudian Italy
Cornelius Vermeule   85

ARCHAEOLOGY, GEOGRAPHY, LANGUAGE, AND
LITERATURE

11. The Corsini Throne and the Man in the Pot
Larissa Bonfante   105

12. The Location of Adulis (*Periplus Maris Erythraei* 4)
Lionel Casson   113

13. A Footnote on Heroic Representations: Helen's Web
Elsbeth B. Dusenbery   123

14. Thoughts on the Significance of the Latin
Component in the Welsh Language
Robert A. Fowkes   127

15. Map Projection and the Peutinger Table
Annalina and Mario Levi   139

16. Literati in the Service of Roman Emperors:
Politics before Culture
Naphtali Lewis   149

17. The Clysma-Phara-Haila Road on the Peutinger Table
Philip Mayerson   167

18. The Temple of Messa on Lesbos
Hugh Plommer   177

19. Old Testament Motifs in the Iconography of the
British Museum's Magical Gems
Morton Smith   187

20. Labyrinth: Anatolian Axe or Egyptian Edifice?
Robert R. Stieglitz   195

Index   199

CONTRIBUTORS

Larissa Bonfante, professor of classics, New York University

Blanche R. Brown, professor of fine arts, New York University

Lionel Casson, professor of classics, New York University

Joe Cribb, Department of Coins and Medals, British Museum

Elsbeth B. Dusenbery, research associate, Institute of Fine Arts, New York University

Robert A. Fowkes, professor of German, New York University

Aleksandra Krzyzanowska, Department of Numismatics, National Museum of Warsaw

Georges Le Rider, formerly administrateur général, Bibliothèque Nationale

Annalina and Mario Levi, New York City

Naphtali Lewis, professor of classics, School of Graduate Studies, City University of New York

Philip Mayerson, professor of classics, New York University

David M. Metcalf, Heberden Coin Room, Ashmolean Museum, Oxford

Hélène Nicolet, conservateur en chef du Département des Médailles et Antiques, Bibliothèque Nationale

James Packer, associate professor of classics, Northwestern University

Hugh Plommer, professor of art and archaeology, Cambridge University

Martin Price, deputy keeper, British Museum

Anne S. Robertson, keeper of the Hunter Coin Cabinet, Hunterian Museum, University of Glasgow

Morton Smith, professor of history, Columbia University

Robert R. Stieglitz, assistant professor of Hebraic studies, Rutgers University

Cornelius Vermeule, curator, Department of Classical Archaeology, Boston Museum of Fine Arts

FOREWORD

This volume of essays is offered to Bluma Trell by her colleagues, to honor her for the important contributions she has made to classical studies and for the generous, contagious enthusiasm with which she has made them.

Bluma Trell is an inspiring, devoted teacher.

In her classroom Greek grammar is thrilling and Greek literature is alive. But the classroom does not contain her as teacher. Students sign up for four hours a week, only to find themselves thrust into a new full-time way of life, one which is compelling, consuming, bluming, and trelling. First the students in each class are divided into the more and less able, then the more able are pressed into tutoring the less, and from then on her office is filled with grouplets of student-tutors helping their friends or reading with their peers beyond what the rest of the.class can do. When the students are hardly beyond lisping through conjugations, they are coaxed into appearing in full-length productions of ancient tragedies in the original Greek. All are pressed into a stream of activities that include lectures, poetry readings, visits to museums in the city, and bus trips to farther places, as well as coffee hours and departmental parties.

Not only before but also after graduation, each student is praised and pressured, encouraged and bullied, educated and induced into the cultural life. The Trell "agency," operating through files carried in the Trell head, brings individuals together with the scholarships, assistantships, graduate schools, and jobs that they need.

All of the foregoing virtues were acknowledged officially in 1974, when she was honored as one of New York University's Great Teachers.

Bluma Trell is an innovative, productive scholar.

She found her path in scholarship as a graduate student, when she joined the group devoted to Architectura Numismatica which was organized by Karl Lehmann at the Institute of Fine Arts, New York University. She wrote her dissertation on "Architectura Numismatica: The Temples in Asia Minor" (New York University, 1942), of which a portion was published by the American Numismatic Society as *The Temple of Artemis at Ephesos,* Notes and Monographs 107 (1945). She alone of the original group organized by Lehmann has pursued the same path ever since, and she has broadened it to a 11 highway, detailing its methods, widening the possibilities of problems undertaken and solutions achieved, and bravely extending it into new areas, so that her name is now evoked inevitably in association with the discipline of *architectura numismatica.*

She has produced a continuous series of lectures and articles, always illuminating and often provocative. She capped her endeavors with a key book, *Coins and Their Cities: Architecture on the Ancient Coins of Greece, Rome, and Palestine* (London and Detroit, 1977), written in collaboration with Martin Price, Keeper of the British Museum, Department of Coins and Medals. She is now off again, once more breaking roads through new territory, studying Phoenician customs and religion in preparation for a book on Punic coinage.

Bluma Trell is a fervent champion of Classical studies.

She was a lawyer before she became a classicist, and she unstintingly uses her legal talents, techniques, and information for the promotion of Classical studies in particular and the humanities in general. To this end she has plunged into faculty governance with passion and success. No caucus is too raucous, no ploy unemployed. In addition, every worthy cause, whether for individuals or for principles, becomes her cause. This too was given official acknowledgment when the administration of New York University asked her to serve for several years as ombudsman.

Colleagues regularly receive in the mail envelopes containing helpful bibliographic items or references, as well as book reviews and footnotes concerning their own works which they may have overlooked. The script is hurried, but the encouragement is unfailing. Three hundred personal friends and students on an organized mailing list are pressed into participating in all ongoing activities. A group of colleagues and former students that she organized in 1945 has persisted until today, meeting with her once a week to sight-read the ancient Greek classics.

She is enthusiastic about the merits of an interdisciplinary discussion group devoted to the ancient world, which was organized over half a century ago by William L. Westermann of Columbia University and others, and its successful continuation in recent years owes much to her efforts. She has served as its secretary, still serves as its chairman, and for several years even personally prepared buffets of Danish open sandwiches for the refreshment of its participants.

For Bluma Trell no effort is too little or too much if it will help to keep the classics alive. No coin collection is too distant to reach and no coin too battered to scrutinize if it will yield evidence in pursuit of answers that serve to illuminate the ancient world.

Blanche R. Brown

ABBREVIATIONS

For abbreviations other than those given below, see the list in *American Journal of Archaeology* 82 (1978) 5-10 (periodicals and series) and in Liddell-Scott-Jones, *Greek-English Lexicon* xxxviii-xlii (inscriptions and papyri).

AMGUS	*Antike Münzen und geschnittene Steine*
ANRW	*Aufstieg und Niedergang der römischen Welt*
AttiMGrecia	*Atti e Memorie della Società Magna Grecia*
BASP	*Bulletin of the American Society of Papyrologists*
BEFAR	*Bibliothèque des écoles françaises d'Athènes et de Rome*
BMC	*British Museum Catalogue*
BMCRE	H. Mattingly et al., *Coins of the Roman Empire in the British Museum* (London 1923–)
BMCRR	H. Grueber, *Coins of the Roman Republic in the British Museum* (London 1970²)
CPJ	V. Tcherikover et al., *Corpus Papyrorum Judaicarum* (Cambridge, Mass. 1957–1964)
IGLMemnon	A. and E. Bernand, *Les inscriptions grecques et latines du Colosse de Memnon* (Cairo 1960)
IGURomae	L. Moretti, *Inscriptiones graecae urbis Romae* (Rome 1968–1973)
IMagn	O. Kern, *Die Inschriften von Magnesia am Maeander* (Berlin 1900)
JNG	*Jahrbuch für Numismatik und Geldgeschichte*
JNSI	*Journal of the Numismatic Society of India*
MEFR	*Mélanges de l'école française de Rome*
NNM	*Numismatic Notes and Monographs*
LRBC	R. Carson and J. Kent, *Late Roman Bronze Coinage* (London 1960)
RIC	H. Mattingly et al., *Roman Imperial Coinage* (London 1923–)
RM	*Rheinisches Museum*
Rph	*Revue de philologie*
SHA	*Scriptores Historiae Augustae*
SNG	*Sylloge Nummorum Graecorum*

NUMISMATICS

1
STYLES IN THE ALEXANDER PORTRAITS ON THE COINS OF LYSIMACHUS

BLANCHE R. BROWN

On entering the realm of numismatics recently as a neophyte, I was fortunate to receive inspiration and guidance from Bluma Trell. That is only one of many long reasons, both professional and personal, for dedicating this article to her with love, admiration, and gratitude.

As an art historian, interested in the history of Early Hellenistic art,[1] I treasure the coins of this period as original works of art in small format, often of high quality. I also treasure the numismatists who have developed techniques for dating coins more closely than is possible with larger works. I restrict myself to royal portrait heads on coins because that is a central, characteristic subject of the period, and because limiting subject matter so closely makes stylistic characteristics emerge more clearly.

In another article I deal with the portrait coins of Ptolemy I, which were the first to be issued by any of the successors of Alexander the Great.[2] From ca. 320/19 to ca. 301 B.C., Ptolemy's coins carried a portrait of Alexander on the obverse (figs. 1, 2), first with Alexander's own type of seated Zeus on the reverse, and then with an archaistic Athena.[3] From ca. 305, a portrait of Ptolemy himself was introduced on the gold coins, with an elephant-drawn chariot on the reverse. From ca. 301, the portrait of Ptolemy was placed on both gold and silver (fig. 3), with an eagle on the reverse.[4] Somewhat later than the introduction of each coin with Ptolemy's portrait came two small issues by Seleucus I, both produced in the East. One, of ca. 303 to ca. 293 B.C. in Ecbatana and one or two other cities, had a portrait of Alexander on the obverse (fig. 4) and Alexander's own type of Nike on the reverse. The other, of ca. 300 B.C. in Persepolis and Susa, had a portrait on the obverse of a man in a panther-skin helmet who is taken to be either Alexander or Seleucus himself (fig. 13), and a Nike erecting a trophy on the reverse (fig. 14).[5] In the present article I deal with the portrait issues that were minted by Lysimachus from ca. 297 B.C.

Fig. 1. Tetradrachm of Ptolemy I, obverse, Alexandria. *Courtesy American Numismatic Society*

Fig. 2. Tetradrachm of Ptolemy I, obverse, Alexandria. *Courtesy American Numismatic Society*

Fig. 3. Tetradrachm of Ptolemy I, obverse, Alexandria. *Courtesy American Numismatic Society*

Fig. 4. Double daric of Seleucus I, obverse, Ecbatana. *Courtesy Dept. of Coins and Medals, British Museum*

Fig. 5. Drachm of Lysimachus, obverse, Lampsacus. *Courtesy American Numismatic Society*

Fig. 6. Tetradrachm of Lysimachus, obverse, Lampsacus. *Courtesy American Numismatic Society*

Fig. 7. Drachm of Lysimachus, obverse, Ephesus. *Courtesy American Numismatic Society*

Fig. 8. Stater of Lysimachus, obverse, Pella. *Courtesy American Numismatic Society*

Fig. 9. Tetradrachm of Lysimachus, obverse, Pergamum. *Courtesy American Numismatic Society*

Fig. 10. Portrait of Alexander the Great, the "Azara Herm." *Courtesy Musée du Louvre*

Fig. 11. Tetradrachm of Lysimachus, obverse, Magnesia. *Courtesy American Numismatic Society*

Fig. 12. Portrait of Demosthenes. *Courtesy Vatican Museum*

Fig. 13. Tetradrachm of Seleucus I, obverse, Persepolis. *Courtesy American Numismatic Society*

Fig. 14. Tetradrachm of Seleucus I, reverse, Persepolis. *Courtesy American Numismatic Society*

Lysimachus did not identify himself on coins at all until he took the title of king in 306/5 B.C.[6] After Alexander died, Lysimachus had received as his domain Thrace and the neighboring territory on the Euxine, where no royal mint had existed before. At first, apparently, the mints that had been used by Alexander continued to supply all the satrapies of his successors. After 317, when the assassination of Philip III and the imprisonment of young Alexander made it clear that the empire was divided, Lysimachus probably took most of his coinage from the mints of Cassander, his friend and ally. Even after 306/5, Lysimachus proceeded cautiously. At first he produced only small silver and bronze coins with the types of Philip II, but imprinted with his own initials and his badge, a lion protome. These he minted at the city of Lysimachia, which he had founded in 309 B.C. After the defeat of Antigonus and Demetrius at Ipsus in 301 B.C., when Antigonus's realm was divided, Lysimachus's share was western Asia Minor, where a number of mints already existed. Then he began producing gold and large silver coins. At first he continued to be cautious, changing only from the types of Philip II to those of Alexander, and still adding his own inscriptions. It was only after his friend Cassander died, in 297 B.C., that he finally introduced types of his own. On the obverse he placed a head of Alexander the Great (figs. 6–9, 11), as Ptolemy and Seleucus had done before him, and on the reverse a seated Athena.

Once under way, Lysimachus produced voluminously, rivaling Ptolemy in the amount of his output. After 301, he used the mints at Lampsacus, Sestus, Abydus, Sardes, Colophon, and Magnesia in Asia Minor, as well as Lysimachia in Thrace. About 297, Colophon was closed after a single issue of the Alexander heads, Mytilene and Teos were added briefly, and a new mint was established at Alexandria Troas (formerly Antigonia). In 293 he added Ephesus, which he renamed Arsinoe after his wife. In 289, when he took Bithynia, he added Cius and Heraclea. His largest production in Asia Minor was in Lampsacus, climaxing during the years 293 to 287.

In 288 Lysimachus invaded Macedonia, and then Amphipolis became his principal mint. After 287, when Demetrius Poliorcetes invaded Ionia and brought considerable unrest to the more southerly regions of Asia Minor, Lysimachus concentrated his coin production in northern Asia Minor, Thrace, and Macedonia, and established new mints in Pergamum and Parium. In Macedonia he added Pella after he took that city from Pyrrhus in 286. About 283/2, single issues were struck somewhere in Thrace, perhaps in Perinthus and Aenus. In 282/1 B.C., Lysimachus died at Corupedium, fighting against Seleucus.

Like the Alexanders on the coins of Ptolemy and Seleucus, Lysimachus's Alexander wears the ram horn of Zeus-Ammon, who was called Alexander's father even during his lifetime. Unlike the

Alexanders of Ptolemy and Seleucus, this one does not wear the elephant scalp or the aegis, and his royal diadem is fully visible, binding his hair, from the earliest issues on.

On most of Lysimachus's coins, Alexander's eye is distended to an exaggerated degree, as though to suggest a more than human illumination. Concerning such distended eyes Kyrieleis has said (in discussing Ptolemaic coins of the next generation) that they express an understanding, recognizable among the Greeks from Homer on, that "im grossen, strahlenden Augen göttliches Wesen kundtut,"[7] and he points out that on Late Classical coins Zeus, Hera, and Helios are shown with large eyes and intense looks. In fact, such a conception is a rather obvious one, which exists among other peoples as well. It is well known that the large, compelling eye was an essential part of Alexander's iconography. It occurs, for example, in the earlier coin portraits, and it seems to have been inherited by Ptolemy for his own portrait as well. But such an exaggeratedly dilated eye as this one appears in coins earlier than Lysimachus's only in two dies of one issue of the early Alexanders of Ptolemy (fig. 2), those of issue 14, which dates ca. 318/17 B.C.[8] In monumental art, the earliest surviving evidence of such an eye appears in the Alexander mosaic, from the House of the Faun in Pompeii, which is taken to be a copy of a painting. The original painting has long been dated ca. 300 B.C., close to the date of the Lysimachus coin. But it has also been put earlier on stylistic grounds, most recently ca. 320 B.C., in which case it would be close to the date of Ptolemy's issue.[9]

The productions of Lysimachus's many far-flung mints have a surprising degree of uniformity. Margaret Thompson has pointed this out, saying, "Throughout the coinage there is a puzzling similarity, almost identity, of style."[10] She notes that the same monogram recurs at different mints, which may be taken to record the actual transfer of personnel, and also that one die was shared by Lysimachia and Lampsacus and another by Mitylene and Lampsacus. She continues,

> There is a marked homogeneity of style in the early period involving the issues of Lysimachia, Lampsacus, Abydus, Magnesia, and Alexandria, and in the late period involving those of Amphipolis and Pella and those of Lampsacus, Magnesia, Alexandria, Pergamum, and Smyrna. Many of these dies must be the work of the same man. It is not impossible that an individual die-cutter travelled from place to place, but on the whole it seems more likely that there were central workshops for the production of dies and that these dies were then distributed to meet the needs of the various mints.[11]

The artistic style that predominates in the Alexander head throughout this wide area, from Asia Minor through Thrace to Macedonia, is not only consistent but also distinctive. It is illustrated here by a

21

splendid example of the first issue of ca. 297/6, from the mint at Lampsacus on the south shore of the Hellespont (fig. 6). This Alexander head comes directly out of the local version of the Heracles head—Alexander's own type—which had immediately preceded it (fig. 5), as is also the case with the Ptolemaic and Seleucid examples, I believe. The comparison illustrated here shows that the physiognomy is followed feature by feature. This, parenthetically, can be taken to prove either that the Heracles head was already a portrait of Alexander, as is often stated, or that the Alexander head is an ideal, heroic conception, as the Heracles head had been before it. In style the Heracles head had been conceived within the orbit of the sculptor Scopas, since its beginnings with Alexander. In Alexander's earliest issues, it was contained and moderate in form, indeed quite backward-looking. But soon afterward, during Alexander's li'etime, it became increasingly high in relief and rich in modeling. On the coins of Lysimachus, the Heracles head (fig. 5) continued to develop along the same lines. Other fourth-century influences seem to have been added to that of Scopas, in both physiognomy and style, and the contrasts of light and dark are quite dramatic. Lysimachus's Alexander head, then, follows the Heracles head not only in physiognomy but also in style, and it carries the dramatic effect still further, to a degree of extravagance which matches the emotional intensity implied by the distended, inspired eye.

Lysimachus's Alexander goes further in this way than the Alexander heads of Ptolemy and Seleucus, except for Ptolemy's maverick Alexanders of 318/7 B.C. (fig. 2), which approach it. In extravagance of form, Lysimachus's Alexander matches, it seems to me, the portrait of Ptolemy himself, the later one with eagle reverse (fig. 3), which had begun only a few years before (ca. 301 B.C.) and was continuing in the same vein contemporary with the Lysimachan coin. In both of them the parts of the head and hair tend to be separated from one another, making a cluster of hyperactive subforms. But while the Ptolemy head is built in terms of plastic structure, the Lysimachan head spreads out more loosely and "pictorially," with an overall alternation of light and shadow. In the Ptolemy head the subforms rise brusquely in distinct knobs, which are all but outlined by dark shadows. The plane of the cheek is quite flat. It meets the planes from nose and eyes at a near angle and turns abruptly at the jaw. In the Lysimachan head everything is curved and everything is in motion. All forms are more rounded, including cheek and chin, and all transitions are rounded as well, often forming concaves which alternate with the convexes, so that forms flow in and out of each other, up and down the small hills and valleys, varying the surface gradually and catching light and shadow in a more evenly distributed, richly contrasting chiaroscuro. In addition, the surface is nuanced minutely throughout, so that it keeps catching the light in a small overall flicker, which unfortunately is not visible in the photograph. The chiaroscuro

22

continues with equal force in the hair, which, unlike the more plastic and linear hair of Ptolemy, is made up of thick tufts, exuberantly rounded also, bouncing vigorously in many directions and splintering the light into strands. The hair maintains its own lively rhythms in counterpoise to the heavier forms of the face, but finds an echo in the rounded outline of the profile, and an accent in the decisive curve of the ram's horn curling concentrically around the ear. Because the surface is modeled so richly, the effect tends to be volatile, changing readily with the changing light that falls on the coin.

This rich, volatile style was produced in Lampsacus without interruption from ca. 297/6 to 282/1 B.C., holding throughout those fifteen years, although the heads became somewhat looser and less dynamic during the later years. The same style prevailed also in practically all of Lysimachus's other mints, from Asia Minor to Macedonia, although often it was not executed as brilliantly as in the example given. The average is more summary and flaccid.

Variations in style do, however, occur. The mint of Pergamum has a distinctive manner, but most often the variations occur within the same mints that produced the style that is described above. The layered relief and rich surface are almost always maintained, and the differences lie in varying degrees of shift from the pictorial mode to a more plastic one. For example, in Ephesus (fig. 7), in many dies the planes are rather broader, the forms of the head more unified. The coins of Pella run a gamut of variants, reaching as far as the strongly plastic head on a gold stater which is illustrated in fig. 8. In that one the forms are leaner and more compact, still very rich, but firm. The surface is still enlivened with modeled nuances that catch light, but the planes are clearly drawn over a strong basic skeleton structure. The eye is more normal in size. The facial type suggests the Alexander of the Azara herm (fig. 10), which is generally thought to be a summary, weathered Roman copy of the head of a statue by Lysippus, and the style also can be considered Lysippic. Apparently in such cases the die cutter turned away from the Scopaic model that had come out of coin tradition and followed a monumental model instead.

Probably the most beautiful variant (fig. 9), as well as the most consistent, was issued by Philetaerus at Pergamum, during the short five years that it was a mint of Lysimachus, from ca. 287 to ca. 282 B.C. Here also the surface richness of the volatile style remains, but it takes the form of a very sensitive and subtly nuanced modeling. The basic form is more plastic and unified, with fewer concave transitions. The convex forms are more clearly delimited and structured. The drawing itself is not exuberant, as it is in fig. 6, but suave and refined. It does not have the effusive liveliness of the Lampsacan coin, but it does have a pervading sense of movement and life which is related to it.

However, there is one variant that takes a new and different tack entirely (fig. 11). It occurs in the city of Magnesia, which produced   23

Alexander heads from 297/6 to 282/1 B.C., practically all of them in the prevailing rich, pictorial style. In the series of Magnesian issues that are numbered 101 to 116 by Margaret Thompson, the exceptional one is no. 105, so that its date would fall in the neighborhood of 293/2 B.C.[12] The facial type is different on the head of this coin. It has a small triangular eye, a sharply angled brow made up of two straight lines, a straight nose, and a tight, horizontal mouth. Also the style is different. The head is relatively hard and severe. The surface is not volatile, as it is in the others, but plastic and tangible, made up of broad simplified areas of cheek which continue to the chin, brow, nose, and neck, each plane rigorously contained. The outlines are neither buoyantly nor subtly curved, but tend to the rectilinear. The small eye is set in a geometric area of shadow. The hair does recall the curvilinear formula of the others, but it is tamer. In general, this head has a spare, sober, contained look. It represents, it seems to me, a clear example of what Gerhard Krahmer called the "schlichte Stil"[13]—translatable as the "plain style"—making a rare appearance among royal portraits on coins of this generation. Krahmer used as a paradigm of his plain style the portrait of Demosthenes, known in Roman copies (fig. 12), which originally was made by Polyeuktos and dedicated in Athens in 280/79 B.C. Others since Krahmer have identified the same style in statues that are datable both earlier and later than the Demosthenes, but always less precisely.[14] Here is a good, though small, original example of the style which can be dated quite closely, at ca. 293/2 B.C.

Herbert Cahn, in his important article "Frühhellenistische Münzkunst," does not deal with the coinage of Lysimachus in general, but only with the Pergamene issue. He cites it as the first in a sequence of coins minted by Philetaerus at Pergamum, where, he says, "die pathetische Richtung der frühhellenistischen Münzkunst ihre vollendesten Werke hervorbracht."[15] Furthermore, he saw this "pathetische Richtung" as being basically characteristic of the new kingdoms of the eastern part of the Hellenistic world and basically inimical to the West.[16] However, if one looks at all the mints of Lysimachus for evidence, one finds rather a consistency than a diversity of style from East to West, from Asia Minor through Thrace to Macedonia, which apparently was abetted by the bureaucratic organization within Lysimachus's domain. Margaret Thompson has demonstrated this numismatically, and the style seen in the Alexander head confirms it artistically. Cahn stresses the primacy of Pergamum, but others may find the coins of Lampsacus, Lysimachia, and related places as consummate an expression of the style, in their way, as the Pergamene is in its way.

Cahn says that the "pathetische Richtung" came out of Scopas, took a distinct step beyond its source, and pointed to the developed style of the Middle Hellenistic period. The time when the "step beyond" was taken Cahn places ca. 325 B.C., early, still within the lifetime of Alexander, as illustrated in coins issued in the city of

Alexandria. He proves his point by comparing the head of Heracles on the Alexandrian coins with one of Alexander's earliest issues.[17] The fallacy there, I believe, is that Alexander's earliest Heracles heads are retardataire, and probably deliberately so, since they seem to quote the precise configuration of the Heracles head on the coins of Perdiccas III (365–359 B.C.)—an argument which I offer more fully, and illustrate, elsewhere.[18] I would say, rather, that Alexander's later coins simply bring the Scopaic style up to date. Increased richness of modeling and emotion appears in the Alexander heads on Ptolemy's coins of issue 14 (fig. 2), only to disappear again quickly. A decisive new step was taken with Ptolemy's own coin portrait (fig. 3) from 301 B.C. and with Lysimachus's Alexander (figs. 6, 9) from 297/6 B.C. In that new step, the heads are treated in an exaggerated, overwrought way which gives the effect of a rather mannered extension of the fourth-century style. It does not seem to point to the pathetic or baroque style of the Middle Hellenistic period, which is characterized by bold, unified forms, because the forms of these coin heads are scattered rather than integrated.

Ernst Pfuhl sought the plain style in Early Hellenistic portraiture as early as 1930, not long after Krahmer's article on the subject, but he dealt with coin portraits only very generally and loosely, making a single summary statement about the whole post-Alexander generation.[19] Cahn, later, saw the plain style as an alternative in coins to what he called the Early Hellenistic pathetic style. He does not cite the exceptional coin of Lysimachus from Magnesia (fig. 11). He illustrates his point with the coin which was issued by Seleucus from Persepolis and Susa ca. 300 B.C.[20] In that head, however, it seems to me, there is too much richness of modeling for such a designation; the eye is too heavily shadowed, the lips and chin too fully curved. In fact it compares strikingly with the Lysimachan Alexander head from Pella (fig. 8), and its leaner face and firmer modeling also can be explained better as being Lysippic in derivation—which, parenthetically, may help to tip the scale in identifying the subject as Alexander rather than Seleucus.[21] On the other hand, I agree with Cahn that the plain style appears on the reverse of the same coin, in the composition of Nike erecting a trophy (fig. 14), of which he says, "Hier ist der 'schlichte' Stil schon ganz zum Durchbruch gelangt. Die Figur wendet sich vom Raum ab, die Bewegung ist eckig, fast abrupt, der Körper kräftig, beinahe hart unterteilt."[22] Furthermore, I believe that the plain style appears again during this generation, and more extensively, among the coin portraits of Demetrius Poliorcetes, an observation which I hope to demonstrate soon in another article.

Cahn localizes the plain style in the West, as he had localized the pathetic style in the East, while allowing for overlap in both directions due to the mobility of artists. He makes an ingenious argument for its inception in Athens, where, he says, it expressed, "als Reaction des Mutterlandes, besonders Athens, auf die plötzliche Ausweitung der

Welt, eine freiwillige Einkapsuling, ein bürgerliches Selbstbescheiden.''[23] However, the numismatic evidence, broadly surveyed, indicates that the plain style was current outside Athens, and in the East as well as the West. The places where the style has been (or will be) identified on coins, so far, are Persepolis, Susa, and Magnesia, as well as Pella, Thebes, and Demetrias, within the mints of Kings Seleucus, Lysimachus, and Demetrius Poliorcetes.

Thus, the Alexander portraits on the coins of Lysimachus provide examples, predominantly, of a richly modeled, dramatic style, which follows the earlier Scopaic line but which takes a recognizable step beyond it in the depth of its relief, the multiplicity of its planes, the complexity of its chiaroscuro, and the intensity of its drama, and also in its rather mannered exaggeration. That step beyond is prefigured in a single issue of Ptolemaic coin portraits of Alexander (fig. 2) of ca. 318/7 B.C. and is paralleled in portraits of Ptolemy himself (fig. 3) from ca. 301 B.C. on. The Lysimachan style tends to a more pictorial mode, however, while the Ptolemaic style retains a more plastic basic structure. In the Lysimachan coins, when a variation occurs within a mint, or is particular to a mint, it tends to modify the pictorial treatment in the direction of greater plasticity, sometimes with specific reminiscences of Lysippus in facial type and style. There is one issue of one mint, ca. 293/2 B.C. in Magnesia, where the plain style appears. Then it is quickly withdrawn, just as happened with the dramatic style ca. 318/7 B.C. in Alexandria. The plain style also occurs on other coins of the early third century, on the reverse of a coin of Seleucus issued ca 300 B.C. in Persepolis and Susa, and on the coins of Demetrius Poliorcetes, particularly those issued in Pella, Thebes, and Demetrias.

NOTES

1. The end in view is a history of Early Hellenistic art. Toward that purpose I worked from 1977 to 1978 under a fellowship from the National Endowment for the Humanities, and from 1978 to 1979 under a fellowship from the John Simon Guggenheim Memorial Foundation. This article is part of a larger study of Early Hellenistic coin portraits undertaken within that period. For access to coin collections I thank the staffs of the Department of Coins and Medals of the British Museum, the Cabinet des Médailles of the Bibliothèque Nationale, the Seattle Art Museum, and above all the American Numismatic Society in New York. For essential guidance and bibliographic help I thank, in addition to Bluma Trell, Margaret Thompson, Nancy M. Waggoner, Orestes H. Zervos, and Martin J. Price.

2. The conclusions about the coins of Ptolemy I that are summarized here are explained more fully in ''Art History in Coin Portraits: Issues of Ptolemy I,'' which will appear in a volume in honor of Achille Adriani.

3. Head of Alexander/seated Zeus: Ioannos N. Svoronos, *Ta Nomismata tou Kratous ton Ptolemaion* (Athens 1904) pl. 2, nos. 5-6, 12-18; vol. i, pt. 2, 5-7;

Orestes H. Zervos, *The Alexander Mint of Egypt*, New York University Diss. (New York 1974), type II, 69-80, 292-313; pl. 1, nos. 8-11; pl. 2, nos. 1-4. Heads of Alexander/Athena: Svoronos, pl. A, nos. 18-21; pl. 2, nos. 7, 10-15, 17-24, 26-28; pl. 4, nos. 8-12, 23-31; pl. 5, nos. 5-24; pl. 6, nos. 1-15, 19-20; vol. i, pt. 2, 7-10, 16, 19-31; vol. ii, 403; Zervos, type III, nos. 81-209, 314-50; pl. 2, nos. 5-10; pl. 3, nos. 1-11; pl. 4, nos. 1-11; pl. 5, nos. 1-10; pl. 6, nos. 1-12.

4. Head of Ptolemy/elephant chariot: Svoronos (n. 3 above) pl. 4, nos. 1-7, 18-22; pl. 5, nos. 1-4, pp. 19-22, 24. Head of Ptolemy/eagle: Svoronos, pl. A, nos. 27-29, 31, 38, 43; pl. 7, nos. 1-27; pl. 8, nos. 1, 6-13, 19-28; pl. 9, nos. 1-24; pl. 10, nos. 1-10, 24, pp. 33, 35-47, 404-5, 407-8.

5. Head of Alexander/Nike: Edward T. Newell, *Coinage of the Eastern Seleucid Mints: Seleucus I-Antiochus III*, with summary of recent scholarship by Otto Mørkholm, Numismatic Studies[1] (New York 1978) pl. 35, nos. 4-7, pp. 162, 170, 174-75; pl. 22, nos. 10-11, 14-19, pp. 109-10, 112. Head in panther-skin helmet/Nike erecting trophy: Newell, pl. 32, nos. 1-17, pp. 154-60; pl. 23, nos. 6-9, pp. 107-8, 113-15.

6. Data given in this paragraph and the next are derived from Margaret Thompson, "The Mints of Lysimachos," *Essays in Greek Coinage Presented to Stanley Robinson*, ed. C. M. Kraay and G. K. Jenkins (Oxford 1968) 163-82, pls. 16-22.

7. Helmut Kyrieleis, *Bildnisse der Ptolemäer*, Archäologische Forschungen 2 (Berlin 1975) 163.

8. Zervos (n. 3 above) 70, 78-79, pl. 2, no. 3.

9. B. Andreae, *Das Alexandermosiak aus Pompeii* (Bongers 1977) 24-28.

10. Thompson (n. 6 above) 166-67.

11. Ibid. 167. Also on die-sharing: Niklaus Dürr, "Bemerkungen zur hellenistischen Münzprägung: II. Lysimachos," *Schweitzer Münzblätter* 23 (1973) 93-94.

12. Thompson (n. 6 above) 174.

13. Gerhard Krahmer, "Stilphäsen der hellenistischen Plastik," *Röm. Mitt.* 38-39 (1923-24) 138-89.

14. For discussion with bibliographic footnotes, see B. R. Brown, *Anticlassicism in Greek Sculpture of the Fourth Century B.C.* (*AIA and CAA Monographs* 26 New York 1973) 64-67.

15. Herbert A. Cahn, *Frühhellenistische Münzkunst* (Basel 1948); also in *Kleine Schriften* (Basel 1975) 121. References below are to the latter. I will be citing Cahn repeatedly because I find his art historical observations in relation to the coins especially interesting, worth quoting, and worth disputing.

16. Ibid.

17. Ibid. 118-21, 126, 128.

18. This point is discussed more fully, and illustrated, in "Art History in Coins": see n. 2 above.

19. Ernst Pfuhl, "Ikonographische Beiträge zur Stilgeschichte der hellenistischen Kunst," *JDAI* 45 (1930) 52: "Ungeachtet aller Unterschiede der stilistischen Richtungen ist es klar, dass das für die Tektonik grundlegende Verhältnis von Haupt und Nebenformen des Köpfes den Demosthenes mit den annähernd gleichzeitigen Münzen und Köpfen der ersten Diadochen verbindet."

20. Cahn (n. 15 above) 117-18.

21. The interpretation of the head as Alexander rather than Seleucus has been made on other grounds by F. Taeger, *Charisma, Studien zur Geschichte des antiken Herrscherkultes* (Stuttgart 1957) 282-83, and recently by R. A. Hadley, "Seleucus, Dionysus, or Alexander?" *NC* 7, 14 (1974) 9-13.

22. Cahn (n. 15 above) 117.

23. Ibid. 128.

2
A NEW COIN OF VIMA KADPHISES, KING OF THE KUSHANS

JOE CRIBB

It is now generally agreed that the coinage of the Kushan kingdom was standardized and reformed by the ruler known on his coins as *Sōtēr Megas* ("the Great Savior").[1] This reform took place between the reigns of Kujula Kadphises, the founder of the Kushan kingdom, and of Vima Kadphises, the consolidator of that kingdom and the conqueror of India. It is, therefore, unexpected that an irregular coinage of the latter of these two kings should be found. Nevertheless, there are twenty such coins in the British Museum.[2] The types of this coinage are the same as those of one of Kujula's issues: the obverse shows an Indian humped bull standing right; the reverse shows a Bactrian camel standing the same way[3] (figs. 1, 2).

Because the inscriptions on these coins were considered unreadable, Sir A. Cunningham, who first published them, attributed them to Kujula as part of his issue with the same types.[4] His attribution has not been questioned since. The following features of these coins, however, make such an identification questionable.

1. They were struck on a weight standard of ca. 4 grams, while the coins of the same type issued by Kujula were struck on a standard of ca. 9.5 grams. There is no relationship between these two standards.
2. The control marks used on them are different from those used on the bull and camel coins of Kujula.
3. The fabric and engraving style are not the same as those of Kujula's coins.
4. The immediately legible parts of the inscriptions on them do not match, either in arrangement and letter forms or in content, those found on coins of the same type issued by Kujula.
5. Marshall, in his excavations at Taxila, found numerous specimens of Kujula's bull and camel coins, but none of these irregular coins.[5]

Fig. 1. Coins of Vima Kadphises, obverse, showing bull. *Photograph by author. Courtesy Dept. of Coins and Medals, British Museum*

Fig. 2. Coins of Vima Kadphises, reverse, showing camel. *Photograph by author. Courtesy Dept. of Coins and Medals, British Museum*

These features point to a different attribution from that proposed by Cunningham and suggest the necessity of reexamining the inscriptions of these coins.

Cunningham read on the obverse *Basilei Basilei* (written *Bupnei Bupnein)*, and on the reverse *maharajasa raja . . .* on some coins and *. . . ra* on another. He offered no reading of the end of the obverse inscription, but, on the basis of his attribution of the coins to Kujula, he suggested the following reconstructions for the reverse inscriptions: *maharajasa raja (tirajasa Kuyula Kaphasa)* and *(maharajasa rajatirajasa Kuyula Ka)ra. Maharajasa raja . . .* is correct, but there is no basis for the reading *. . . ra.* or for his reconstructions. The comparison of all the coins and the correlation of the visible parts of their inscriptions has made it possible to establish complete readings of both the obverse and reverse inscriptions.

It is clear from Cunningham's reading that the obverse inscription (fig. 3) is in badly written Greek. As written on the coins, the inscription appears to be *Bupnei Bupnein Haoou*. The *u* which Cunningham read in *Bupnei* is in fact an *a* tilted backwards; it is frequently written in this way on the regular coins of Vima. The *p* in the same word is a ligatured *si*, again paralleled on Vima's regular coins. The *n* is a misengraved *l* with an extra stroke added. The final letter *i* is the drastically narrowed form of the letter *ō* which occurs on many Indo-Scythian coins.[6] The word *Bupnei* is therefore to be read as *Basileō*, and the context makes clear that this is the Greek word *Basileōs* with its final *s* omitted. Similarly, the second word in the inscription *Bupnein* is a blundered version of *Basileōn*. The last word of the inscription was not read by Cunningham, but is in fact *Haoou*. This word does not appear to be a Greek word, although, like the rest of the inscription, it is written in corrupt Greek letters. Its use in a Kushan coin inscription suggests it is the name or title of a Kushan ruler. The only similar word among the names and titles used by the Kushan kings on their other coins and in their inscriptions is *Zaoou*, the Greek form of the Kushan title *Yabgu,* meaning "Tribal Chief" and used by Kujula on his "Augustus's head" type coins.[7] Only the initial letter of the form *Haoou* differs from the transliteration used by Kujula, and this presumably either is a variant transliteration or the letter *H* is a blundered form of the letter *Z*; in the context, either possibility is credible. The obverse inscription can therefore be interpreted as a blundered version of the Greek legend *Basileōs Basileōn Zaoou,* which would be translated "of the King of Kings, the Tribal Chief."

Cunningham's reading of the reverse (fig. 4) is correct for the first two words, but his conjecture of the rest has no foundation. The first two words are clear on most of the coins, and are *Maharajasa rajatirajasa.* On several of the coins the beginning of the next word is also visible. It is *devaputrasa* (meaning "son of heaven"). On two of the coins the end of *devaputrasa* is legible, and in both cases it is

Fig. 3. Inscriptions, obverse, on coins of Vima Kadphises.

Fig. 4. Inscriptions, reverse, on coins of Vima Kadphises.

31

followed by further syllables, which are in their turn followed by the beginning of the first word of the inscription, *maharajasa*. On one coin the end of the inscription is the two-syllable *vema;* on the other it is the four-syllable *vemasa kho*. These are obviously a shorter and longer version of the same inscription. The shorter has just *vema*. The longer also has this word, but gives it with the genitive ending *-sa* and adds another syllable, *kho*. This syllable does not seem to be a complete word, but the context implies that it is the beginning of the word *Khoshana* (meaning "Kushan").

These last two words have a clear meaning. The context demands that they should be the names or titles of a Kushan king, and this cannot be anyone other than Vima Kadphises. The form *Vema* for his name is attested by inscriptions both on coins and on stone,[8] and the title *Khoshana* could apply to any king of the Kushans. The reverse inscriptions on these coins should therefore read *maharajasa rājatirajasa devaputrasa vema/sa kho* and be translated "of the Great King, the King of Kings, the Son of Heaven, Vima, the Kushan."

The proposed readings of the obverse and reverse inscriptions of these coins fully justify the reasons given for questioning the attribution to Kujula suggested by Cunningham. Many of the aspects of this series that led to a reexamination of their inscriptions are in fact features of the regular coins of the king to whom they can now be attributed. The weight standard on which these coins were struck is the reformed standard of *Sōtēr Megas* which was used by Vima for striking his regular coins.[9] The fabric of these coins is close to the fabric of the drachms of Vima's regular coinage. The use of Greek and Kharosthi inscriptions starting at the top of the coin and forming a continuous circle round the edge of it is normal on Vima's coins. (This feature is found elsewhere only on the bilingual coins of *Sōtēr Megas* and on the Nike reverse Indo-Parthian coins.) The style and forms of the Greek and Kharosthi letters match exactly those used on Vima's other coins. All these attributes confirm what the inscriptions of these coins proclaim: they are an irregular issue of the Kushan king Vima Kadphises.

The existence of an irregular issue of coins by Vima Kadphises represents a considerable contribution to the sparse primary source material relating to him. The information derived from these coins alters previous ideas about the titles used by the Kushan kings. Also, if it is possible to establish the circumstances of the issue of this irregular coinage, then the coins will add several pieces to the jigsaw puzzle of the history of the Kushan kings.

Three titles occur on these bull and camel coins which are not used by Vima on his regular issues. They are *devaputra* ("son of heaven"), *Khoshana* ("Kushan"), and *Zaoou* (= *Yabgu*, "tribal chief"). *Devaputra,* a common title in Kushan royal inscriptions and used by Vima on his portrait statue at Mat,[10] appears on coins only in this irregular issue and on the bull and camel coins of Kujula. *Khoshana,* a title also used extensively by the Kushan kings, is used here for the first time by Vima. The remaining title, *Yabgu,* is not known to have been used by any Kushan king other than Kujula, who used Greek and Kharosthi versions of it freely on his coins.[11] Kujula did not, however, use the title on his bull and camel coins, which were issued after he had adopted the royal titles *maharaya rayatiraya.* Thus the combination of the titles *maharaja rajatiraja* with *Yabgu* is a novel feature displayed by this coin, and its use by Vima on them is certainly not expected. One other example of this combination exists on a small group of silver coins of uncertain attribution Marshall found in Taxila as part of a hoard of coins from the lower Indus Valley.[12] Most of the coins of this hoard were Indo-Parthian, but three of them bore on the obverse the portrait of a Kushan king. Although none of the inscriptions was complete, the following titles were clear in the Kharosthi legends: *maharaja, rajatiraja, kushana,* and *yavuga.* These coins have been attributed to both Kujula and Vima.[13] The use of these titles was the principal argument for the attribution of the coins to Kujula, but the portrait and headgear of the king on the obverse are of a type which is stylistically closer to known representations of Vima. The parallel between the combination of titles now known to be used on the bull and camel coins of Vima and that used on the silver coins gives greater strength to the argument in favor of Vima. This attribution to Vima would help explain the traces of a Greek inscription visible on the silver coins, which, like that on Vima's bull and camel coins, is continuous and starts at the top of the coin. Furthermore, it appears to be a corrupt Greek version of a legend which begins *Basileōs Basileōn,* in the same way as that on the bull and camel coins. If, as the similarities between them suggest, these coins are in fact issues of the Kushan king Vima, it is possible to propose that during his reign he issued not one but two irregular coinages. Apart from these two instances, *Yabgu* is absent from the titles of the Kushan kings when the royal titles are used; the implication is that the Kushan kings stopped using it after their assumption of royal titles. So far, no reason for its retention on the bull and camel coins of Vima or on the silver coins attributable to him has been proposed.

The production of an irregular coinage appears to be caused on most occasions by an event disrupting the normal demand for or supply of coins. Examples of such occurrences are the sudden increase in demand for coin to pay troops and the need for coin arising during a military campaign in foreign territory, when the army is at too great a distance from the normal source of supply for practical convenience. One occasion which conforms to the conditions which necessitate the issue of an irregular coinage is documented for the reign of Vima Kadphises. The Chinese history by Fan Ye known as the *Hou Han Shu* describes Vima as the conqueror of India,[14] and if, as is proposed above, the silver coins from the lower Indus Valley were issued by him, they would provide confirmation of this state- 33 ment. Perhaps the existence of the other irregular coinage of his reign is evidence for his military activities in a different direction.

The upper Indus Valley, where coins of the bull and camel types were issued by Vima's father, Kujula, is probably the place of issue of Vima's irregular coins of the same types. Marshall found many specimens of Kujala's coins in Taxila, and they were closely copied in all respects from the coins of his predecessor in Taxila, Jihonika (Zeionises),[15] who, according to the Taxila Silver Vase inscription,[16] was satrap of that area. In spite of the relationship with Taxila and the upper Indus Valley, none of Vima's coins of this type has actually been recorded as being found there; the only recorded find spot for a coin of this issue is at Khotan in Chinese Turkestan.[17]

If Vima's bull and camel coins were issued in the context of military activity, the areas with which the coins are connected by their types and by find spot may have been the location of such action. The position of these areas suggests that any military activity with which the coins are connected must have been in the form of an invasion of Chinese Turkestan by the Kushans, who used the upper Indus Valley as their base. Similar activity in this region is implied by the finds of other Kushan coins in Khotan[18] which belong to the reign of Vima's successor, Kanishka—about twenty copper drachma and hemidrachms, all of the type issued by Kanishka in the upper Indus Valley.[19]

Fig. 5. Chinese character *yu*.

There are several reasons other than the find mentioned above for relating the bull and camel coins of Vima to the city of Khotan.

1. The control mark in the reverse field of most of these coins is the Chinese character *yu* (fig. 5), which is the first half of the Chinese name for the city of Khotan, *yu t'ien* (fig. 6), during this period.[20]
2. The coins are struck on a weight standard of ca. 4 grams, which is the same as that used for the Sino-Kharosthi coins which were struck in Khotan during the first and second centuries A.D.[21]
3. The Kharosthi inscriptions on these Sino-Kharosthi coins also show a remarkable stylistic similarity in content, arrangement, and epigraphy to those of Vima.

Fig. 6. Chinese name for the city of Khotan.

On the basis of such evidence, a relationship between the coins of this irregular issue of Vima and the city of Khotan in Chinese Turkestan seems certain. It is probable that their existence indicates some military activity by Vima in that area.

Kushan military involvement in Chinese Turkestan is not only suggested by numismatic evidence but attested by Chinese literary sources as well. The *Hou Han Shu* reports two major Kushan campaigns in that area. The first took place during the time of the Chinese general Pan Ch'ao, who was the commander in chief there from A.D.

73 to 102. The Kushans began to assert themselves in Chinese Turkestan after they had helped Pan Ch'ao in his successful attack on Turfan. In A.D. 86, they broke off relations with him after their request for the hand in marriage of a Han princess had been refused. In 90 their army fought an indecisive battle against the Chinese, and, as it was unable to obtain supplies, withdrew to Kushan territory. The second occasion was during the period A.D. 107–27, when the Chinese army in Central Asia had been withdrawn and the local kingdoms were in revolt. According to Fan Ye, a Kushan army took the opportunity of replacing the king of Kashgar with their ally Ch'en Pan in A.D. 114–16. No mention is made in Chinese historical works of other incursions into Chinese Turkestan by the Kushans.[22]

In his paper on the date of Kanishka given at the conference on that topic in London in 1960, A. K. Narain, following the suggestions of several other scholars, proposed that these two invasions could be linked with the reigns of Vima and Kanishka.[23] The connection between these Kushan kings and the events reported in the *Hou Han Shu* is strengthened by the numismatic evidence presented above. Recent work done on the local coins of Khotan further supports this proposal. A coin of this series, which has long been recognized as being closely copied from the bull and camel coins issued by Kujula, has now been dated to the year A.D. 60.[24] (The issuer of this coin has been identified as the Khotanese king Hsiu Mo Pa, who, according to the *Hou Han Shu,* ruled only in A.D. 60 and the following two or three years: his name can be read on a coin in the Hermitage Museum in Leningrad.) It is clear, from his use of the royal titles *maharaya rayatiraya,* that Kujula issued these coins toward the end of his reign. Therefore, it would be reasonable to place the date A.D. 60 either at the end of or after his reign.[25] Allowing some time for the period during which the *Sōtēr Megas* coins were issued, such a date for the end of Kujula's reign makes it quite possible that the Kushan king ruling in A.D. 88–90 was his son and successor, Vima, and also that the Kushan ruler in A.D. 114–16 was the next Kushan king, Kanishka.

These conclusions, drawn from the evidence of both the irregular coins of Vima and the local and Kushan coins found in Khotan, pose obvious implications for the question of Kushan chronology. The placing of the periods A.D. 88–90 in the reign of Vima and A.D. 114–16 in the reign of Kanishka must still be reconciled with Narain's proposed date of ca. A.D. 103 as the first year of Kanishka's reign. The findings presented here do not make that date any more exact, but they do reinforce Narain's rejection of the traditional date of A.D. 78 and the more recent suggestions—ca. A.D. 128, 144, 225, 278, and so on[26]—for the start of the Kanishkan era.

The proposed identification of Vima as the Kushan king who invaded Chinese Turkestan in A.D. 88–90 suggests an explanation for the gold coin of Vima which shows him riding in a chariot (fig. 7).[27] Two of Vima's gold pieces are clearly special issues outside the

Fig. 7. Gold Kushan coin, obverse, showing Vima riding in a chariot. *Photograph by author. Courtesy Dept. of Coins and Medals, British Museum*

normal series; one is this coin, while the other shows him riding on an elephant.[28] The latter coin is generally held to be commemorating his Indian victory.[29] The elephant is the regular military vehicle of the Indian, and Vima is shown holding weapons. It is possible that the former was made to commemorate his "victory" over the Chinese. On the coin Vima is shown riding in a chariot drawn by two horses and with a central umbrella, accompanied by a charioteer. These attributes not only suggest a Chinese general's chariot of the period, but also make Vima's chariot totally dissimilar to that portrayed on the coin of the Roman emperor Tiberius (*BMCRE* no. 1) which the engraver used as his model. Vima's lack of a Chinese victory would not necessarily have deterred him from commemorating one; his army fought an indecisive battle, suffered no actual defeat, and only withdrew because it lacked supplies. For propaganda purposes, such a campaign could easily be called a victory. The type used on this coin certainly refers to a triumph,[30] and the placing of Vima in a Chinese chariot clearly indicates that this triumphal issue relates to his military campaign against the Chinese army in Chinese Turkestan.

NOTES

1. For a full discussion of the *Sōtēr Megas* coins and of their significance in relation to other Kushan coins, see D. W. MacDowall, "*Sōtēr Megas,* the King of Kings, the Kushan," *JNSI* (1968) 28-48.
2. The British Museum specimens include those published in *BMC* 112, nos. 15 and 16. There are also eight examples listed in R. B. Whitehead, *The Catalogue of the Coins in the Panjab Museum, Lahore* i *The Indo-Greeks* (Lahore 1914) [hereafter *PMC* 180, nos. 20-23.
3. See *BMC* 112, nos. 7-14; *PMC* 180, nos. 16-19.
4. A. Cunningham, "The Coins of the Kushans or Great Yue-ti," *NC* (1892) 28, nos. 4 and 5, pl. 14.12, 13.
5. J. Marshall, *Taxila* (Cambridge 1951) 818, nos. 235-39.
6. For example, the coins of Azes II and of Aspavarma.
7. See *BMC* (n. 2 above) 123, nos. 1-10; *PMC* (n. 2 above) 181, nos. 24-28.
8. Vima's portrait statue at Mat has his name in the same form, *Vema.* In the Greek coin inscriptions his name is transliterated *ooēmo* (see n. 10 below).
9. D. W. MacDowall gives a full account and analysis of Kushan weight standards in "The Weight Standards of the Gold and Copper Coinages of the Kushan Dynasty," *JNSI* (1960) 63-75.
10. The inscription on this statue is discussed by K. Rosenfield, *The Dynastic Art of the Kushans* (Berkeley 1967) 144.
11. See *BMC* (n. 2 above) 120-23.
12. See Marshall (n. 5 above) 211, 212, and 820, nos. 258-60.
13. A full account of the various attributions of these coins is to be found in D. W. MacDowall and N. G. Wilson, "References to the Kusanas in the Periplus and Further Numismatic Evidence for Its Date," *NC* (1970) 232-33.
14. E. Zurcher, "The Yueh-Chih and Kaniska in the Chinese Sources," in A. Basham, ed., *Papers on the Date of Kaniska* (Leiden 1968) gives details of all the references to the Kushans in the *Hou Han Shu.*

15. See *BMC* (n. 2 above) 111, nos. 3, 4; *PMC* (n. 2 above) 158, nos. 84-90.
16. See S. Konow, ed., *Corpus Inscriptionum Indicarum: Kharosthi Inscriptions* ii.1 (Calcutta 1929) 81-82.
17. See M. A. Stein, *Ancient Khotan* (Oxford 1907) 575, pl. 89.1. Apart from this irregular coin, three copper tetradrachms of Vima's regular coinage have also been found in Khotan.
18. See ibid. 575-76.
19. The attribution of the coins of Kanishka of the type found in Khotan to the Kashmir area has been made by D. W. MacDowall in a paper on Kushan mints given to the Royal Numismatic Society; this paper has not yet appeared in print.
20. Fig. 6 illustrates the form of the name of Khotan used in the *Hou Han Shu*. A second century A.D. lead coin found in Khotan (Stein[n. 17 above] pl. 89.5) shows a form of *yu* identical to that used as the control mark on these coins.
21. For details of the weights of the coins of this series, see A. F. Rudolf Hoernle, "Indo-Chinese Coins in the British Collection of Antiquities," *The Indian Antiquary* (1899) 46-56.
22. See n. 14 above.
23. "The Date of Kaniska" in Basham (n. 14 above) 206-43.
24. This coin was published but not fully read by E. V. Zeymal in "Sino-Kharosthi Coins," *Strany i Narody Vostoka* (1971) 109-20, no. 2.
25. Kujula's numerous other issues on which he only uses his tribal title *Yabgu* point to a great part of his reign having elapsed before he adopted royal titles.
26. For details and discussion of the various proposals for the date of Kanishka, see E. V. Zeymal, *Kushan Chronology* (1968) and Basham (n. 14 above).
27. *BMC* (n. 2 above) 175 and pl. 32.13.
28. Rosenfield (n. 10 above) pl. 1.17.
29. Rosenfield 22-23.
30. Rosenfield also proposes a triumphal interpretation of this type.

3

A HOARD DATING THE DESTRUCTION OF A TEMPLE AT PALMYRA

ALEKSANDRA KRZYZANOWSKA

Archaeological discoveries often gain in importance when it becomes possible to date them or determine their character by means of coins. An example of such a case is reported here.

For many years the Polish archaeological mission has been carrying out excavations at Palmyra in Syria. The work has concentrated on a part of the city called "Diocletian's Camp"; an extant inscription verifies that a large military camp occupied the place at the time of that emperor.[1] The remains of a temple of the goddess Allath have been discovered in the northwestern part of this area. The dedication to that goddess was proved beyond doubt by an inscription preserved on the gate.[2]

During the 1975 campaign, the temple building itself was found, its temenos defined, and exploration of the inside commenced. In the course of work within the temple walls, which were preserved to the level of the column bases, a most interesting cult statue of Athena-Allath was found which had been purposely damaged, the marks of the blows being clearly visible. Fragments of a smaller statue of the same goddess were also found. A small hoard of bronze coins was discovered under a piece of the broken head of the smaller statue. Next to it lay a small ordinary household pot bearing traces of patina, a positive indication of its former role as container of the coins. The whole find was situated next to the interior wall, preserved about 0.5 m. above the floor level, which set off the innermost part of the building, where the cult statue once stood in a niche. A fragment of the pot was stuck on the right side of the niche, under a floor slab that had been torn away and touching the above-mentioned wall; next to it, slightly scattered, lay the coins.[3] Apart from the coins and statue, numerous fragments of clay lamps, some broken, some undamaged, were found. All of them bore signs of use, having traces of smoke at the outlets. They date to the fourth century.[4]

All forty-four bronze coins of the hoard (see table) were struck in the second half of the fourth century, with the highest percentage 39 dating from 346/7, to the time of Valentinian I and Valens. Coins of earlier issues are fewer, and only the coins struck under Constantius II are present in a significant quantity: Constantius II, nine coins, about 20 percent; Constantius II or Julian II, four coins, about 9 percent; Jovian (?), one coin, about 2 percent; Valentinian I and Valens, twenty-six coins, about 60 percent; uncertain emperor, four coins, about 9 percent. When grouped according to mint provenance, the hoard presents the following pattern: Antioch, eighteen coins, about 40 percent; Alexandria, two coins, about 5 percent; Constantinople, two coins, about 5 percent; Heraclea, two coins, about 5 percent; Thessalonica, three coins, about 7 percent; uncertain, seventeen coins, about 38 percent.

The coins which date the moment of the hoard's burial clearly are those of Valentinian and Valens. The presence of the considerable number of coins struck under Constantius II may be explained by the fact that the copious coinage of that emperor was in circulation for many years after his death. The mints represented in the hoard clearly point to its local provenance, with Antioch holding first place at 40 percent. The percentages for the other mints throw some light on coin circulation in the area. We could expect Cyzicus or Nicomedia to be represented also. However, considering that 38 percent of the coins are so badly preserved as to be illegible, we cannot be certain if those mints really are not represented in the hoard.

The hoard, therefore, does not present any anomalies and seems to be typical for that area and time. Palmyra was no longer a flourishing city, and its most prosperous years belonged to the remote past. We can assume that many a citizen could own such a modest property as our hoard. It could well have been a soldier's possession—the camp was in the neighborhood. In any case, the real value of the coins was definitely small at the time and, were it not for its location, it would hardly deserve a separate description.

Its special value lies in the fact that it was discovered amid the debris of the intentional destruction of the interior of the pagan temple. The hoard gives a *terminus post quem* for this disaster. After the floor slab was torn away the coin pot must have been disclosed, but it was not noticed and the falling head of the statue broke the pot. The coins scattered and remained as witnesses to the date of the disaster. The date can be defined more accurately with the help of one further coin found directly on the stone floor nearby. This coin provides a *terminus ante quem*—it is a bronze coin of Flacilla, struck in Antioch in 383/8 (*RIC* 62).

Therefore, the numismatic evidence dates the end of the Allath temple of Palmyra to the years between 378 and 388. Within the period of those ten years there was a day when a crowd of Christian fanatics broke into the temple and destroyed everything—smashing statues and breaking the oil lamps. They did not, however, destroy the coins which now provide their evidence.

NOTES

1. T. Wiegand, *Palmyra, Ergebnisse der Expeditionen von 1902 und 1917* (Berlin 1932) 85-107; J. Cantineau, *Camp de Diocletien: Inventaire des inscriptions de Palmyre,* fasc. 6 (Beirut 1931).
2. M. Gawlikowski, *Le temple palmyrenien: Palmyre VI* (Warsaw 1973) 92.
3. M. Gawlikowski, "Le temple d'Allath à Palmyre," *Revue Archéologique* 2 (1977) 253-74.
4. M. Krogulska, "Une lampe à symbole juive du temple d'Allath à Palmyre," *Études et Travaux* (in press).

THE PALMYRA HOARD

COIN	EMPEROR	MINT	DATE	REFERENCE
1	Constantius II	Constantinople	341-46	*LRBC* i 1064
2	Constantius II	Constantinople	351-54	ii 2040
3	Constantius II	Thessalonica	355-61	ii 1689
4	Constantius II	Antioch	355-61	ii 2638
5-9	Constantius II	?	346-61	
10-13	Constantius II or Julian II	?	355-61	
14	Jovian?	Antioch	363-64	ii 2648?
15	Valentinian I	Heraclea	364-67	*RIC* 3a
16	Valens	Heraclea	364-67	3b
17	Valentinian I	Thessalonica	364-67	16a
18	Valentinian I or Valens	Thessalonica	364-67	16
19-22	Valentinian I	Antioch	364-67	10a
23-24	Valens	Antioch	364-67	10b
25-28	Valentinian I or Valens	Antioch	364-67	10
29	Valentinian I	Antioch	364-67	12b
30-31	Valens	Antioch	364-67	12a
32-33	Valentinian I or Valens	Antioch	364-67	12, 2c
34	Valentinian I	Alexandria	364-67	1a
35	Valentinian I or Valens	Alexandria	364-67	3
36-39	Valentinian I or Valens	?	367-75	
40	Valentinian I or Valens	?	365-78	
41	uncertain	Antioch	2d half 4th cen.	
42-44	uncertain	?	2d half 4th cen.	

4

UNE DRACHME D'ALEXANDRE DE PHÈRES SURFRAPPÉE EN CRÈTE

GEORGES LE RIDER

J'ai donné en 1966 une liste de villes dont des monnaies avaient été surfrappées en Crète du Ve siècle au début du IIIe.[1] Cette liste peut être complétée aujourd'hui par une addition intéressante que m'a signalée M. L. Cancio et qu'il me permet aimablement de publier ici: je l'en remercie vivement.

Il s'agit d'une drachme d'Alexandre de Phères utilisée comme flan à Phaistos ou à Praisos. Voici tout d'abord la description de la monnaie crétoise (fig. 1). *Droit*: tête de divinité à dr., de style plutôt rude. *Revers*: tête de taureau de face; à g. traces de légende, dont seul l'*iota* est net; grènetis. 5,47 g.; ↓

Au droit comme au revers, on distingue les vestiges de types antérieurs: on aperçoit au droit, au-dessus de la tête phaistienne ou praisienne, le sommet d'une autre tête et certains détails de la chevelure; au revers, on lit en haut à droite les lettres ΞΑΝΔΡ et, devant le *nu*, il faut reconnaître l'extrémité d'un mufle de lion.

Fig. 1. Drachme crétoise, droit et revers.

La monnaie qui a servi de flan ne peut être, semble-t-il, qu'une drachme d'Alexandre de Phères, qui régna de 369 à 358.[2] Une pièce semblable, de la collection de Luynes (n° 1867; 6,00 g.), est reproduite ci-dessous (fig. 2): on y voit au droit la tête à dr. d'Ennodia, ornée d'une couronne et de boucles d'oreille (le nom de la déesse est inscrit dans le champ: EN derrière la nuque, NO sous le cou, Δ sous le menton), et, au revers, un mufle de lion à droite avec la légende ΑΛΕΞΑΝΔΡΟΥ.

Un seul autre exemple de monnaie thessalienne surfrappée en Crète était connu jusqu'à présent: celui d'une drachme de Larisa utilisée comme flan à Phaistos.[3] La surfrappe des monnaies du Péloponnèse, de Grèce centrale, de Thessalie par les villes crétoises ne posait à cette époque aucun problème métrologique, puisque ces divers ateliers se conformaient au même étalon, l'étalon éginétique.[4]

La drachme crétoise qui vient d'être décrite doit-elle être attribuée à Phaistos ou Praisos? L'hésitation est permise. Le type de droit semble être l'imitation de la tête de la divinité qui orne les monnaies

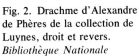

Fig. 2. Drachme d'Alexandre de Phères de la collection de Luynes, droit et revers.
Bibliothèque Nationale

43

de Praisos illustrées par Svoronos, *Num. de la Crète antique,* pl. 28, 12-15 (cf. *Monnaies crétoises,* pl. 27, 2-6). Mais la tête de taureau, au revers, est issue du même coin de droit que certains revers de Phaistos (Svoronos, pl. 24, 4; *Monnaies crétoises,* pl. 24, 6), sur lesquels les lettres ΦΑΙ sont distinctes.

Sur notre exemplaire, la légende est beaucoup moins nette, comme si les premières lettres avaient été effacées à dessein. On pourrait considérer que le coin, gravé à Phaistos et d'abord mis en service dans cet atelier, aurait ensuite été transféré à Praisos: il existe plusieurs exemples de villes crétoises qui se sont partagé un même coin.[5] Je laisserai donc l'attribution de notre pièce en suspens.

Qu'elle soit phaistienne ou praisienne, il faut noter que cette émission crétoise date les dernières années du IVe s. ou du début du IIIe s. Il s'est donc écoulé un laps de temps assez long entre la frappe de la drachme d'Alexandre de Phères et son utilisation comme flan en Crète:[6] l'usure qui a pu résulter de ces nombreuses années de circulation explique peut-être le poids un peu faible de l'exemplaire crétois.

La drachme d'Alexandre de Phères illustrée a pour type de droit la tête de la déesse Ennodia. Le culte d'Ennodia (ou Enodia) en Thessalie a fait l'objet d'une étude fondamentale de L. Robert.[7] D'autres monnaies de Phères nous montrent l'image complète de la déesse: à cheval, assise en amazone, tenant une torche dans chaque main, ou parfois seulement une torche dans la main droite.[8] Ce type monétaire permet d'identifier à coup sûr comme Ennodia la déesse de nombreux reliefs thessaliens.

Ainsi que le souligne L. Robert, il est regrettable que les numismates aient appelé ou continuent d'appeler cette déesse Hécate, alors que son nom est inscrit si clairement sur certaines pièces: "elle est Enodia à Phères et en général en Thessalie; à l'étranger (autres villes de Thessalie ou Argos, Issa etc.) elle peut garder son vrai nom local (Enodia) ou y recevoir son ethnique (Pheraia, seul ou avec le nom) ou enfin porter à la fois l'ethnique de provenance et un nom plus général qui l'assimile à une divinité panhellénique (Artémis Pheraia)."[9] Le nom d'Hécate est une invention des modernes.

On remarquera que l'exemplaire de Luynes illustré est contremarqué au droit, derrière la tête d'Ennodia. Le type de la contremarque n'est pas clair: peut-être est-ce une tête de taureau de face.

NOTES

1. *Monnaies crétoises du Ve au Ier siècle av. J.-C.* (Études crétoises 15) 125-28; voir la planche annexée à la p. 128.
2. Cf. H. D. Westlake, *Thessaly in the Fourth Century B.C.* (London 1935) 126-59.
3. *Monnaies crétoises* (n. 1 above) 97, no. 65, pl. 24.7.
4. Sur les problèmes métrologiques posés par les surfrappes, voir G. Le Rider,

"Contremarques et surfrappes dans l'Antiquité grecque," *Numismatique antique, problèmes et méthodes,* Annales de l'Est (1975) 46-47.

5. L. Robert, *Villes d'Asie Mineure* (1962²) 188-91, 366-77; *Monnaies crétoises* (n. 1 above) 52, n. 4, et 97, n. 1 (où est évoqué un autre cas d'attribution difficile à Phaistos ou à Praisos).

6. Cf. *Monnaies crétoises* 181-82.

7. L. Robert, "Une déesse à cheval en Thessalie," *Hellenica* 11-12 (1960) 588-95.

8. Cf. Robert (n. 7 above) 594, n. 1. Souvent, quand seule la tête de la déesse est représentée, une torche est placée dans le champ.

9. Ibid. 591, n. 4.

5
ARCHITECTURAL DESIGNS ON PAPAL COINS
DAVID M. METCALF

What more appropriate way is there to honor Bluma Trell than with a review of some of the most handsome coins with architectural designs that have ever been struck? I refer to the papal scudi of the late seventeenth and early eighteenth centuries. They were large (dollar-sized) silver coins which exploited the greater force and precision of striking that could be achieved by machine presses. All ancient and medieval coins, of course, were struck by a man with a hammer, and a sharp and level impression was very difficult to achieve above a certain size of flan.

The scudi, it must be admitted, are to some extent medallic in character, and this is a fault rather than a virtue in coin design. Even though they were related by weight to the smaller silver denominations, so that a given sum of money, whether made up of large coins or small, would be equally heavy in the purse or pocket, the public has always found talers, scudi, crowns and the like to be inconveniently large. But their flans offer splendid scope to the designer.

We owe the coins illustrated and discussed here to a distinguished line of engravers of papal coins and medals—the Hameran family. (The coins are now in the Heberden Coin Room of the Ashmolean Museum and are part of the Grissell Milne bequest.) The eldest was Johann Andres Hameran, a Bavarian who settled in Rome and worked as an engraver for Paul V (1605–21). His son Alberto (1620–77) did the same for Clement IX and Clement X. The grandson, Giovanni (1649–1705), succeeded Alberto, and produced some fine architectural designs on coins which he signed *I. H.* His sons Ermenigildo (1685–1744) and Ottone (1694–1768) achieved even more distinctive results: their work may be recognized from the initials *E. H.* and *O. H.* respectively.

Our earliest piece, however, is unsigned, and is not a coin but a medal in bronze (fig. 1). It illustrates a major exercise in town planning: the Piazza del Popolo, with its twin churches of S. Maria di Monte Santo and S. Maria de' Miracoli, and the three main roads leading into the city. The medallist has created a strong sense of

Fig. 1. Papal medal with Piazza del Popolo. *Courtesy Ashmolean Museum, Oxford*

Fig. 2. Scudo of Innocent XI with facade of St. Peter's. *Courtesy Ashmolean Museum, Oxford*

Fig. 3. Scudo of Clement XI with aerial perspective of S. Teodoro al Palatino. *Courtesy Ashmolean Museum, Oxford*

perspective, chiefly by means of the high relief of the central column, and by the device of the numerous figures in the piazza (including the statutory dog). The medal is firmly dated 1662, once on the reverse and twice on the obverse: this is the year when the foundation stone of the left-hand church was laid. What we are looking at, then, is the sketch of an architect's intentions, not a picture of the finished work. Rainaldi's wish to place the pediments of the porticoes against a high attic was, in the outcome, modified by Bernini. If one can judge from the medal, the original scheme would have united the square and the streets more effectively.

The scudo of Innocent XI, 1677 (fig. 2), shows the facade of St. Peter's in an immensely successful design by Giovanni Hameran. The design uses the available space as fully as it possibly can and presses hard against the legend without, somehow, making either seem cramped. The arms of Monsignor Raggi serve to tie the design to the surface of the coin and prevent it from being merely an architectural drawing. The engraver's "hand" is seen in the contrast between the bold, flat lines of the columns and portico (balancing the weight of the lettering) and the delicate stippling in the doorways. The distance of the dome from the observer is skillfully conveyed by the slightly lower relief of the engraving. The facade is shown without the towers which Maderno had planned and which caused Bernini so much trouble.

Our next coin, a scudo of Clement XI dated 1703 (fig. 3), gives an aerial perspective of the church of S. Teodoro al Palatino, showing the rotunda, the large forecourt, and the double staircase of the entrance. It has been suggested that the design is by Giovanni Hameran, but it is unsigned and is far inferior to his other work, lacking both weight and technical inventiveness.

Ermenigildo's view of S. Maria Rotonda (the Pantheon) on a half-scudo of Clement XI of 1711 (fig. 4) is not much better. The design is

Fig. 4. Half-scudo of
Clement XI with S. Maria
Rotonda (Pantheon).
*Courtesy Ashmolean
Museum, Oxford*

Fig. 5. Scudo of Clement XI
with Piazza della Rotonda.
*Courtesy Ashmolean
Museum, Oxford*

Fig. 6. Half-scudo of
Clement XII with S. Giovanni
dei Fiorentini. *Courtesy
Ashmolean Museum, Oxford*

too small for the field, and the lettering is somewhat small. The
facade, which is off-center on the flan, is not very effectively balanced
by the curved mass of the rotunda. Bernini's turrets are made to
appear small and mean. The arms in the exergue are not incorporated
into the design as they are on the scudo of St. Peter's. The marvelous
interior of the Rotonda would have been a worthy challenge to
Giovanni's skill as a coin designer.

Ermenigildo's masterpiece is the scudo of Clement XI from 1713,
showing the Piazza della Rotonda with the obelisk and fountain at
the center, against a background of three sides of the square (fig. 5).
The houses on the far side are agreeably irregular in their architecture, offsetting the symmetry of the coin's design. There are stalls in
the square and figures inside the doorways; there are also figures in
the piazza, emerging from a side street and even seated at two of the
windows. The overall result has great charm and quality. It is hard to
say what sets this design apart, since other compositions—for example, the medal of the Piazza del Popolo—are equally animated.
Perhaps it is the spectators at the windows who add psychological
depth to the scene.

Finally, one of the latest of the papal coins with architectural
designs: a half-scudo of Clement XII, dated 1736 (fig. 6). The facade
of the church of S. Giovanni dei Fiorentini, which Galilei under-
took in 1734, is here commemorated by Ottone Hameran, the brother
of Ermenigildo. The architecture is too pretty for modern taste, but
the handling of it by the engraver is extremely polished, combining
great delicacy in the details with a firm treatment of the main outlines.
The foreground perhaps looks rather empty, and the design as a whole
inevitably invites comparison with the scudo showing St. Peter's.
What are the qualities which make the latter so satisfying? In what
ways had taste changed in sixty years? I leave the pleasure of pon-
dering these questions to the reader.

49

6

UNE MONNAIE DE BRONZE FRAPPÉE À PELLA (DÉCAPOLE) SOUS COMMODE

HÉLÈNE NICOLET

Mrs. Bluma Trell connaît bien cette monnaie de Pella (fig. 1) qu'elle a pu examiner lors de ses recherches à Paris et dont elle a illustré le revers dans une étude sur les nymphées.[1] Elle m'encourage néanmoins à lui consacrer la notice numismatique qui n'a pas encore été publiée à son sujet: la rareté des monnaies de la Décapole syrienne et de celles de Pella en particulier peut justifier un bref retour sur cette pièce unique.[2]

Fig. 1. Monnaie de bronze frappée à Pella sous Commode, droit et revers. *Cabinet des Médailles de la Bibliothèque Nationale*

DESCRIPTION

Droit: buste drapé de Commode, à droite. La tête est imberbe et laurée, les pans du diadème forment deux boucles et les deux extrémités flottent sur la nuque. Légende: AY.K.Λ.AYP à gauche, KOMOΔOΣ à droite. *Revers:* monument en forme d'arc de cercle fermé à la base par un mur droit qui se confond avec la ne d'exergue. Au fond, une niche à fronton triangulaire, flanquée d'arcatures à deux étages; dans la niche, la statue drapée d'un personnage appuyé sur un bâton ou un sceptre. De part et d'autre du fronton, M-C. Tout autour, entre le monument et le grènetis, une longue légende qui commence à l'exergue: ΦΙΛΠ.Τ. / Κ.ΠΕΛΤ / Π.ΝΥ. / Φ.ΚΟ.ΣΥ. Bronze, diamètre: 33 mm., poids: 33,16 g.

DATE DE LA MONNAIE

Le droit, avec l'effigie imberbe de Commode et le prénom de Lucius qu'il porte encore—non abrégée, la legende serait: *Autokrator Kaisar Loukios Aurelios Komodos*—nous indique que la pièce a été

51

frappée entre 176 et mars 180: avant 176 en effet il était nommé Lucius Aelius Aurelius Commodus; après la mort de son père Marc Aurèle, le 17 mars 180, Commode porte le prénom de Marcus, et son effigie, barbue, se rapproche de celle de l'empereur précédent.

Le revers de la monnaie porte une date: MC (240) qu'il faut interpréter selon une ère locale, propre à la ville ou à la région. H. Herzfelder et H. Seyrig ont considéré que la plupart des villes de Syrie du Sud adoptèrent une ère pompéienne partant de -63, date de l'annexion de la Décapole par les Romains.[3] Selon cette ère, notre pièce de l'an 240 aurait été frappée en 177/8, ce qui s'accorde avec le portrait et la titulature de Commode au droit; mais une date légèrement postérieure n'est pas exclue: nous le verrons plus loin, l'ère de Pella était peut-être comptée à partir de -61.

LE TYPE DU REVERS

Le monument représenté au revers de cette monnaie est un nymphée—fontaine monumentale dont les fonctions utilitaire et ornementale paraissent bien liées. Sur son identification, aucun doute, et nous partageons entièrement la conviction de Bluma Trell;[4] on se trouve donc devant la nécessité de comparer cette représentation et celle postérieure de quarante-trois ans, qui apparaît sur les deux bronzes d'Elagabal publiés par Henri Seyrig.[5] La juxtaposition des deux revers montre la ressemblance générale des monuments: nymphée ''sigmoïde'' dans les deux cas, même bassin en demi-lune, avec les bouches versant l'eau représentées dans le bord concave; même élévation complexe, de niches et de colonnades, au-dessus. Mais dans le détail de ces dernières on est surtout frappé par les différences. Dans le champ d'une pièce un peu plus petite, le graveur d'Elagabal a représenté un monument apparemment beaucoup plus somptueux, avec ses deux étages, ses ailes terminées en façade par quatre colonnes groupées par deux, comme le sont aussi celles de la loggia centrale, supportant le fronton triangulaire. Le monument de Commode en paraît quasi rudimentaire.

Comment interpréter ces différénces non négligeable? On doit, semble-t-il, écarter d'emblée l'hypothèse selon laquelle il s'agirait pour la monnaie de Commode d'un monument autre que le nymphée de Pella, suffisamment célèbre pour qu'il ait sa place dans la légende monétaire et la localisation de la ville.

S'agit-il alors d'une ''simplification'' en quelque sorte accidentelle, due seulement au manque d'habilité ou à la négligence d'un graveur peu soucieux de reproduire fidèlement un bâtiment trop imposant? Si le nymphée tel que le montrent les monnaies d'Elagabal existait déjà au temps de Commode, la réduction est cruelle; une telle simplification a pu avoir lieu—mais on ne peut exclure cependant une troisième hypothèse, à mes yeux plus vraisemblable: à savoir que le nymphée de Commode aurait été partiellement au moins reconstruit sous Elagabal. Ces travaux d'embellissement, favorisés peut-être par une générosité princière, auraient alors été commémorés sur l'émission monétaire d'Elagabal (fig. 2).

Fig. 2. Monnaie de bronze frappée à Pella sous Elagabal, droit et revers. *Cabinet des Médailles de la Bibliothèque Nationale*

LA LÉGENDE DU REVERS

La nouvelle monnaie de Pella présente, comme l'émission au nymphée sous Elagabal et le grand bronze au type de l'acropole de la ville sous Commode,[6] une légende longue, abrégée, que l'on peut restituer ainsi: $\Phi\iota\lambda(\iota\pi\pi\acute{\epsilon}\omega\nu)$ $\pi(\rho\grave{o}\varsigma)$ $\tau(\hat{\varphi}$ ou $\hat{\eta})$ $K(?)$ $\Pi\epsilon\lambda(\lambda\alpha\acute{\iota}\omega\nu)$ $\tau(\hat{\omega}\nu)$ $\pi(\rho\grave{o}\varsigma)$ $\nu\nu(\mu)\phi(\alpha\acute{\iota}\varphi)$ $Ko(\acute{\iota}\lambda\eta\varsigma)$ $\Sigma\nu(\rho\acute{\iota}\alpha\varsigma)$.

Le nom de ''Philippéens'' que portent les habitants de Pella a été mis en relation avec le nom du promagistrat romain L. Marcius Philippus, gouverneur de Syrie en 61 et en 60 avant J. C., peu après la conquête de la Décapole par Pompée.[7] Cette explication, proposée par H. Herzfelder, approuvée par H. Seyrig, est née du rapprochement avec la légende de certaines monnaies impériales de Gaba:[8] celles-ci portent aussi, avant $\Gamma\alpha\beta\eta\nu\hat{\omega}\nu$, les mentions $K\lambda\alpha\nu(\delta\iota\acute{\epsilon}\omega\nu)$ et $\Phi\iota\lambda$- ou $\Phi\iota\lambda\iota\pi(\pi\acute{\epsilon}\omega\nu)$. A. H. M. Jones suggérait d'expliquer ce dernier nom par le rôle joué en Syrie par L. Marcius Philippus, plutôt que par celui du roi Hérode Philippe, selon l'ancienne interprétation de Eckhel.[9]

Ces Philippéens se distinguent de leurs homonymes par la localisation géographique: pour développer Π, T, K, on attendrait par exemple le nom d'un fleuve commençant par un K. L'emploi sur une autre émission monétaire du type de la Tyché de la ville, au pied de laquelle un nageur personnifie le fleuve, n'est sans doute pas simple emprunt, dépourvu de signification, du type bien connu d'Antioche. L'acropole de Pella dominait la vallée d'un affluent du Jourdain.[10] Mais Pline, qui note l'abondance des eaux à Pella, dans son énumération des villes de la Décapole, ne le nomme pas.

Des deux formes attestées par les monnaies pour l'ethnique des Pelléens, *Pellaioi* et *Pellēnoi*, c'est la première qui figure sur les deux émissions contemporaines de la nôtre, l'une au type d'Athéna, l'autre au type de Tyché assise devant un fleuve (année MC). Ensuite vient sur notre pièce la mention du nymphée précisant le nom des Pelléens—mention qui indique, comme l'a exposé de façon lumineuse Henri Seyrig, la proximité du sanctuaire important situé sur le territoire de la ville. Cette mention fait partie de la désignation officielle de la ville—notons qu'elle figure aussi sur l'émission monétaire (fig. 3) où le nymphée lui-même n'est pas représenté mais une autre vue architecturale, plus imposante encore, celle de l'acropole de Pella couronnée par un grand temple (cf. n. 6). Dans la légende de cette

Fig. 3. Monnaie de bronze avec représentation de l'acropole de Pella, droit et revers. *Cabinet des Médailles de la Bibliothèque Nationale*

53

monnaie en effet, au revers, Herzfelder lisait, après ΠΕΛΛΑΙΩΝ, ΠΙΝ
. . ΚΣΥΡΙ qu'il paraît maintenant naturel de compléter en $\pi(\rho\grave{o}\varsigma)$
N($\nu\mu\phi\alpha\acute{\iota}\omega$).[11]

L'ÈRE DE PELLA

Il est depuis longtemps reconnu[12] que l'ère de Gaba était comptée à
partir de -61 ou -60 et cela, indépendamment de la relation indiquée
par A. H. M. Jones avec L. Marcius Philippus. La coïncidence entre
l'adoption de cette ère à Gaba et la modification du nom officiel de la
ville est frappante. D'autres cas en sont bien connus: ainsi en Syrie
toujours, Gadara libérée et reconstruite par Pompée inscrit ses monnaies impériales de la légende ΠΟΜΠΗΙΕΩΝ ΓΑΔΑΡΕΩΝ et les date
selon une ère de -64. Aussi pourrait-on se demander si des faits du
même genre ne se seraient pas produits à Pella en l'honneur de
L. Marcius Philippus, et s'il ne faudrait pas calculer les dates de nos
monnaies selon une ère "philippéenne" comme à Gaba, plutôt que
"pompéienne." À Gaba, comme l'avait bien vu F. de Saulcy,[13] la
monnaie d'Hadrien datée ZOP, conservée à Paris et très lisible,
permet d'affirmer que l'année initiale de l'ère de Gaba n'est pas
antérieure à -60. Pour Pella, il semble que les monnaies datées ac-
tuellement connues montrent que cette année initiale ne peut être
comprise qu'entre -63 et -61. La monnaie de l'an BMC (242) (au rev.,
Athéna debout, Herzfelder 4) au droit de laquelle Commode est dit
Antōninos, ne peut en effet être antérieure à la mort de Marc-Aurèle
en mars 180. L'an 242 de Pella, selon l'ère pompéienne de -63,
correspond à 179/80: on doit alors estimer, avec Herzfelder, que cette
émission a été frappée entre avril et septembre 180 de notre ère. Mais
elle pourrait aussi bien être postérieure à 180. L'autre branche de la
fourche chronologique est donnée par les frappes monétaires de l'an
MC (240) de Pella au nom de *Loukios Aurēlios Komodos,* qui, elles,
ont pu être frappées *au plus tard* en avril de 180.[14] Elles excluent donc
une ère de -60, mais non notre hypothèse selon laquelle Pella aurait
adopté une ère de L. Marcius Philippus et modifié son nom un peu
plus tôt que Gaba, en -61, lors de la première année de charge du
promagistrat romain qui selon Appien resta deux ans en Syrie.

On est ainsi amené à proposer pour notre monnaie de Commode au
nymphée la date 179/80, celle de 181/82 pour les monnaies au type
d'Athéna de l'an 242, celle de 185/86 pour la pièce remarquable au
type de l'acropole. C'est à l'époque de Commode que la numismatique de Pella apparaît comme la plus riche et variée, sans qu'il soit
pour l'instant possible de mettre ce fait en relation avec une histoire
détaillée de la ville.

NOTES

1. B. Trell, "Epigraphica Numismatica: Monumental Nymphaea on Ancient Coins," *BASP* 15 (1978 = Studies Presented to Naphtali Lewis) 147-61 et pls. 1-2.
2. Entrée au Cabinet des Médailles de la Bibliothèque Nationale en 1973.
3. H. Herzfelder, "Contribution à la numismatique de la Décapole," *RN* (1936) 285-96 et pl. 6; H. Seyrig, "Temples, cultes et souvenirs historiques de la Décapole," *Antiquités syriennes* vi, 34-53 et pls. 12-13 (= *Syria* 36, 1959, 60-78).
4. Trell (cit. n. 1) 150. S'agit-il du nymphée dont "des traces" ont été reconnues lors d'une exploration archéologique conduite par R. H. Smith, du Collège de Wooster, Ohio (U. S. A.), en 1967? "Les tessons qu'on ramasse en surface montrent que la ville s'était développée à la période romaine. Le forum peut avoir été dans le *wadi* et avoir été entouré de rues à colonnades, de temples, de thermes et d'un nymphaeum dont il reste des traces aujourd'hui" (Chronique archéologique de la *Revue Biblique* 1968, 105-6, Communication de Robert H. Smith sur Pella).
5. Seyrig (cit. n. 3) p. 52, nos. 23 et 24, illustrés pl. 13, 23-24 (ici pl. 5.2, l'exemplaire conservé à Paris).
6. Herzfelder (cit. n. 3) 5 (an 246 de l'ère de Pella), ici pl. 5.3 (Paris); belle reproduction du revers agrandi de cette monnaie dans B. Trell et M. Price, *Coins and Their Cities* (London and Detroit 1977) 172, fig. 56.
7. Appien *Syr.* 51.
8. Par exemple F. de Saulcy, *Numismatique de la Terre Sainte* 340 (Titus), 341 (Trajan, Hadrien).
9. A. H. M. Jones dans son compte-rendu de A. Momigliano, *Ricerche sull' organizzazione della Giudea sotto il dominio romano* (63 a.C-70 d.C), *JRS* (1935) 228-31.
10. Citons encore Smith (cit. n. 4) 105: "Le *tell* principal est un monticule de 450 x 280 m, qui s'élève à 35 m au-dessus du Wadi Jirm, dans lequel coule une source abondante située à la base du *tell*. Le monticule semble être en grande partie artificiel. Son point le plus élevé est à 30 m au-dessous du niveau de la mer. Au sud du wadi se trouve une grande colline naturelle appelée Tell el Husn, qui se dresse majestueusement jusqu'à une hauteur de 90 m." Le nom moderne du site de Pella est Tabaqat Fahl.
11. Le début de cette légende monétaire mentionne aussi la proximité du fleuve (?) dont le nom commencerait par un kappa—cette fois sans article: $\Phi\iota\lambda\iota\pi(\pi\acute{\epsilon}\omega\nu)\,\tau(o\hat{v}$ ou $-\hat{\eta}_S)$ K(?).
12. B. V. Head, *Historia Nummorum* (Oxford 1911²) l'indique p. 786.
13. de Saulcy (cit. n. 8) 341 et 342.
14. Voici la récapitulation de ces équivalences:

	ère de -63	-62	-61	-60
année locale 240	A.D. 177/78	A.D. 178/79	A.D. 179/80	A.D. 180/81
année locale 242	A.D. 179/80	A.D. 180/81	A.D. 181/82	A.D. 182/83

7

NUMISMATIC EVIDENCE FOR THE SOUTHEAST (FORUM) FACADE OF THE BASILICA ULPIA

JAMES PACKER

At the beginning of the nineteenth century, only Trajan's Column marked the position of his renowned Forum in Rome. The column stood in a small, irregular piazza bounded on the north by two churches, the Madonna of Loreto and the Name of Maria, and the so-called Imperial Palace, which partially incorporated the latter shrine and provided the visual link between the two sanctuaries. To the south stretched the massive Convent of the Holy Spirit, while private houses of the late seventeenth or early eighteenth centuries closed the square to the east and west.[1]

Of Trajan's celebrated Basilica Ulpia, only the fame remained. But that alone was sufficient to prompt the French, when they occupied Rome in 1808, to undertake excavation of the monument. They demolished the Convent of the Holy Spirit, but—with some regret—decided to respect the churches and the palace on the opposite side of the square.[2] Exposing the central section of the Basilica Ulpia, they uncovered the foundations of the projecting porch and also two lateral porches, some fragments of the *giallo antico* stair which ran continuously along the whole southeast facade, giving access to the porches, and abundant pieces of the gray granite shafts of the interior columns.[3]

Unfortunately, the remains were very fragmentary,[4] and the southeast wall of the building—its facade on the Forum, is vital for any comprehensive understanding of the structure—had completely disappeared. Luckily, as early students of the basilica soon discovered, various coins which were struck to commemorate the completion of the Forum and its monuments represent that side of the building.[5] Yet, since these coins were never compared with one another, those who attempted theoretical reconstructions of the Ulpia in the nineteenth and early twentieth centuries failed to note the variations in such representations.

These portraits appear on the reverses of aurei and sestertii which display at least five general types.[6] The first, Type I, includes the   57

Fig. 1. Type I, obverse and reverse. *Courtesy American Numismatic Society*

Fig. 2. Type I, obverse and reverse. *Courtesy American Numismatic Society*

Fig. 3. Type I, obverse and reverse. *Courtesy American Numismatic Society*

Fig. 4. Type I, obverse and reverse. *Courtesy American Numismatic Society*

Fig. 5. Type I, obverse and reverse. *Courtesy American Numismatic Society*

Fig. 6. Type I, obverse and reverse. *Courtesy American Numismatic Society*

Fig. 7. Type I, obverse and reverse. *Courtesy American Numismatic Society*

Fig. 8. Type I, obverse and reverse. *Courtesy American Numismatic Society*

greatest number of examples (figs. 1-8).[7] In most instances (save where the coin is too worn), a circular, beaded border frames the southeast facade of the Ulpia, rendered frontally at approximately the observer's eye level. Three thick lines, broken at intervals to indicate the projecting porches, represent the front stairs. Each porch has two columns. Within the rectangular feature above the columns of each side porch (a combination of the entablature and attic), there is a generously proportioned recessed panel, perhaps a sculptured relief.[8] Inside the central porch, just below the entablature, is a small circular boss, probably a peculiarity of the die.[9] Two apparently freestanding columns, one on each side of the building, carry ressauts which support *signa*.[10] There seems to have been a frieze between these columns and the porches, but none of the coins in this group shows its character clearly.

The porches carry ornamental sculptures: a *biga* on each of the side porches; a *quadriga* on the central one. The heads of the horses which pull the chariots turn toward one another, and the *triumphatores* are clearly visible. With raised right arms, all three seem to salute the spectator.[11] Two figures (fully draped females?) flank the *quadriga*. Each carries an attribute (a palm branch?) in her right hand.[12] They appear to stand in the space between the central and the side porches, but this distortion arose largely from the fact that the engraver did not have the space to locate all the necessary figures above the central porch. None of these coins affords a good view of the second story behind the statuary, but all represent its entablature by a thick double line surmounted by nine cross-shaped antefixes, their arms curving slightly upward. The roof which, though low, would have been clearly visible from the Forum does not appear. As in all the coins showing this facade, the inscription, set closely under the building's front steps, reads BASILICAVLPIA.

Another coin, which we may classify as Type Ia (fig. 9),[13] closely resembles the preceding examples—with certain minor differences.[14] Three very thick lines indicate the stairs. The bases and obviously Corinthian capitals of the porch columns show up clearly, and the boss under the entablature of the central porch is lower than those of Type I and is displaced to the left. The columns on each side of the building stand out, but only the left ressaut is visible. The drivers in the *bigae* and the *quadriga* are missing, and the positions of the horses of the latter differ slightly from those on the previously discussed coins. The heads of the outer horses face away from the center of the porch, those of the middle horses towards it. The draped figures which flank the *quadriga* are crisply defined, and a long, slender attribute (a palm branch?) rests in the right hand of the left figure and the left hand of the right figure. Above the entablature of the second story are eleven antefixes of the type already described.

In Type II (figs. 10, 11), the colonnades of the porches are squat and heavy rectangular blocks represent the entablature-attics of the porches.[15] A frieze of crossed shields occupies the space between the porches. The drivers of the *bigae* and the *quadriga* are omitted, but an Ionic colonnade shows plainly behind the triumphal statuary.[16] It supports a double line, above which are twelve antefixes of the usual sort.

The single coin of Type III is intermediate between those of Types II and IV.[17] As in Type II, the heavy porch attics rest on stubby columns, but in Type III they are more nearly equal in width and almost completely obscure the frieze of crossed shields between the porches. Within the columns of the central porch are two columns of an internal colonnade and above is a crisp rendering of the *triumphator* in the central *quadriga. Signa* stand both at the corners of the side porches, flanking the *bigae,* and on the ressauts above the columns at each end of the building. Only six antefixes are visible above the thick line which indicates the entablature of the second-story Ionic colonnade.

On the sestertii of Type IV (figs. 12, 13), the porches resemble those of Type II, save that the columns and the entablature-attics are lighter.[18] As in Type III, there are smaller columns between those both of the central porch and of the porches at the sides.[19] The frieze of crossed shields between the porches shows up well, and the triumphal statuary closely resembles that shown on coins of Type II. As there, the Ionic colonnade is distinct, and a single line represents the upper sections of the building. The inscriptions differ from those of earlier examples. In addition to the words BASILICA VLPIA and below them SC, which run under the building, there is, around the edge of the coin, another phrase which reads SPQR OPTIMO PRINCIPI.[20]

Our last coin, Type V (fig. 14), differs considerably from any of the others.[21] The basilica's general form appears to be assimilated to that of a massive triumphal arch. Two lines render the steps, and the columns of the porches and the two freestanding columns at each side of the building clump together in groups of five on either side of a central open space below the central porch's entablature-attic. Behind the first row of columns is a second, visible between the columns of the front order. The capitals and bases of the columns are thick lines, the former giving a strong impression of the Corinthian order. Within the attics of all three porches are large rectangular recesses separated by standing male figures (surely Dacians). The latter seem to take the place of the frieze of crossed shields shown on coins of Types II and III, but in fact they were probably at the corners of the porches and, in trying to represent them, the die maker was forced to omit the frieze of shields.

The triumphal statuary on the porches also differs radically from that on any of the other coins we have reviewed. The horses of the central *quadriga* form pairs which face toward the corners of the porch, and the driver, raising his right arm in a salute, is clearly 61

Fig. 9. Type Ia, obverse and reverse. *Courtesy British Museum*

Fig. 10. Type II, obverse and reverse. *Courtesy American Numismatic Society*

Fig. 11. Type II, obverse and reverse. *Courtesy American Numismatic Society*

Fig. 12. Type IV, obverse and reverse. *Courtesy British Museum*

Fig. 13. Type IV, obverse and reverse. *Courtesy American Numismatic Society*

Fig. 14. Type V, obverse and reverse. *Courtesy British Museum*

shown. The two figures flanking the *quadriga* appear to be soldiers dressed in the usual short military tunic(?).[22] In place of the *bigae*, there are two equestrian figures on each lateral porch. Those on the left each raise an arm in the direction of the *quadriga*. Three lines on either side of the building represent the Ionic colonnade behind the statuary; the section of the building above the colonnade is again a single line. Eleven antefixes, each indicated by three large dots arranged in a triangle, complete the building.

The obverses of all the coins portray Trajan's right profile. He wears a toga (although in two examples his neck and shoulders are bare) and a laurel wreath, the ribbons of which cascade down his neck.[23] The inscriptions on the coins vary, but all date from Trajan's sixth consulship in A.D. 113.[24]

Thus the numismatic evidence, combined with the information from the excavations concluded between 1812 and 1814, gives a rather complete picture of the facade. It was approached by a stair of five treads (which the die makers regularly abbreviated to two or three lines). The three projecting front porches divided it into seven bays (including the porches), framed at either end by freestanding columns carrying ressauts. Most of the coins show the central porch as wider than the two which flank it, and the French excavations proved that the former had four columns (regularly reduced by the die makers to two); the latter had two apiece.

The treatment of the four bays bracketed by the porches and ressauts cannot be understood from representations of the building on any of the coin types. Following De Romanis, later restorers assumed that each was embellished with pilasters whose placement corresponded to the spacing of the columns of the internal colonnades.[25] Even in this century, De Romanis's suggestion has been taken up by Gatteschi and Gismondi.[26] Strack, however, postulated that the rear colonnades shown on some of the coins indicate that there was an open colonnade framed by the projecting porches and the freestanding columns at the ends of the structure—precisely the arrangement shown on the *Forma Urbis*.[27] Thus, in the light of the total lack of any evidence to the contrary, we may assume that the facade of the Ulpia was entirely open to the Forum. The continuous stair frequently mentioned above was, consequently, both utilitarian and ornamental.

All the porches supported high attics occupied by large, rectangular recesses framed by Dacian prisoners, and there was sculpture atop all three. At the ends of the facade on each ressaut were two *signa*. A *quadriga* crowned the center porch, a *biga* each of the side ones. Trajan presumably drove the *quadriga*, and the horses were posed so that the outside ones faced the corners of the porch, while the inner two looked toward its center.[28] In each *biga* the driver (one of Trajan's chief aides?) raised his right arm, and the heads of the two horses inclined toward one another.[29] A frieze of crossed shields decorated the attics of the bays between the porches, and a low Ionic colonnade

64

opened up the building's second story. The die makers all depicted the entablature above it as a single or double line, and, omitting the roof altogether, they showed a row of antefixes which must have crisply defined the building's profile against the sky.[30]

Thus we arrive at a surprisingly detailed portrait of the Ulpia's southeast facade. The use of this information, in conjunction with the architectural remains uncovered in the early nineteenth century and at the beginning of the 1930s, will make possible a reasonably accurate reconstruction of the basilica's general ancient appearance. And a reconstruction of this kind, although necessarily conjectural in some parts, should prove of prime interest to all students of Roman art and architecture.[31]

NOTES

1. A. Uggeri, *Della Basilica Ulpia nel Foro Traiano . . .* (Rome 1840) pl. 1, shows the general appearance of this square prior to 1812; his pl. 6 gives a schematic plan of the area in that period.

2. The best general account of the postantique history of the Forum is that of M. Bertoldi, "Ricerche sulla decorazione architettonica del Foro Traiano," *Studi miscellanei del Seminario di Archeologia e Storia dell'Arte Greca e Romana dell'Università di Roma* 3 (1962) 4-8. A. DeTournon, *Études statistiques sur Rome* (Paris 1831) 253, notes that the excavators agreed that the churches could not be demolished, even to set off Trajan's Column in the exact center of a new enclosure.

3. Antonio Nibby, in F. Nardini, *Roma antica, Roma riscontrata ed accresciuta delle ultime scoperte e con note ed osservazioni critiche antiquarie di Antonio Nibby* ii (Rome 1818) 348-58 (plan of A. De Romanis facing p. 348) and in *Roma nel 1838* ii (Rome 1839) 183-221, describes the excavations.

4. Nardini-Nibby (n. 3 above) 348: "Questo scavo. . . . ci abbia mostrato il Foro presso che totalmente distrutto, almeno in questo spazio."

5. Ibid. 355, recognizes the value of the numismatic evidence. Some of the earliest reproductions of these coins appear in F. Richter, *Il restauro del Foro Traiano* (Rome 1839) pl. 9 and L. Canina, *Monumenti inediti dell'Istituto di Corrispondenza Archeologica* 5 (Rome 1849-53) pl. 30.

6. Coins of Types I-III are aurei; those of IV, V are sestertii. I have collected much of the information in the following discussion through the help of the American Numismatic Society, which generously gave me access to its sales catalogue file. With the exception of the coin described as Type III (on which see n. 17) and those reproduced as figs. 9, 12, and 14, the coins discussed in this article are from the materials in that file. All the coins save the one Type III are numbered consecutively.

7. The bibliographical information for coins of Type I is as follows: 1. Adolph Hess, *Catalogue* 207 (Dec. 1, 1931) 43, pl. 24, no. 1040; 2. *Münzen und Medaillen* 4 (Nov. 3, 1945) 27, pl. 10, no. 419; 3. Santa Maria, *Catalogue* 1603A (June 26, 1950) 20, pl. 4, no. 85; 4. Glendening & Co., *Catalogue: Greek, Roman, English and Scottish Coins [of] the Late V. J. E. Ryan, Esq.* (Feb. 20, 1951) 26, pl. 6, no. 1725; 5. Otto Helbing, *Antike Münzen* (Dec. 9, 1932) 5, pl. 4, no. 66; 6. J. Vinchon, *Monnaies d'Or* (Oct. 29, 1962), pl. 1, no. 23; 7. *Münzen und Medaillen, Fixed Price List* (Feb., 1966) 4, pl. 2, no. 36; 8. *Münzen und Medaillen, Sammlung Walter Niggler,* pt. 3, *Römische Münzen* (Nov. 2-3, 1967) 20, pl. 8, no. 1219.

65

8. Seen best in figs. 6, 7, 8.

9. Bluma Trell suggested this possibility to me.

10. P. Strack, *Untersuchungen zur römischen Reichsprägung des zweiten Jahrhunderts* i (Stuttgart 1931) 204 and *BMCRE* iii 99, 207, note these side columns. M. W. Stoughton, "Architectural Representations on the Coinage of Trajan," unpublished seminar paper in the Library of the American Numismatic Society (1966) 13, identifies them "as the last supports of the enclosing colonnade." But see p. 64.

11. These gestures are most clearly seen in fig. 4.

12. The attribute of the figure to the left appears best in figs. 5, 6; that of the right figure in figs. 4, 5.

13. Fig. 9 (from the British Museum). This coin appears to be of the same type as that described in *BMCRE* iii 99 (no. 492), pls. 17, 15. It is cited by P. Zanker, *AA* 85 (1970-71) 520, n. 62.

14. In the following discussion, I note only the details by which the several types differ from the previously described coins.

15. Fig. 10: Jacob Hirsch, *Catalogue* 20 (Nov. 13, 1907) 59, pl. 18, no. 551; fig. 11: *Münzen und Medaillen* 15 (July 1-2, 1955) 53, pl. 27, no. 763.

16. Of the early writers, only T. L. Donaldson, *Architectura Numismatica* (original ed. 1859; reprt. Chicago 1966) 253, has noted this colonnade.

17. This coin, probably an aureus, appears in E. Nash, *A Pictorial Dictionary of Ancient Rome* (New York and Washington 1968²), 450, pl. 548. Nash implies that it is the coin cited in *BMCRE* iii as no. 492, pl. 17, no. 15, but the two plainly come from different dies.

18. This coin (fig. 12) is of the same type as that shown in *BMCRE* iii 207, pl. 38, no. 8, and like it is in the British Museum; *Münzen und Medaillen, Sammlung Walter Niggler* (2-3 Nov. 1967) 20, pl. 9, no. 1224 = no. 13. Zanker (n. 13 above) 520, n. 62, cites both, and the latter is the clearest representation of the southeast facade of any of the coins treated here.

19. See p. 64 and nn. 25, 26.

20. On fig. 12, the left corner of the building intervenes between the first and second words; on fig. 13, the building's corners produce the following breaks: SPQROP TIMOPRIN CIPI.

21. Fig. 14: *BMCR* iii 208, no. 983. See also H. Cohen, *Description historique des monnaies frappés sous l'empire romaine* ii (Paris and London 1882) 22, no. 44. Like coins of Type IV, those of Type V have an inscription around the edge which reads: SPQR OPTIMO PRINCIPI. As Cohen notes, the British coin illustrated in fig. 14 spells the latter word PRNCIPI.

22. The scale of these soldiers is too small to know whether the die maker intended to show them in their everyday uniform—in which case they would have been wearing tunics—or in formal parade dress—a cuirass (molded or segmental) and a kilt of leather or heavy cloth. On these distinctions see I. A. Richmond, "Trajan's Army on Trajan's Column," *BSR* 13 (1935) 6 and L. Rossi, *Trajan's Column and the Dacian War* (Ithaca 1971) 83-84, 88.

23. Figs. 12, 14.

24. Strack (n. 10 above) 205; *BMCRE* iii, pls. 80, 81. On figs. 1-9, the inscription reads: IMP TRAIANO AUG GER DAC PM TRP COS VI PP; on figs. 10-11: IMP TRAIANVS AUG GER DAC PM TRP COS VI PP; on figs. 12-14: IMP CAES NERVAE TRAIANO AUG GER DAC PM TRP COS VI PP.

25. For De Romanis's restored plan of the area of the basilica, uncovered in the excavations completed in 1812-14, see n. 3 above. L. Canina took up this notion, rendering it persuasively in several publications: *Architettura antica*, pt. 3, *Architettura romana* (Rome 1830-40) pl. 90; *Edifici di Roma antica* (Rome 1848) pl. 121.

26. G. Gatteschi published numerous editions of his famous drawings, but one of the more accessible is *Restauri della Roma imperiale* (Rome 1924). His design for the

66

southeast facade of the Ulpia appears as pl. 69. I. Gismondi never wrote an essay explaining his ideas for a restoration of the Ulpia, but they are illustrated in his frequently reproduced plan of the imperial fora and in his well-known model of ancient Rome (executed between 1933 and 1973 by Pierino Di Carlo), now exhibited in Rome's Museum of Roman Civilization. In the plan he renders a closed facade (apparently without pilasters); in the model there is an arcade, designed after that on the facade of the Basilica Julia in the Roman Forum. The plan was published originally in G. Lugli, *Roma antica, il centro monumentale* (Rome 1946) pl. 5 (facing p. 256). A good contemporary photograph of the facade of the Ulpia from the model appears in L. B. Dal Maso, *Rome of the Caesars,* trans. M. Hollingworth (Florence 1975) 65.

27. Strack (n. 10 above) 204; G. Carettoni et al., *La pianta marmorea di Roma antica* (Rome 1960) 89, pls. 3, 28.

28. With respect to the appearance of the horses of the two *bigae* and the *quadriga,* the coins give contradictory evidence. Type I coins (figs. 1-8) show all the horses looking toward the centers of the porches; in Types Ia, II, IV (figs. 9, 11, 13), the two outer horses of the *quadriga* face the corners of the porch. On the other coins, the precise poses of the horses are not clear. We have no way of knowing which pose is the correct one.

29. The coins of Type V are again the exceptions to this description, replacing the *bigae* on each of the side porches with two equestrian statues turned toward the central *quadriga.* The designer of these two coins was presumably working from a description of the Ulpia rather than from any firsthand knowledge of the structure.

30. Bluma Trell has suggested to me that, following the conventions of buildings represented on Roman coins from the East, these features may not have been antefixes but merlons or perhaps crenelations. For examples of similar features, see M. J. Price and B. L. Trell, *Coins and Their Cities: Architecture on the Ancient Coins of Greece, Rome, and Palestine* (London and Detroit 1977) figs. 225, 229, 243, 501.

31. Both P. H. von Blanckenhagen, "The Imperial Fora," *JSAH* 13, no. 4 (1954) 26, n. 1, and H. Plommer, "Trajan's Forum: A Plea," *Proceedings of the Cambridge Philological Society* 186, n.s. 6 (1960) 62, lament the lack of a final publication of the Forum of Trajan based on the excavations of the early 1930s.

8

PAINTINGS AS A SOURCE OF INSPIRATION FOR ANCIENT DIE ENGRAVERS

MARTIN PRICE

One of Bluma Trell's many endearing qualities is her persistence in pursuing avenues of research that have never before been explored. To have been her companion on such journeys has been an honor indeed, and by way of recompense I offer to her this short essay, the result of just such an excursion, in the hope that it will underline once again that buildings were not the only designs which were chosen to be placed on ancient coins.

To those familiar with the vast array of ancient coin types, it will not come as a surprise to learn that buildings actually play a rather small part in the total repertory. Far more extensive is the array of statuary that has been preserved in these miniature representations. Sculptures in the round which have survived, whether as originals or in copies, may be compared with the coin types to show without question that the engraver drew his inspiration directly from this medium. Cult images may be recognized on coins from the appearance of the same figure in the same pose within its shrine and also alone, often depicted in great detail as the main coin design. In this way the coins are a rich source for the study of statues which have no longer survived.

In this essay, however, it is another art form which must hold our attention, one which has sometimes been quoted as the origin of certain coin designs, but an art of which our knowledge today is woefully inadequate, relying as it does on the chance survival of wall paintings in tombs or in well-preserved houses such as those of Pompeii and Herculaneum. Not a single work by Apelles, Zeuxis, or Nicomachus has survived. Yet these were the giants of painting of the fifth and fourth centuries B.C. Their names were as familiar and important to the ancients as Leonardo da Vinci or Raphael are to us today. Original works of the great sculptors of the fifth and fourth centuries B.C. survive to allow us to study them at first hand, but the great frescoes of the Stoa Poikile in the Agora at Athens, for example, which even in Pausanias's day were seriously deteriorating, have 69 crumbled into oblivion, never to be resurrected.[1] Yet it must be remembered that painting was as major an art in the Hellenistic and Roman periods as it was in the Renaissance. Pliny names 405 famous painters in his account of the subject, but only 225 sculptors.[2] Philostratus devoted a book to descriptions which purport to have been inspired by some seventy famous paintings. Finally, if money reflects interest, M. Agrippa is reported to have paid to the city of Cyzicus the sum of HS 1,200,000 for two paintings.[3] There can be no doubt that painting was as likely a source for coin types as sculpture or architecture. Since our knowledge of ancient painting is so slight, how much more important is it to try to establish whether lost paintings have survived in miniature coin designs. Two recent discoveries—paintings in the so-called tomb of Philip II at Vergina (attributed by the excavator, without much plausibility, to Nicomachus)[4] and in the tomb of the late Roman painter Flavius Chrysanthius[5]—underline that the future may provide important evidence to fill the gaps in our knowledge. In the meantime, we can but attempt to establish criteria for comparing the designs of coinage with monumental paintings.

There are three aspects of painting technique which are shared by both coins and large reliefs and which distinguish them from sculpture in the round. First, perspective is achieved by placing the planes of action in tiers. This gives a perfectly intelligible sense of distance and at the same time allows the artist greater freedom in depicting figures which would otherwise be obscured. For example, the engraver of a coin of Synnada, Phrygia (fig. 1), shows the action of a hunt in the amphitheater—a lion chasing a stag in the center of the ring, a *bestiarius* halting the charge of a boar with his spear in the front, and an *ursarius* making a leap over a bear in the distance. This is exactly how the painter would have shown it, giving the impression of a bird's-eye view, but with no further evidence it would be foolhardy to suggest that the Synnada coin was derived from a painting. Although it is clear that there are similarities of technique in the execution of a painting and in the cutting of a shallow relief coin die, care must be taken not to assume that such similarity must imply the existence of a common origin.

Secondly, narrative is possible in paintings and reliefs by depicting a frieze of continuous scenes in a way that is hardly possible in freestanding sculpture. Similarly, the restricting area of a coin die does not lend itself to narrative. Thus, when it does appear, the possibility that the design may have been borrowed from an original in another medium should be considered. Such a case is the depiction of the story of Noah made at Apamea in Phrygia (fig. 2). Thirdly, paintings and, much more rarely, reliefs often make a point of naming the person illustrated, which provides a key to scenes that might not otherwise be immediately intelligible. Thus the Noah story, which must have been unfamiliar to the Greeks in Asia Minor, requires that his name be written on the Ark.

Fig. 1. Hunt in an amphitheater on a coin of Synnada in Phrygia. *Courtesy British Museum*

Fig. 2. Story of Noah on a coin of Apamea in Phrygia. *Courtesy British Museum*

70

These three aspects of technique may be helpful in deciding whether a particular design on a coin owes its inspiration to a painting, but it should be emphasized that coin engravers must have been capable of creating their own designs, using similar techniques, and that the presence of any one or other of these does not imply that a painting or a relief must have been the origin of the coin type. Indeed, many of the paintings that have survived are but simple figures or groups which, when transferred to the miniature relief of a coin flan, cannot be distinguished from sculpture.

One of the first coin types[6] to be linked with a painting is a distinctive design found at Deultum in Thrace depicting Perseus rescuing Andromeda (fig. 3). This occurs three times at that mint, under Macrinus, Gordian III, and Philip I.[7] In each case the details of the representation are similar: Andromeda stands on a higher plane than Perseus with a snake-monster at her feet. Perseus stands with his right foot on a rock and his right hand raised to the elbow of Andromeda's outstretched left arm. The scene immediately recalls that of a painting from Pompeii (fig. 4), although in the latter there is one major difference—the complete absence of the monster—and several minor differences. Pompeii had been destroyed long before the issues of the coins, but the similarity is sufficiently striking to permit the suggestion that the coins and painting were derived from a common original. There is, however, no reason to suppose that the original was itself a painting. Indeed, consideration of the details of the composition would suggest that the original was a sculpture in the round. In particular, the manner in which Perseus's raised arm supports that of Andromeda, a gesture that is distinctly unnatural, looks as if the original required such a support for the outstretched arm, and therefore was a sculpture. With the appearance of this unusual group in the coinage of the city on three separate occasions, it is fairly certain that there existed at Deultum a statue of this type sufficiently well known to be adopted as a design on the coinage.

Of the coins so far illustrated, only that depicting the story of Noah might claim to have been derived from a painting. The scene occurs four times in the coinage of Apamea. Under Severus Alexander, Gordian III, and Philip I, the design is so closely similar in the treatment of figures, birds, and Ark that we may assume either that the later issues were copying the earlier issue or that all were copying a common original. The last issue, under Trebonianus Gallus,[8] reverses the design, and slightly alters the roof (lid) of the Ark (κιβωτὸς), but otherwise repeats all the general details. The narrative element, through which the figures are shown both within the Ark and on dry land and the successful and unsuccessful doves are shown together, is more suited to paintings and reliefs than to the miniature treatment of a coin design, for which one or the other element might have sufficed to symbolize the story. The name of Noah included by all the engravers on the Arks is a further detail which might lend some   71

Fig. 3. Perseus and
Andromeda on a coin found
at Deultum in Thrace.
Courtesy British Museum

Fig. 4. Perseus and
Andromeda on a Pompeian
wall painting. *Courtesy
British Museum*

substance to the idea that the general details of the design were
borrowed from a monumental painting.

This example illustrates the difficulty of deciding from a coin alone
whether a design must have originated from a painting, even if several
depictions of the same scene are used for coinage at different times.
Another coin of Apamea in Phrygia, showing Marsyas and Athena,
was regarded as a "certain case" by Macdonald, because the head of
the goddess mirrored in the pool "is a feature that only a painter
would have introduced into the composition."[9] But since the
engraver of the coin also introduced it into his design, there seems to
be no reason to suppose that a relief sculptor would have been unable
to do so. Such an argument must be resisted. Indeed, of all the
examples suggested by Macdonald, who is the main proponent of the
influence of painting on coin designs, the only one at all persuasive is
that depicting the story of Hero and Leander.

This design appears three times at Abydus (fig. 5) under Commodus, Caracalla, and Severus Alexander, and once at Sestus under
Caracalla (fig. 6). The Abydus design emphasizes details which

72

strongly suggest that a painting, or at least a relief, was the original. The window in the tower, prominently preserved on all the coins, is empty, but it is clearly here that we should imagine Hero leaning out anxiously with her lamp, as she does in other representations.[10] The coin of Sestus is similar in composition and in the detail of the window, but differs from the Abydus coins in the position of Leander's arms, of Hero's hand as it rests on the parapet, and in the absence of Eros. It is at least possible to say that the Sestus coin is not copying, except in the most general way, the earlier coin of Commodus at Abydus. It is far more likely that they are independently copying a common original, and it is the window in the tower that underlines that common origin. The charming figure of Eros on the Abydus coin reflects directly the passage in Statius where Cupid is made to observe that he carried his torch before the swimming Leander.[11] Such a detail may be more than coincidence. On the Sestus coin Leander appears to be reaching for the rocks, safe after his perilous journey. On the Abydus piece his weapons and clothes are visible on the Asian shore, and he seems to be looking into the distance to where Hero stands. Such elements of narrative may well indicate an original that showed several scenes of the story. In that case a painted original would seem to be a strong possibility. It is, however, impossible to say whether Ovid or Statius knew of such a painting, and since we do not know that such a painting existed, we can only offer it as one possible suggestion for the origin of this attractive scene.

In order to find a coin type which comes close to representing a known painting, we must turn to the Roman Republican series.[12] The reverse of a denarius struck by L. Plautius Plancus in 47 B.C. depicts a winged Victory holding a palm branch and leading a team of four horses (fig. 7). Somewhat surprisingly, the engraver has shown only half the body of the leading horse. This would not be particularly significant if we did not know from Pliny that the moneyer's brother, L. Munatius Plancus, had placed in the Capitol a painting by Nicomachus showing Victory leading a *quadriga*.[13] The coincidence between the painting and the coin type is too great to be ignored, even if the commemoration of one brother's pious action by another on a coin seems distinctly unlikely. It is to be noticed that the family cognomen has been placed with the type on the coin, and it seems at least possible that the moneyer had adopted a type that would be recognizable as representing the family name. A painting by Nicomachus, of sufficient merit to be mentioned by Pliny, could well be a family heirloom, and if so, would certainly be distinctive enough to be used as the symbol of the Plancus family.[14] The coin shows a lively group of horses similar in many ways to the signed dies of late-fifth-century engravers at Syracuse. We do not know whether Nicomachus's painting was in this vein, but the manner in which the leading horse disappears behind the border of the coin is perhaps a conscious attempt to indicate that the design has been taken from an

Fig. 5. Hero and Leander on a coin of Abydus. *Courtesy British Museum*

Fig. 6. Hero and Leander on a coin of Sestus. *Courtesy British Museum*

Fig. 7. Winged Victory and a team of four horses on a Roman Republican coin. *Courtesy British Museum*

73

Fig. 8. Heracles and Auge on a coin of the Ionian League. *Courtesy British Museum*

Fig. 9. Hector and Patroclus on a coin of Ilium. *Courtesy British Museum*

Fig. 10. Cult image, Temple of Dikaiosyne, on a coin of Prymnessus. *Courtesy British Museum*

original that itself continued further—to show, in fact, the chariot to which the horses belong.

A similar detail is to be remarked on the fine medallion of the Ionian League depicting the meeting of Heracles and Auge (fig. 8). Incongruously placed upright at the side of the design is Heracles's bow-case. To a certain extent it balances the rather heavy mass of the rock on which he is sitting, but this would seem to be a minor consideration compared with the strange way that it stands alone. The artist might have used such a device to lead the eye to the left, thus indicating that the design had been inspired by an original which depicted more of the story. Today, however, without the evidence of such an original, to suspect that we have here a design derived from a painting can only be speculation.

Perhaps the nearest that we can reach towards assuming a painted original for a coin type is at the city of Ilium (fig. 9). We can be sure at least that the houses and civic buildings of that city were richly decorated with paintings, and many of these must have depicted scenes from the Trojan cycle. The coin in question has a feature similar to that of the medallion of the Ionian League—a shield is shown leaning against the border of the design in a notably unnatural manner. Here, too, it may be suggested that the coin type was but part of a more monumental original design, and that the naming of the figures of Hector and Patroclus could also be taken to be part of that original and serve as an indication that the original was a painting.

However tantalizing it might be to know with fair certainty that if die engravers used buildings and statues as models for their coin designs they would also have used paintings, we must restrain ourselves from assuming too readily that an attractive coin design must have been borrowed from a painting. This is to give no credit to the skill of the engraver. At Prymnessus one remarkable design (fig. 10), which occurs twice, under Gordian I and Gallienus, shows the cult image of Dikaiosyne from the city's main temple raised aloft by winged Nikai. Below, two Erotes sit astride fish-tailed monsters with centaur foreparts. One is holding a torch. On the head of the image the eagle of Rome alights with spread wings. It would be easy to imagine such a scene enlarged to monumental size to adorn a wall of the city's Bouleuterion, but it would be pure fantasy to do so, and would, indeed, involve an assumption that the coin engraver could not have designed such a die to do honor to the city's cult image. Without the original for comparison, it must be conceded that any identification of a coin with a painted original involves a series of assumptions. It is perhaps more satisfactory to enjoy the work of the die engravers than to build false impressions of hypothetical originals.

74

NOTES

1. Pausanias 1.15.
2. Pliny, *N. H.* 35.1ff.
3. Pliny, *N. H.* 35.26.
4. *BCH* (1978) 708-9; *Arch. Reports* (1977-78) 47.
5. *Anatolian Studies* (1978) 33-34.
6. J. Svoronos, *ArchEph* (1889) 97.
7. J. Jurukova, *Die Münzprägung von Deultum* (Berlin 1973) nos. 61, 411, 445.
8. *SNG* von Aulock no. 3513.
9. G. Macdonald, *Coin Types, Their Origin and Development* (Glasgow 1905) 171.
10. *NC* (1971) 129-30.
11. Statius 1.2.87-89.
12. M. Crawford, *Roman Republican Coinage* (London 1974) 468, no. 453. I am grateful to A. Burnett for drawing my attention to this coin. Another suggested equation of coin (*RIC* vii Constantinople 19) with a description of a painting (Eusebius *Vita* 3.3) is less convincing. See *Journal of the Society for Ancient Numismatics* 3 (1975) 47-48.
13. Pliny, *N. H.* 35.108.
14. A reminder, perhaps, of the events surrounding the acquisition of the picture by a Munatius Plancus ancestor. There appears to be no reason to assume, as Grueber (*BMCRR* 516-17, n. 2), that L. Munatius Plancus had acquired the painting only shortly before dedicating it on the Capitol.

9

A RARE GREEK IMPERIAL COIN
OF GANGRA IN PAPHLAGONIA
ANNE S. ROBERTSON

Over twenty years ago, A. D. Bellinger wrote of Greek imperial coins, "If these coins are artistically the step-children of the Greek numismatists, economically they are the step-children of the Roman."[1] In recent decades, Bluma Trell has labored valiantly to upgrade Greek imperials from the status of Greek stepchildren, particularly through her work on architectural coin types.[2] I hope she will welcome this present attempt to treat them as more than Roman stepchildren by putting them—or at least one of them—into the family setting of Roman imperial currency.

In his *Greek Coins in the Hunterian Collection* (i–iii, 1899–1905), Sir George Macdonald listed a rare coin (fig. 1) of Gangra in Paphlagonia (ii 235) and illustrated only its reverse (pl. 45, 14). Its description is as follows:[3]

Obv. AYT· K·M· AYP/ ANTΩNINOΣ
Bust of Caracalla, laureate, cuirassed, r. (Bust seen from back)

Rev. APXEO
ΠΑΦΛΑ   ΓΑΝΓΡΑ
(above)   (in exergue)

Two buildings or gate-towers, with steeply pitched roofs, that on l. being taller. On either side a tall tower, each with door.

AE   Wt. 15.56 g.   Size 31 mm.   Axis ↓

Fig. 1. Greek imperial coin of Gangra in Paphlagonia, obverse and reverse. *Courtesy Hunter Coin Cabinet, University of Glasgow*

Macdonald observed that Gangra "appears to have been a fortress, round which in the early days of the Empire, there grew up a town that received the name of Germanicopolis. The legend on the reverse is probably an abbreviation of ἀρχαιόπολις or ἀρχαιοτάτης Παφ-λαγονίας. By the early third century A.D., Paphlagonia was in truth the archaic or ancient name of the district in which Gangra stood."

Fifty years ago, Sir Ian Richmond discussed in detail the buildings or structures on the reverse of the Hunter coin and on the reverse of a   77 similar coin from Gangra, now in Berlin.[4] Richmond, working from casts of the reverses of the Hunter and Berlin coins (which are from different dies), described the structures as, from left to right: a tall, flat-roofed tower with ground-floor door; a section of the city wall, shown higher than the left-hand tower, possibly due "to a desire to indicate that the left-hand tower is shown in perspective," and the back of the city wall "shown returning towards the centre of the coin in sharp perspective, reduced"; "two central buildings"; and, at the extreme right, a flat-roofed battlemented tower with ground-floor door. He added that the two central buildings, not battlemented, were not gates, had steeply pitched overhanging roofs, and appear to have been separated by a narrow alley. He suggested that the two buildings may have represented the city forum in section and the basilica.

The cast from the Hunter coin used by Richmond was less clear and sharp than the cast now available. On the latter it looks as if there was, between his "two central buildings," a wooden door with latticework top, or else a railed walkway between the two "buildings," which would then be gate towers. This does not, however, explain the "alley" or space between the latticed structure and the "building" on the left, nor the differences in the height, doorways, and other details of the "two central buildings." Richmond interpreted the latticework as the tiled roof of a lower lean-to, but, had he been writing later in his career, he might not have dismissed the possibility of the "two central buildings" being gates because of the steeply pitched roofs without battlements (or—his word—merlons). Roman imperial gate towers, it is now known, did commonly have tiled pitched roofs, instead of flat tops with battlements.

Of the city of Gangra, no remains have been uncovered and recorded in modern times, so that there is no archaeological evidence with which to compare the Gangra coin type showing city buildings. In any case, it probably would be fruitless to try to extricate the true likeness and character of these buildings from what was essentially a "bird's-eye" view of a city in the eastern empire with city walls, entrances, towers, and so on. It would be more profitable to note parallels and a possible source of inspiration for the bird's-eye view of a city type either in Greek imperial coinage or in the rest of Roman imperial coinage.

In the repertoire of Greek imperial coin types, there have survived fewer coins with bird's-eye views of a city than of other structures, especially temples. One of the very few really convincing (and engaging) city views was that on bronze medallions of Philip I (A.D. 244–48) from Bizya in Thrace, an example of which was acquired by the British Museum in recent years.[5] The reverse shows a monumental gateway, encircling city walls and towers, and a "back gate," but the internal buildings are sketchily represented by two stoas, a temple, and possible public baths. This is shorthand for a city, and the

Gangra reverse type was telescoped even more, being simply the *disiecta membra* of a city.

Attempts have sometimes been made to show that reverse types of Greek imperial coins were copied from specific reverses of Roman imperial coins. There is no known example of a Roman coin of the first to third centuries A.D. with a bird's-eye view of a city except the simple city type of Emerita in Spain, which was used on the gold and silver of Augustus,[6] and which was, indeed, also used on contemporary local bronze of Emerita.[7] The known bird's-eye views on Roman imperial coins before about A.D. 260 were almost invariably of circuses, as, for example, on coins of Titus, Trajan, Severus, and Caracalla.[8] The bird's-eye view of a city type seems, on Greek imperial coins, to have been homegrown and not inspired by Rome.

The obverse of the Gangra coin in the Hunter collection gives an imperial title whose Latin form, IMP C M AVR ANTONINVS, with the addition of (PIVS) AVG, was used on Roman coins of Caracalla from A.D. 198, in the reign of his father, Severus (A.D. 193–211); and on Roman coins of Elagabalus, great-nephew of Severus, from A.D. 218–22. The obverse type of the Gangra coin shows a youngish bust, with head laureate r., and a distinctive cuirass, much of which is visible, viewed from the back. This distinctive cuirass seen from the back was popular on late Antonine coins from the Roman mint. It also appeared on sestertii of Severus,[9] but hardly ever on the sestertii of Caracalla minted in Severus's reign,[10] and rarely, if at all, on sestertii of Elagabalus. Its life at the Roman mint seems to have been coming to an end by about A.D. 211.

A long-standing confusion between the young Caracalla and Elagabalus, and their coins, has been resolved by Roman numismatists in recent decades, with the aid, for example, of the high TR P numbering attained on Caracalla's coins (TR P = A.D. 198 to TR P XX = A.D. 217 in his sole reign), and of the title BRIT(ANNICVS), held by Caracalla but not by Elagabalus. This confusion has not yet been fully resolved in the Greek imperial series, where doubt still persists at times about the attribution of coins to the young Caracalla or to Elagabalus.[11] How alike the two men were, with common ancestors in the parents of the two sisters, Julia Domna and Julia Maesa, who were mother and grandmother to Caracalla and Elagabalus respectively, may be seen from their portraits on Roman coins.[12] In cases where likeness and imperial title on Greek imperial coins might be appropriate to either the young Caracalla or to Elagabalus, it might be helpful to find a diagnostic feature on Roman contemporary coins, like the distinctive cuirass, which on the Gangra coin was surely worn by the young Caracalla.

The Hunter example of the Gangra coin has a weight below that of most Roman sestertii of the early third century A.D. (which did, however, vary considerably in weight), but its die axis can be paralleled on contemporary Roman issues. The axis is not always recorded for Greek imperial coins, but it might prove of interest to discover a pattern, chronological or geographical, to regular relationships between obverse and reverse dies.

The obverse and reverse dies of the Hunter example of the Gangra coin were evidently engraved by the same hand or in the same workshop. The letters on both sides are exactly similar, as are also the borders of dots and the central sinkings. The reverse type looks like local work, but the obverse type has an official appearance. It may, as has been suggested, have been copied from a Roman imperial coin, but, as already noted, an exact model for the distinctively cuirassed bust is hard to find on Roman coins of Caracalla. It may, on the other hand, have been derived from an *imago* of the imperial personage, such as must have been needed initially at Rome itself, or in any other mint in the empire. It would not, in fact, have been beyond the bounds of possibility to send out obverse dies (or even hubs) from Rome or another central point. However, in the case of the Gangra coin, the close kinship of the obverse and reverse dies makes this unlikely.

In the mint of Rome itself, special treatment of obverse dies, as distinct from reverse dies, has been postulated by Roman numismatists as a result of recent intensive study and analysis of the officina system. A system of six officinae or workshops in the Roman mint was fully established by the reign of Philip I (A.D. 244–48), with each officina signing its work (I-VI, or A-S), and each using a single reverse type. The arrangement of a six-officina system may be traced to as early a date as the late first century A.D., although without the use of officina marks.

In the course of these officina studies, it was noted that one reverse die was often used with two or more obverse dies. This has suggested that, in the Roman mint, each officina retained its own authorized reverse die, but returned an obverse die, after each period of work, to a central repository or office in the mint for safekeeping and reissue for each subsequent spell of work. This practice would prevent the illegitimate use of a die with the name, titles, and likeness of an imperial personage.

It would not be surprising if, in the Greek imperial series, a stricter official control was exercised over the use of obverse dies than of reverse dies. Although Asia, for example, was one of the largest and richest of the Roman provinces, it was still a Roman province—even if once proud and ancient cities clung to old names for parts of a province, as did Paphlagonia. As a Roman province, Asia had a large body of imperial civil servants, including finance and tax officers, operating within a service whose career structure required their transfer about the Roman Empire to carry out imperial policy, some of whose elements at least were of general application. The watchdog presence of such imperial civil servants in Asia might explain any discrepancy between an official-looking obverse (which they might have to authorize) and a local-looking reverse, as on the Gangra coin.

Any discussion of the dies used in Greek imperial coins in Asia has to face differences in the conclusions drawn by various scholars. Louis Robert, for example, considered that dies were shared within a fairly small radius,[13] while Konrad Kraft demonstrated die-linking over a wide area, with a limited number of centers or workshops in Asia responsible for their production.[14] Apparent differences may have been due to the varying importance to the Roman government of individual cities and districts at different periods, to the emperor's travels through certain areas, or to his visits, long or short, to one city or another.

There were certain cities whose importance was long-lasting, as, for example, Antioch in Pisidia, whose Greek imperial coins have been the subject of meticulous study by Aleksandra Krzyzanowska.[15] Antioch, originally a Roman (Augustan) colony, was on one of the most important routes to the Further East, and emperors such as Severus, Gordian III, and Philip I, engaged on campaigns against the Parthians and the Persians, passed through, their visits being recorded by abundant Greek imperial issues in bronze from the Antioch mint. This coinage was issued with weights approximating those of Roman imperial bronze, and with obverse and reverse types strongly romanized and influenced, if not dictated, by Roman imperial policy. About 80 percent of the reverse types reflect the conventional substantive types familiar on Roman imperial coins, a higher proportion than from any other city in Asia. The remaining 20 percent represent local architecture and culture.

Between Antioch in Pisidia, on a route which imperial travelers and armies and civil servants could hardly avoid using, and Paphlagonia, on the southern shore of the Black Sea, which could be very easily bypassed, there lay an infinite variety of Greek imperial cities whose Roman imperial importance fluctuated throughout the reigns from Augustus to Gallienus. No wonder the whole repertory of Greek imperial coins in Asia alone manifests a bewildering complexity.

Die-linking between reverses may demonstrate either the sharing of dies or the supplying of dies by local or regional workshops or centers, which chose their own designs or types so far as these were not inspired or ordered by Roman imperial policy or officials, as at Antioch in Pisidia. The sharing of obverse dies might demonstrate something rather different: the sphere of activity and geographical range of imperial civil servants who might have to authorize or initiate the use of obverse dies (or hubs) with the changing titles and likenesses of imperial personages.

During the first to third centuries A.D., the mint of Rome and other major imperial mints with periodic activity (like Lyons in the west and

81

Antioch in the east) had to provide an abundant and unceasing flow of gold and silver coin for paying the imperial civil service and the higher ranks of the army, and for state contracts (and, from Severus onwards, for private soldiers' pay, which had been steadily increased since the reign of Domitian). The gold and silver currency was needed in both the western and eastern empires, and much of it was probably delivered direct in bulk.

Until the time of Severus, bronze currency was also required for the payment of rank-and-file legionaries and auxiliaries. In the west this at times involved the delivery directly to army units of newly minted, uncirculated bronze, like the Asses of Domitian of A.D. 86 found in North Britain, or the newly minted bronze of Marcus Caesar of A.D. 140–44, and of Pius of A.D. 154–55, found on the Antonine Wall,[16] about two thousand miles from Rome, in the opposite direction from, say, Paphlagonia. New military bronze and other bronze coins acquired through normal circulation came in due course to form the small change of the provincials of the western empire. From the reign of Augustus onwards, such bronze coins stood in relation to gold and silver as a purely token currency.

In the eastern empire, especially in Asia, military bronze was not as much needed as a bulk delivery, since legions and auxilia were less often permanently stationed there in large numbers. Small change, apart from any arriving by the normal processes of circulation, had to be supplied by the cities. Such Greek imperial issues would not have been simply tolerated by the Roman imperial government as a rather engaging and harmless antiquarian phenomenon, flourishing "in a state of complete metrological anarchy."[17] Their production must have been encouraged, if not even initiated, as a matter of imperial policy to avoid the expense of distributing immense quantities of "civilian" bronze to provincials so far from Rome. The form or extent of such encouragement or instruction may be unknown, but the agents must have been carrying out the emperor's policy.

Through imperial finance and tax officers, whose net was thrown provincewide, machinery in fact existed for authorizing the production of Greek imperial coins anywhere and for the use of approved obverse dies. Reverse dies and types could have been less strictly supervised and left at times to local or regional initiative. How widely Greek imperial coins circulated must have been a question of their acceptance by those in need of small change (like, perhaps, British trade tokens). Conclusions about circulation will become more and more firmly based as the accurate recording of coin finds in eastern provinces of the Roman Empire continues to become more widely established.

Throughout the whole Roman Empire, the continued maintenance of an adequate supply of currency in gold, silver, and bronze was a constant concern of the emperors of the first to early third centuries A.D. It is on record that "Trajan melted down all the worn-out currency."[18] This does not imply a general demonetization of old coin, which in the vast empire would have been an impossible task. It simply made explicit a continuous process of small-scale demonetization, as certain issues of coins and certain denominations (for example, the good silver denarii of the earlier centuries of the empire), were quietly withdrawn from circulation and returned to the mint or mints for melting down.

The continuous process was largely achieved by money changers, who served as bankers and also performed the function of bureaux de change.[19] On civil service instructions, money changers would simply not recirculate any coins on a "forbidden" list, but would hand them over for reminting in return for new coins.

Greek imperial coins would be subject to this process of small-scale demonetization, for they provided the cheapest source of bronze for subsequent issues. Continuing work on the scientific analysis of Greek imperials should throw light on this, as on other sources for the metal.

In recent decades, the dauntingly wide but infinitely promising field of Greek imperial coinage has attracted a growing number of Greek numismatists. I hope that they will not mind—I hope that Bluma Trell will not mind—this small attempt by a Roman numismatist to bring these "stepchildren" into a Roman family group and to ask them some questions appropriate to that family group. Each Greek imperial series has a voice with which to answer, though the answers given may vary from time to time and place to place within the vast imperial framework. Even a tiny voice like that of the Gangra coin has a contribution to make.

NOTES

1. "Greek Mints under the Roman Empire," *Essays in Roman Coinage Presented to Harold Mattingly* (Oxford 1956) 137ff.
2. For example, in her own numerous articles and most recently in Price and Trell, *Coins and Their Cities: Architecture on the Ancient Coins of Greece, Rome, and Palestine* (London and Detroit 1977).
3. Cf. Waddington, Babelon, and Reinach, *Receuil géneral de monnaies grecques d'Asie Mineure*, 1, i (Paris 1904) 168, nos. 60-61.
4. "The Town of Germanicopolis-Gangra in Paphlagonia," in *NC* (1929) 310ff. The Berlin coin has been listed and illustrated in Price and Trell (n. 2 above) no. 259, fig. 517.
5. M. J. Price, "Greek Imperial Coins; Some Recent Acquisitions by the British Museum," *NC* (1971) 122, and pl. 24.3.
6. *BMC* i 53; pl. 5, nos. 9-11.
7. E.g. Hunter Catalogue iii 669-70; pl. 99, no. 17.
8. *BMC* ii 262, no. 190; pl. 50, no. 2 (the Colosseum): iii 180; pl. 32, nos. 2-4; v 216; pl. 35, no. 4; v 477-78; pl. 75, nos. 2,3.
9. *BMC* v 128, 138, 144, 148; pl. 22, nos. 2, 6; pl. 23, no. 11; 24, no. 13; 25, nos. 4,5,7.
10. *BMC* v 411; pl. 61, no. 2.

11. Cf., for example, R. E. Hecht, *NC* (1968) 27.

12. Cf., for example, *BMC* v, pl. 40, nos. 1-5; pl. 86, nos. 13-20.

13. *Villes d'Asie Mineure* (Paris 1935), and review by J. G. Milne in *NC* (1938) 63-64; 2d ed. 1962.

14. *Das System der kaiserzeitlichen Munzprägung in Kleinasien—Materialen und Entwürfe* (Berlin 1972), and review by Ann Johnston in *NC* (1974) 203ff.

15. *Monnaies coloniales d'Antioch de Pisidie* (Warsaw 1970).

16. Anne S. Robertson, *Proc. Soc. Ant. Scot.* 103 (1971) 130ff.; in *ANRW* 2, no. 3 (1975) 381ff.; and in *Scripta Nummaria Romana: Essays Presented to Humphrey Sutherland* (1978) 186ff.

17. T. B. Jones, "A Numismatic Riddle: The So-called Greek Imperials," *Proc. Amer. Phil. Soc.* 107 (August 1963) 308ff.

18. Dio Cassius 68.15.

19. The earliest reference to a money changer in Roman literature is in Suetonius, *Galba* 9: *Nummulario, non ex fide versanti pecunias, manus amputavit, mensaeque eius affixit.* The most famous references are in the New Testament Gospels, all four of which record the overturning of money changers' tables in the Temple at Jerusalem by Christ.

10
THE BASIS FROM PUTEOLI: CITIES OF ASIA MINOR IN JULIO-CLAUDIAN ITALY

CORNELIUS VERMEULE

The rectangular base of Aegean marble found late in the seventeenth or in the eighteenth century at Pozzuoli and long in the Museo Nazionale, Naples, was studied in great detail by J. Sieveking, V. Spinazzola, and a succession of scholars in the nineteenth century, notably the great epigraphers. The long, rear side of the monument appeared in scholarly "overviews" written for a wider public, both in Italy and in the English-speaking world. Mrs. E. S. Strong gave the side with six cities a full plate in her Italian history of Roman sculpture in 1923 and a page of text with a postage-stamp-sized photograph in her 1928 survey of Roman art published in America. In England, Mrs. Strong was joined by C. T. Seltman in including the same side again, with a half-plate illustration, in the fourth volume of the *Plates* for the *Cambridge Ancient History* (1934).

In 1953, Mason Hammond, in the course of his definitive publication of the early Hadrianic historical "balustrades" in the Roman Forum, concluded that a standing Tiberius stood on the Puteoli base. Finally, in 1978 George M. A. Hanfmann studied the city-goddess identified as Sardis on the left front corner of the base in his volume, *Sculpture from Sardis*. Thus, when other references and publications are adduced, the Puteoli base may have gone somewhat out of popular fashion since World War II, but aspects of the monument continue to attract scholarly attention.

While little can be added to the iconographic, epigraphic, and even aesthetic investigations of the past, newly assembled numismatic evidence of the last three decades can be applied to yet one more study of the Puteoli base. Since application of the numismatics of the Greek imperial cities of Asia Minor has been a lifetime avocation of Bluma L. Trell, a few pages connecting the fourteen city-divinities of this base with the coins of Lydia, Aeolis, and Ionia are offered as an essay in what Professor Trell began to do, in wider fashion and certainly better, under the aegis of Karl Lehmann when the present writer was still a schoolboy.[1]

Fig. 1. Puteoli base, front. Left and right: Sardis, Magnesia-near-Sipylus. *Courtesy Museum of Fine Arts, Boston*

Fig. 2. Puteoli base, right side. Left to right: Philadelpheia, Tmolus, Cyme. *Courtesy Museum of Fine Arts, Boston*

Fig. 3. Puteoli base, rear. Left to right: Temnus, Cibyra, Myrina, Ephesus, Apollonis, Hyrcanis. *Courtesy Museum of Fine Arts, Boston*

Fig. 4. Puteoli base, left side. Left to right: Mostene, Aegae, Hierocaesareia. *Courtesy Museum of Fine Arts, Boston*

THE CITIES AND THE BASE

In A.D. 17 a great earthquake devastated twelve cities in Lydia and Aeolis, most of them located in the Hermos valley. Tiberius put the resources of imperial and senatorial bureaucracy at their disposal. About five years later, the cities joined together to set up a monument to the emperor, a colossal statue surrounded by statues of themselves personified, in the Forum of Julius Caesar in Rome. Two more cities were ravaged by calamities at a later date, Cibyra in Phrygia in A.D. 23 and Ephesus in Ionia probably in A.D. 29. Statues of these cities were doubtless added to the group. It seems questionable whether the great ensemble survived the Forum's destruction by fire in A.D. 80, at the height of the Flavian era, and the supposition of disappearance may have lessened the figures' impact on the arts in their own home cities in the second and third centuries A.D. Domitian (81–96) probably began rebuilding in the Forum of Caesar, and the work was completed under Trajan (98–117), an emperor mindful of the importance of the provinces and their personifications in architecture and art.

Late in 29 or 30, the priests or corporation of Augustus at Puteoli decided to dedicate a statue of Tiberius, on the base of which were reproduced the city-personifications of the monument in Rome (figs. 1–4). This was both a complement to the emperor's munificence, already recorded on a sestertius of 22–23, and a visual record of the fact that Puteoli had extensive commercial links with the ruined cities of Asia Minor and therefore a strong stake in their recovery.

THE STATUE OF TIBERIUS

For the types of figures which stood on top of the base we must look to cistophoroi of Claudius (41–54) with the standing emperor crowned by Asia, the ROMETAVG reverse, if not to the seated, sacrificing figure of the CIVITATIBVS ASIAE RESTITVTIS sestertii of Tiberius. That the base held a standing statue, regardless of the aspect of the colossus in Rome (mentioned by Phlegon in Hadrian's time and, therefore, perhaps still extant), might be confirmed both by the shape of the base, too narrow or shallow on its front-to-rear axis for a seated figure, and by the careful analysis of the top of the block in its present condition by Mason Hammond over twenty-five years ago.[2]

The cuttings on the top, including the slightly depressed, roughly rectangular area in the center, admit a separate plinth covering the whole base and fixed at the central depression with extra cement or lead, in addition to the clamps near the corners. If such is positively the case, then a seated statue could have been placed in profile from the point of view of the main inscription flanked by Sardis and Magnesia-near-Sipylus, or two statues could have stood on top. The numismatic iconography of the age, from late Republican coins through the big sardonyx cameos to the cistophoroi of Claudius, would suggest a standing Tiberius in toga or possibly even in half-draped, heroic guise, crowned by the turreted, fully draped personification of Res Publica, Roma, Asia, Oikoumene, or the like. As early as 43–42 B.C., on denarii of the Roman Republican official Q. Cornuficius struck in Africa, we find the magistrate with implements of sacrifice being crowned by a standing goddess, in this instance Juno Sospita.[3]

Augustan and Julio-Claudian monumental painting or sculpture and numismatic art abound in instances in which the emperor, high magistrate, or victorious military man is flanked in a one-to-one relationship or is being crowned by an abstract personification symbolic of his successes or by a geographical personification representing the areas of his triumphs or aspirations. These expressions of imperial commemoration, as the medallion of Cyzicus crowning Commodus-Heracles in 192 (fig. 5), may provide solutions for the statue or statues at Puteoli, if not the colossus in Rome.

Fig. 5. Medallion of Cyzicus crowning Commodus-Heracles. *Courtesy Museum of Fine Arts, Boston*

A later illustration of what might have appeared on top of the base is provided by a large bronze coin of Thyateira in Lydia (fig. 6), struck in the name of Elagabalus (218–22). The emperor, in this instance in military costume, gives his hand to the local divinity Apollo Tyrimnaios over a rectangular altar.[4] The presence of an altar could also explain the peculiar rectangular depression in the center of the top of the Puteoli base.

In *Notizie degli Scavi di Antichità* (1933), Roberto Paribeni published the inscriptions found in the Forum of Caesar (pp. 431–55). None of them relates to the Tiberian statues of the rescued cities, but Sabratha in Africa remembered Diva Sabina with a large statue late in 138, showing that the rebuilt area remained a place where overseas cities honored the imperial family. The nearby Forum of Augustus was the place where famous Romans from King Aeneas Silvius to Trajan were commemorated with statues in the niches and with inscribed plaques (pp. 455–77).

Fig. 6. Bronze coin of Elagabalus, Thyateira in Lydia. *Courtesy Museum of Fine Arts, Boston*

REPRESENTATIONS OF THE CITIES

The figures of cities are considered in the order followed by J. Sieveking in the most definitive publication, the text to Brunn-Bruckmann, plate 575. This sequence goes from left to right, counterclockwise around the base (starting with Sardis at the left front corner and ending with Hierocaesareia next to her on the left short side), save that on the rear, or side with the most figures, Myrina and Ephesus in the center are described ahead of Temnus and Hyrcanis on the corners and they, in turn, ahead of Cibyra and Apollonis in the

89

background. Sieveking's system, then, follows an aesthetic rather than a literal sequence.

To simplify matters, the normal order, followed for instance by S. Reinach in his *Répertoire de Reliefs Grecs et Romains* i (Paris 1909) 228, appears below with Arabic numbers following Sieveking's arrangement, which has been designated here by Roman numerals. The same system is continued in the numismatic commentary.

Sieveking's aesthetic rearrangement of the one-by-one numbering system of the figures on the rear or long side of the Puteoli base points up the fact that the order of the cities on all four sides follows no recognizable system. Sardis and Magnesia-near-Sipylus balance each other either side of the inscription as perhaps the most traditionally "classical" of all the cities. Perhaps also they were the ones most affected by the earthquake. Elsewhere, it is clear, on short sides and long rear, the cities are positioned to create an aesthetic balance. The cities turn their heads to left and right so as to lead the viewer around the base counterclockwise, in the manner of all modern descriptions. As statues on coins also demonstrate, latitude in such details was probably exercised by the sculptors of the base in transferring the statues in Rome into the reliefs on the block of Aegean marble at Puteoli. It would be idle to speculate how the statues stood around Tiberius in the Forum of Julius Caesar, but, suitably inscribed to avoid anguish in identification and slight to any visiting Asiatics, they must have exhibited the same visual sensitivities seen in the positioning of the cities of Asia Minor on the Puteoli base.

I-1. Sardis stands in a girt peplos and mantle, the cloth drawn up as a veil over the head, which also wears a mural crown, and falling over the left shoulder and arm. A small rhyton (a Lydian or Phrygian survival) appears in the left hand. The lowered, bare left arm and hand are above, the latter touching the head of a nude child at her side. The child's right hand reaches up to touch that of the city-goddess, like one of the children in the processions on the Ara Pacis Augustae. The folds of the drapery around the legs reveal the influence of Pasitelean art, notably the so-called Electra of the "Orestes-Electra" groups. The child has been identified as the local hero Tylos. G. M. A. Hanfmann has reminded us that "this is a monument of Tiberian classicism shaped after Prokne," meaning that the famous fifth-century group by Alkamenes on the Athenian Acropolis influenced the overall iconography of Sardis. The hero-minor god Tylos has been equated with Triptolemos,[5] which accords with the numismatic evidence for the iconography of the city-goddess Sardis. Tylos was the son of Ge, likewise prominent in Greek imperial coinage.

II-2. Magnesia-near-Sipylus looks like a stock figure out of Praxitelean art of the fourth century B.C. She wears a mural crown, a long

chiton, and a himation wrapped about the lower limbs, the end
brought up over the head to form a veil. The attribute in the raised
right hand is small, possibly floral or agricultural, but basically
uncertain, and the partly lowered left hand either may have held
another attribute or may have grasped the edge of the himation,
as it seems to fall from the left shoulder. Looking at this figure and
at Temnus (VIII-6), it is tempting to speculate that all the statues
were modeled on terracottas and small bronzes brought for the
purpose to Rome from western Asia Minor.[6]

III-3. Philadelpheia is one of the heavier figures of the fourth century,
looking like the Themis of Rhamnous. She wears the most ample
of long, wrinkled chitons and a heavy himation. Her attributes
have disappeared. Her headgear does not seem to be either a
mural crown or her veil, although the line of drapery behind the
neck at her own left may admit this hypothesis. Like all these
figures, firm placement of her feet on the plinth or lower molding
indicates derivation from the statue of the city set up around
the colossal Tiberius in the Forum of Caesar in Rome. (Even
Myrina [VI-8], who crosses her legs, betrays her statuesque
origins since she leans on Apollo's tripod.) Philadelpheia is one of
the "Adaptations and Contaminations of the Praying Woman
Type," to give her Margarete Bieber's classification.[7]

IV-4. Tmolus appears as an active young Dionysos, with his full
complement of attributes, in the general schema of the pouring
satyr identified with Praxiteles. A large grapevine with branches,
leaves, and grapes twists up to the upper molding, and his hand
grasps the branch near the top. His *nebris* or goatskin runs from
his right shoulder, across his chest, and over the back and left
arm, two cloven hooves hanging near his animal-skin boots at his
left side. Only the socket for the extended left wrist and hand
remains. A broad fillet must have encircled his brow. There are
many bronzes which could have come from Asia Minor or
Alexandria to Rome to supply the model, such as a statuette now
in Boston.[8]

V-5. Cyme has the free-form plumpness of the Farnese "Flora,"
again a post-Sullan or Pasitelean restyling of something from the
post-Pheidian period. The chiton is girt with what Bieber called a
"Roman belt," and its folds, as well as those of the himation,
cascade in a rich, rough fall of ridges and furrows. The object in
the lowered right hand may be a vessel or even a small tympanon,
and the remains of a cornucopia were held, it seems, in the left.
Although worn and chipped away, the headgear of this
Cybelelike figure ought again to be a mural crown. A group of
"Aphrodites," from workshops in or exporting to Rome, offer 91

parallels, as do the "Adaptation(s) of the Venus Genetrix Type" which include the Farnese Flora.[9]

VI-8. Myrina has a familiar form and will emerge as the most characteristic figure for her locale, being a large marble version of a terracotta statuette, like the example in Aegean marble from southern Italy, now in Boston.[10] The tripod at her left side, symbolic of the city's devotion to Apollo (the oracle at Gyrneia was nearby), has a cauldron, a big prize crown, or even an omphalos in its bowl. Her left hand held a laurel branch, which runs along her left arm, and the end of her extended right hand is broken and worn away. The iconographies of Cyme and Myrina are not influenced by Strabo, who said these cities were named after Amazons (13.3.6), but the types for some other figures, notably Aegae (XIII-13), suggest that either the sculptors of the statues or the men who labeled the Puteoli base mixed up their urban prototypes.

VII-9. Ephesus is a short-skirted Amazonian Artemis, again a fourth and first century B.C. updating of a middle to late fifth-century type, with the most complete possible set of attributes to define her city, including the large river Kayster, the small river Marnas, or the Aegean harbor (Oceanus) as a mask under the left foot. She holds wheat and poppies in her raised right hand, while the attribute of her left has disappeared, although traces of a branch seem to appear on breast and knee. The "flames" on top of her mural crown may allude to destruction after the earthquake, or they may be, though it seems less likely to me, a collection of stags' antlers or a wicker basket. The slipped, girt chiton, small cloak like a *paludamentum* on the left shoulder and around the lower limbs, and high boots match the pose which is associated in Roman imperial art with Virtus, perhaps under the influence of the city's preeminent position in Roman Asia. The cult image of Artemis Ephesia on the fluted Ionic column in the background confirms what city is intended.

VIII-6. Temnus, although already cited in connection with terracottas of the fourth century B.C., is the most Graeco-Roman or Greek imperial of the figures. The city-divinity is a half-draped, booted, mural-crowned Demos or Genius Populi Romani with Dionysiac thyrsos added in the left hand to symbolize the richness of the plain at the western end of the Sipylus range. The sculptural sources for this figure were precisely those used a century later for Antinous, and it is easy to see how a series of statuettes in terracotta or bronze were handed down to early Roman imperial times, popularized by mass production, and finally turned into the statue flanking that of Tiberius in the Forum of Julius Caesar in Rome. Honos, as the figure escorting the triumphal *quadriga* on the Arch of Titus in Rome, was also a later iconographic counterpart.[11]

IX-11. Hyrcanis appears in the dress of a short-skirted, conservative Artemis of the fourth century B.C., her headgear having been identified by a succession of authorities as the Macedonian *kausia*. Her mantle hangs down from her left shoulder in an artistic device designed both to cover her left arm and the left edge of her chiton and to mark the transition to the figure of Mostene (XII-12) on the left short side, as one faces the inscribed front of the base. Unfortunately, other attributes, save for the boots, have vanished. One of her Late High Classical counterparts is male: Orpheus of the famous three-figure reliefs originating in Athens.[12] Both develop from Amazonian types.

X-7. Cibyra is an unusual Amazon or Artemis, or an Athena in field dress. Her helmet has a rich plume; her chiton covers both breasts, unlike the Virtus pushing Domitian off to war on the Cancelleria relief;[13] a sword belt crosses from the right shoulder to the left side, and she carries shield and spear on the left arm, in a schema repeated with more motion in the Cancelleria relief. The device of placing Cibyra and Apollonis (XI-10) behind Temnus-Myrina and Ephesus-Hyrcanis, or as secondary to Myrina (Cibyra) and Ephesus (Apollonis), has saved their visible attributes from (in the first instance) any, and (in the second case) total, destruction. The city's presence on the base was due not only to the earthquake of 23, but also to Strabo's report that the Cibyratae were descendants of the Lydians (13.4.17).

XI-10. Apollonis also wears a short but modest chiton and boots, a mural crown on her head. Her pose is designed to balance that of Cibyra. The animal on her right hand, its tail on the right arm of Hyrcanis, must be Cybele's lion, for the Great Mother of these mountains was worshiped locally, and the lion on the arm was a feature of the Ionian rather than the Attic Cybele in sculpture. By way of contrast, the sculptor has undercut the strands of her hair over her (left) ear somewhat more than any of the other figures preserved. This may reflect a Pergamene prototype on large or small scale.

XII-12. Mostene has the dignity of a Roman Juno[14] and updates the costumes of the Erechtheion Korai, later Muses (Bieber, pl. 76), or Kephisodotos' Eirene with Ploutos, and is designed to balance Cyme in mirror reversal and aesthetic plumpness. She wears a long peplos with loose, heavy overfold. Her headgear must have been a mural crown, and agricultural produce provided the attri-

93

butes: fruit in the folds of the garment below the left hand and sheaves of wheat or pinecones in the lowered right. Thus Mostene, like Cyme, became a veritable Flora and would seem to reflect taste in imperial Rome rather than in the river valleys of central Lydia.

XIII-13. Aegae sweeps forward like a Nike of Samothrace on the prow of a ship,[15] right breast and right leg exposed, a mural crown on her head. Her attributes, evidently a trident in the raised right hand and a dolphin in the crook of the left arm, suggest marine commerce. Strabo notes that the city is "situated in the mountainous country that lies above the territory of Cyme" (13.3.5). Since this Attalid city has nothing to do with the sea, the iconography here could only reflect a Pergamene, Roman Republican, or Augustan victory monument, or be a confusion with something in an Aeolic coastal city like Cyme or Myrina.[16] Perhaps one of the unidentified temples in the triad at the northwest corner of Aegae's citadel, an architectural group which included a shrine to Demeter and Kore, was dedicated to Aegae as a marine Tyche.

XIV-14. Hierocaesareia is a conservative Artemis-Tyche of fourth century B.C. type, a mural crown on her head and a large cornucopia on the left arm. Her chiton pinned on the right shoulder and full himation around the lower body, on the left shoulder, and over the left arm suggest the stately aspects of the hunting Artemis rather than an Amazon, although Artemis in freestanding statuary nearly always wears her cloak in a rolled bundle around the middle.[17] Only Apollonis (see above) appears to wear such a sash, or a bundle of folds like the Capitoline Amazon.[18]

THE NUMISMATIC EVIDENCE

Publication of the H. von Aulock collection of coins and medallions of Asia Minor and contiguous islands since the 1950s has provided a spectacular corpus of new coins and larger medallions available for comparison with the Puteoli base. Older published collections, like those in London and Paris, are cited, and lesser-known cabinets, like that in Boston, have been surveyed. All are taken together to give a thorough, if not necessarily exhaustive, conspectus of available numismatic evidence.

One fact is quickly noticed. If the statues were dedicated about 22–23, with possible additions in 23 or 24 and 29 or 30, and the base were commissioned and executed in 30–31, the majority of cogent coins date much later than the monuments in Rome and at Puteoli, namely, in the second and third centuries A.D. This gap in the

94

chronologies from monuments to coin types is acceptable procedure in applied numismatics, as Bluma Trell has so often shown. The archaeological, architectural, antiquarian, or historical consciousnesses of cities in the Greek imperial world were sharpened in the Hadrianic and Antonine periods or later, chiefly about the time Pausanias was setting forth on his travels from Asia Minor to Greece.

Fig. 7. Alliance coin of Caracalla, Sardis and Ephesus. *Courtesy Museum of Fine Arts, Boston*

I-1. Sardis (Sardeis, Lydia), coins: *SNG* (von A.) 3121–3177, 8253–8262. The Homonoia coins with Ephesus under Caracalla (211–17) show the turreted city-goddess in chiton and himation, the "Daedalic" Kore on the right hand, scepter-staff in the left[19] (no. 8258) (fig. 7). Since Demeter is also a major goddess of the city (as no. 3164, a large *aes* of Valerian, 253–60, where she stands next to the "Daedalic" Kore), could this veiled, crowned personification which leads off the group on the base have been inspired by a statue group of Demeter with Triptolemos, based, of course, as Hanfmann has observed, on Prokne and Itys from the Athenian Acropolis, a work identified with a man named Alkamenes? The small rhyton in the left hand of the figure on the Puteoli base is unusual and without surviving parallels in monumental relief or on the coins. The rhyton is doubtless a reference to Lydian luxury, and the group on the base can only be connected with the coinage in a general way. A bronze of the Flavian period has a single version of the majestic Demeter,[20] and the goddess is shown in profile on a second *aes* of Julia Domna, wife of Septimius Severus (193–211).[21]

The small *aes* of Tiberius with Sardis kneeling on the obverse before the togate emperor commemorate the earthquake, and Hanfmann has noted that "we cannot be sure that this design reflects an actual group of statues erected at Sardis."[22] Sardis is here the conventional city-goddess with turreted crown, chiton, and himation around her lower limbs, obviously the safest form of standard personification. She is offering Tiberius ears of corn, but these are omitted on at least one die.[23] The design copies that of the rare Augustan aureus of 14–13 B.C., struck by the magistrate Cossus Lentulus, with the togate emperor receiving Res Publica on the reverse,[24] but such scenes were also popular in high relief and undoubtedly as groups of statues. It is even possible such a group fitted on top of the Puteoli base, with the most general geographical or political personification as the kneeling figure.

II-2. Magnesia-near-Sipylus (ad Sipylum, Lydia), coins: *SNG* (von A.) 2997–3007, 8232–8233. A standing Cybele ("Meter Sipylene") in her shrine on a quasi-autonomous coin of the time of Gordianus III (238–44) suggests that this goddess may have provided the inspiration for the base, since the numismatic figure

95

clearly relates to a cult image set up in the city (no. 2999), but a standing, draped, mural-crowned city-goddess greets the cuirassed Tiberius on a coin of his reign (no. 3000), one surely struck to commemorate the emperor's munificence. The coin's flan is too small to afford further details than the crown, chiton, and himation. The fact that the city-goddess personification on the Puteoli base is veiled as well as crowned furthers the relationship with Cybele, and Cybele's head appears on the city's coinage as early as the second century B.C.[25] However, Demeter on quasi-autonomous issues of the late second or third century A.D. also suits the description.[26]

III-3. Philadelpheia (Lydia), coins: *SNG* (von A.) 3057–3086, 8240–8242. The mural-crowned bust of the city-goddess appears on quasi-autonomous coins around A.D. 200 (no. 3062). Otherwise the closest goddess might be Cybele, who appears enthroned, between the years 200 and 260 (no. 3067), on an alliance coin with Smyrna. The attributes are the usual. She is also represented in this fashion on a small bronze of Trajan, 98–117.[27]

IV-4. Tmolus (Tmolus-Aureliopolis, Lydia), coins: *SNG* (von A.) 3240–3241. On a coin of Antinous, late in Hadrian's reign, 117–138 (no. 3240), Tmolus is bearded and wears a short chiton; he still holds the knotted staff in his right hand. The coin, medallic in size or at least a sestertius, of Commodus (177–92) for Aureliopolis (no. 3241) features an excerpt from the Dionysiac *thiasos* on the reverse, an indication of the god's connection with the city. On a middle *aes* of Faustina II, wife of Marcus Aurelius (138–61–80), the bearded Tmolus is naked and holds the infant Dionysos. The *nebris* is a prominent feature of the city-god's costume.[28] Since the figure on the base is clearly not bearded, he is closer to Dionysos and, therefore, a symbol of the city before its iconography was thoroughly refined and fixed by the coinage.

V-5. Cyme (Aeolis), coins: *SNG* (von A.) 1621–1657, 7691–7703. The city-goddess is an Amazon on quasi-autonomous coins of the time of Vespasian, 69–79, a globe and trident as attributes (nos. 1645, 1646).[29] She is also an Amazon on the city's latest coinage under Valerian, a dolphin at her feet like Lysippic and later statues of Poseidon (no. 1657).[30]

VI-8. Myrina (Aeolis), coins: *SNG* (von A.) 1659–1668, 7704–7707. A sestertius-sized *aes* of Elagabalus, 218–22 (no. 7707), shows Dionysos greeting the city-goddess, who is an Amazon with Tyche or mural crown and battle attributes, pelta shield and double axe. She is thus a figure much more like Cibyra and Hierocaesareia. As has been mentioned more than once, Myrina the city-personification on the Puteoli base seems most like the famous terracottas and least like the urban iconography of this or the neighboring cities.[31]

VII-9. Ephesus (Ionia), coins: *SNG* (von A.) 1824–1935, 7816–7890. The cult image of the Artemis Ephesia stands on a slender, fluted Ionian column behind the Amazonian city-goddess on the Puteoli base. The Artemis Ephesia does not as yet seem ready to represent the city as a whole, although she has done so on the gold of Mithradates's time, 87–85 B.C. (no. 1869) and does so when grouped with the emperors (as Marcus Aurelius and Lucius Verus, 161–69, no. 1891) or when representing the city on Homonoia coins, as the example of Gordianus III (238–44) with Perinthus in Thrace or that of Caracalla's time cited in connection with the numismatic iconography of Sardis (fig. 8).

Fig. 8. Alliance coin of Gordianus III, Perinthus and Ephesus. *Courtesy Museum of Fine Arts, Boston*

Amazons, to my knowledge, do not appear on the coinage of Ephesus. A large *aes* of the emperor Severus Alexander (222–35), struck by Cibyra (X-7) in alliance with Ephesus,[32] shows elaborately helmeted or crowned Amazonian figures with their city cult images on their hands (Hekate or Kore and Artemis Ephesia), the urban personifications facing each other across an altar. When Pergamum in Mysia commemorated an alliance with Ephesus on the reverse of another, even larger, bronze struck in the name of the young Commodus (177–92), the local hero Androklos was delegated to hold the image of Artemis Ephesia on his hand, while Pergamos held out the Pergamene cult image of Asklepios. As in statuary, Androklos looks like Meleager, which is natural since both were famous hunters (von Aulock, no. 1424, which is Boston no. 1975.357; fig. 9).[33]

Fig. 9. Alliance coin of Commodus, Pergamum and Ephesus. *Courtesy Museum of Fine Arts, Boston*

A standing and a seated Tyche, the latter holding the Artemis Ephesia on her hand, symbolize the city and its alliance festival with Pergamum and Smyrna on a rare *aes* of sestertius size, struck under Antoninus Pius about 140.[34] This medallic coin, of highest die-designing quality, shows how difficult it is to fix the imagery of a major Greek imperial city. In selecting an urban personification, there were numerous choices.

VIII-6. Temnus (Aeolis), coins: *SNG* (von A.) 1671–1680, 7708–7709. Only the busts of Dionysos on the early coins, third to second century B.C., confirm the city's identity with the young god of wine (nos. 1671–1673).[35]

IX-11. Hyrcanis (Hyrkaneis, Lydia), coins: *SNG* (von A.) 2974–2977, 8228. The reclining river god Hermos, youthful and with a "Macedonian" shield at his left side, appears on a coin of Otacilia Severa and Philip II, 244–49 (no. 2977).[36] The shield also symbolizes Macedonia on the city's quasi-autonomous coinages.[37]   97

Other than these vague epigraphic or visual allusions to Macedonia and local geography, which tie in with the Macedonian headdress of the figure on the Puteoli base, there appears to be no directly connected coin type.

X-7. Cibyra (Phrygia), coins: *SNG* (von A.) 3699–3756, 8394–8400. A quasi-autonomous bronze of the time of Domitian (81–96) has the bust of Senatus on the obverse and a running Amazon on the reverse (no. 8395).[38] The most spectacular related numismatic evidence is a big medallion of Macrinus and Diadumenianus (217–18) with a facing city-Amazon in full regalia on the reverse, a sphinx on a tripod at her side (no. 3738). A similar piece for Macrinus alone shows the Amazon in partial profile, as on the Puteoli base, a wicker basket *kibotos* (or *kivotos*) as a play on the city's name in evidence in the field.[39] On a Homonoia medallion of the young Marcus Aurelius, however, it is Hekate in full dress who represents the city (no. 3757).

XI-10. Apollonis (Apollonidea, Lydia), coins: *SNG* (von A.) 2897–2905. The only even vaguely related coin of Apollonis is a semi-autonomous bronze of the time of Lucius Verus (161–69) with a bust of the city-goddess wearing the mural crown (no. 2902). It could be the same figure seen on the Puteoli base, since both wear the urban headgear. Since the earliest, noncistophoric Hellenistic coinage[40] features a turreted head of Cybele on the obverse, the Amazonian city-goddess on the Puteoli base may be a partial manifestation of Cybele holding her lion.

XII-12 Mostene (Lydia), coins: *SNG* (von A.) 3028–3031, 8238. A coin of the early second century A.D. has a bust of Roma on the obverse and a goddess with double axe in the left hand, sheaves of wheat in the extended right on the reverse (no. 3028). The double axe is the city's most characteristic feature.[41]

XIII-13. Aegae (Aigai, Aeolis), coins: *SNG* (von A.) 1592–1601, 7667–7676. A Homonoia coin with Myrina, of the emperor Commodus, ca. 185, shows a short-skirted city-goddess with oinochoe and scepter, while Myrina with scepter and "trauben" looks like her appearance on the Puteoli base (no. 7676).[42] The connections with the sea seen in the figure of Aegae on the base do not, but could, enter onto related Greek imperial coinage; inland location is no obstacle to the use of marine types. Ge and Thalassa with her dolphin appear on a large *aes* of Laodiceia in Phrygia under Caracalla (fig. 10).[43]

XIV-14. Hierocaesareia (Hierokaisareia, Lydia), coins: *SNG* (von A.) 2951-2959. A coin of Agrippina the Younger, with

Fig. 10. Coin of Caracalla, Laodiceia in Phrygia. *Courtesy Museum of Fine Arts, Boston*

standing Artemis Persica on the reverse (no. 2959), although in long chiton,[44] indicates, as throughout the coinage, that it is Artemis who personifies the city on the Puteoli base. She also appears in short garb on coins struck from Nero (54–68) to Hadrian (117–38)[45] and has been adapted as a city-goddess on the base, with mural crown and cornucopia. A coin of T. Julius Ferox, proconsul, 116–17, has the turreted city-goddess on the obverse, bringing the connection with the base through the full circle.[46] Finally, a coin of Trajan with head of the Demos (?) on the obverse has the canonical, Hellenistic hunting Artemis on the reverse.[47]

CONCLUSIONS

The Puteoli base with its statue of Tiberius on top, either seated as Roman coins show or standing crowned by a geographical personification, gives a faithful picture of the twelve, later fourteen, statues of cities which stood around the image of the emperor in the Forum of Julius Caesar in Rome. These statues were products of the selective, academic classicism of the Augustan and Julio-Claudian periods, being based on post-Pheidian, Praxitelean, Pergamene, and Pasitelean models. Unfortunately, Greek imperial coins of these cities do not provide many parallels or prototypes for these statues, since most historical, pictorial coins were later than the reign of Tiberius, and since the monument was a creation in Roman Italy rather than Greek Asia Minor.

As to models for the cities, I would suggest that delegations from these cities brought or sent to Rome small marbles, bronze statuettes, terracotta figurines, or plaquettes in various materials representing what Roman officials and Greek municipal magistrates thought to be characteristics of each city. These images were not necessarily based on the major or patron divinities of the cities. The labels beneath each statue and on the Puteoli base told the whole story. The carvers of the base may have mixed up these identifications, or the delegates bringing the figurines to serve as prototypes may have become confused, as in the instance of "maritime" Aegae, which was really far removed from the sea. (An iconographer in Rome could have confused this city with Cilician Aegae on the Gulf of Issus, although the names of the two are spelled differently in Greek capitals on their coinages.)

In brief, applied numismatics serves best to show how the iconography of regional geography did not become even loosely organized until the ages of Trajan and Hadrian, a visual situation demonstrated by J. M. C. Toynbee in the 1930s, just as Bluma Trell was beginning her own pioneering studies of the related Greek and Greek imperial architectural settings.

NOTES

1. Thanks are due, directly and indirectly, to Kristin Anderson, Miriam Braverman, Herbert Cahn, Mary Comstock, George Hanfmann, Robert Hecht, John and Ariel Herrmann, Silvia Hurter, Leo Mildenberg, Martin Price (who greatly improved the manuscript), Emily Townsend Vermeule, and Florence Wolsky for help with this article. Photographs were collected or taken between 1948 and 1978 during studies in England, Italy, Greece, and Turkey. A. C. Cooper in London, the photographers of the Museum of Fine Arts, Boston, and Complete Photo in Cambridge, Massachusetts, deserve a full measure of credit for the visual aids. All of the coins illustrated are courtesy of the Museum of Fine Arts, Boston, Theodora Wilbour Fund in Memory of Zoë Wilbour.

In addition to the books and articles cited throughout, most of which contain detailed bibliographies, the following can be consulted about the Puteoli base: D. Magie, *Roman Rule in Asia Minor to the End of the Third Century after Christ* (Princeton 1950) i *Text* 499-500; ii *Notes* 1358-59, no. 23 (with all of the ancient sources); J. M. C. Toynbee, *The Hadrianic School* (Cambridge 1934) 122-23, pl. 28, no. 1, in connection with Hyrcania's derivation from Macedonia or a common prototype; E. Strong, *Art in Ancient Rome* i (New York 1928) 158; E. Strong, *La scultura romana da Augusto a Costantino* i (Florence 1923) 93-94, pl. 18, opposite p. 81, who dates the earthquake to the year 29; C. T. Seltman, *The Cambridge Ancient History: Plates* iv (Cambridge 1934) 138-39, with speculation about a similar monument at Smyrna; *CIL* 10, no. 1624.

2. Cf. *BMCRE* i, pl. 23, nos. 16, 17; pl. 34, no. 4; M. Grant, *Roman History from Coins* (Cambridge 1968) pl. 18, no. 1, the sestertius of 22-23. For Hammond's analysis, see *Memoirs of the American Academy in Rome* 21 (1953) 163-65.

3. E. Sydenham, *The Coinage of the Roman Republic* (London 1952) 212, nos. 1352-55, pl. 30.

4. Boston no. 64.1451, from Münzen und Medaillen Sale 28 (Basel 1964) no. 426; *Romans and Barbarians* (1976) 92, no. C 78.

5. *RE* Zweite Reihe 7.1730-31.

6. See Museum of Fine Arts, Boston, *Greek, Etruscan, and Roman Art* (Boston 1972) 155, figs. 137-38; D. Burr, *Terra-cottas from Myrina* (Bryn Mawr 1934) 64, pl. 31, no. 78.

7. M. Bieber, *Ancient Copies* (New York 1977) pls. 139-40.

8. M. B. Comstock, C. C. Vermeule, *Greek, Etruscan, and Roman Bronzes* (Greenwich, Conn. 1971) 489, no. 100A.

9. Bieber (n. 7 above) pls. 74, 28.

10. M. B. Comstock, C. C. Vermeule, *Sculpture in Stone* (Boston 1976) 38, no. 52.

11. See M. Bieber, *"Honos* and *Virtus,"* *AJA* 49 (1945) 25-34, figs. 1, 10, etc.

12. Bieber (n. 7 above) pl. 3, fig. 13.

13. Bieber (n. 7 above) pl. 45, fig. 265.

14. Bieber (n. 7 above) pl. 29.

15. Cf. Boston (n. 8 above) pl. 71, no. 74, a Nike on an orb.

16. See R. Stillwell, *The Princeton Encyclopedia of Classical Sites* (Princeton 1976) 19 (G. E. Bean) map 7.

17. Bieber (n. 7 above) pls. 43-50, as a "sash."

18. Bieber (n. 7 above) pl. 2.

19. Also M. B. Comstock, *BMFA* 65 (1967) 168-69, fig. 14.

20. *BMC* no. 73, pl. 25.7.

21. *BMC* no. 147, pl. 27.1.

22. Appendix to *Sculpture from Sardis* (Cambridge, Mass. 1978) 181.

23. *BMC* nos. 98-101, pl. 26.4.

24. *Numismatica* i (1960) 1-7.

25. *BMC* no. 4, pl. 15.3.

26. *BMC* no. 16, pl. 16.2.

27. *BMC* no. 67, pl. 22.6.
28. *BMC* no. 1, pl. 33.1.
29. Also *BMC* no. 99, pl. 22.7.
30. Also *BMC* no. 115, pl. 22.14, quasi-autonomous coins of this final period.
31. Cf. Burr (n. 6 above) 69, no. 95, pl. 36, which is M.F.A. no. 87.389; also p. 68, no. 92, pl. 35, which is M.F.A. no. 87.388.
32. E. Babelon, *Inventaire sommaire de la Collection Waddington* (Paris 1898) 344-45, no. 5839, pl. 15, fig. 21.
33. *Romans and Barbarians* (1976) 91, no. C 71; the alliance coin of Perinthus cited above is pp. 90-91, C 62.
34. R. E. Hecht, *NC* (1968) 28, no. 4, pl. 8.
35. Also *BMC* nos. 7, pl. 28.12, 10, pl. 29.2.
36. Also *BMC* nos. 24-25, pl. 13.7.
37. *BMC* no. 1, pl. 13.1.
38. Also *BMC* no. 23, pl. 16.7.
39. *BMC* no. 52, pl. 17.5.
40. *BMC* no. 2.
41. Also *BMC* no. 5, pl. 17.9.
42. Also *BMC* no. 31, pl. 18.12.
43. M. B. Comstock (n. 19 above) 172-73, fig. 20b.
44. *BMC* no. 22, pl. 11.7.
45. See *BMC* no. 15, pl. 11.4.
46. *BMC* no. 19, pl. 11.6.
47. *BMC* no. 24, pl. 11.9.

ARCHAEOLOGY, GEOGRAPHY, LANGUAGE, AND LITERATURE

11
THE CORSINI THRONE AND THE MAN IN THE POT

LARISSA BONFANTE

The marble Corsini Throne (figs. 1, 2), recently explained as an archaistic creation carved by an artist trained in the neo-Attic style in Rome at the time of Caesar,[1] presents many interesting problems, among them the survival of artistic motifs from a much earlier time.

The shape is that of an ancient Etruscan orientalizing type of chair, often represented in Etruscan tombs of the seventh and sixth centuries. It was not funerary, however, but a perfectly normal item of everyday furniture. The original chairs were probably made of wicker—like modern chairs of similar shape—or wood; fancy models were covered with decorated bronze plates. In the tombs at Cerveteri, full-sized models were carved out of the rock.[2] In the North Etruscan city of Chiusi, miniature rounded chairs were used for terracotta or bronze cinerary urns in human shape in the seventh and sixth centuries and for larger, life-sized stone urns at a later date.[3] Similar chairs were also represented farther north, in the region of the Veneto in northeast Italy, the Alps, and beyond (modern Switzerland, Austria, and Yugoslavia) on the engraved bronze buckets or situlae which give the art of this area the name of "situla art."[4]

In fact, the most surprising feature of the Roman Corsini Throne is the influence of this art, dating from five hundred years earlier and located far to the north of Rome. For the style and subject of the relief decoration of this archaizing monument imitates that of these ancient bronze situlae, which also represented soldiers, processions, hunts, and games. For example, boxers using a strange kind of barbell-shaped object appear on the situlae as well as on the Corsini Throne, with the prize—a helmet—between them (fig. 3).[5]

The chief inspiration for this monument, then, is that of these northern situlae, some of which Julius Caesar's men must have brought back to Rome from the Gallic campaigns in the mid-first century B.C., at the time the Corsini chair was carved in the neo-Attic archaizing style of this period. The use of Pentelic marble, and the style of the decorative borders in low relief, confirm this date.[6]

105

Fig. 1. Corsini Throne, front. *Courtesy Gabinetto Fotografico Nazionale, Rome*

Fig. 2. Corsini Throne, back. *Courtesy Gabinetto Fotografico Nazionale, Rome*

Fig. 3. Situla from Watsch.

Fig. 4. Detail of Corsini Throne, the "Corsini Dunker." *Courtesy Gabinetto Fotografico Nazionale, Rome*

Fig. 5. Red-figure cup. *Courtesy Institute for Advanced Study, Princeton, N.J.*

107

The problem I would like to present in honor of Bluma Trell, who is good at puzzles, has to do with a strange figure in this throne's relief decoration (fig. 4). Some scholars interpreted it, not as a single figure, but as a pair of wrestlers, one of whom is shown—in awkward perspective—pinning his struggling opponent to the table. The legs of the second would then be shown flailing up from the table. I originally agreed with this view, but several colleagues objected to the interpretation.[7] They are right, and I stand corrected. What is being represented is one man, shown with his head stuck inside a pithos or a well head, his hands holding on to the rim. The remarkable size of the hulking, muscle-bound figure, as well as its strange proportions and awkward stance, must be attributed to the artist's lack of ability, which caused it to be misunderstood as a group of two men.

The meaning and origin of such a figure are hard to understand. A group of two wrestlers would fit in quite naturally with the aristocratic theme of the whole decoration, which features noble activities such as games and sports events. But a man with his head in a pithos—or well head—does not fit into the context of situla art.

When we look for analogies for what we might call the "Corsini Dunker," we find the following possibilities.[8]

1. A man or a satyr plunging into a pithos to get the wine in the bottom: the context is that of a symposium or Dionysiac scene on Attic vases; the mood humorous (fig. 5).[9]

2. In archaic art, a very popular story is that of Eurystheus hiding in a huge jar, like Ali Baba, in terror of the Erymanthian boar which Heracles is bringing back, alive and kicking. Numerous examples occur on relief metopes,[10] and on Attic black-figure and red-figure vases, on which Eurystheus's name is sometimes even inscribed.[11] In Etruria, on two Caeretan hydriae, the artist has made an interesting change: he has substituted the underworld figure of Cerberus for that of the boar.[12]

But what can a Greek genre scene, or a Greek myth—even if transformed on Italic soil—have to do with the very Roman context of the Corsini chair?

3. A third analogy that, like the hydriae, is from Italy, occurs on Hellenistic Etruscan urns representing a purely local myth: a wolf-bodied or wolf-headed creature rising from a well, to the consternation of those around him.[13] Perhaps, it has been suggested, this was the Etruscan monster named Olta.[14] Though closer in date, and on Italian soil, this example does not seem to help us.

4. More promising is another mysterious Italic myth represented on a Praenestine cista of the fourth or third century: Minerva is dunking a naked, armed figure of Mars into a pot of boiling liquid—apparently giving him a bath of immortality, like Achilles.[15]

5. The most surprising comparison, recently connected with the ritual of immersion represented on the Praenestine cista, takes us north again, beyond the region of situla art. This is the Celtic Gun-

destrop cauldron, dated around 100 B.C. and, therefore, not far from the first-century date of the Corsini chair. It shows "persons plunging or being plunged willy-nilly into vases."[16] Jean Gricourt has recently suggested that it represents a god successively giving soldiers a ritual plunge which turns them into heroized horsemen, preparing them for another life. He connects this "vat of resurrection, rejuvenation, or immortality" with the ritual the Celtic hero Cuchulain undergoes, as well as with other magic pots or wells, including Medea's.[17]

The chair found in Rome, perhaps still *in situ* or close to it, was intended for use in some religious ritual. Its function is indicated by the important central motif of the sacrifice at the altar (fig. 1), which, unlike other scenes represented, fits into a specifically Hellenistic or late Roman Republican context.[18] Erika Simon has suggested that the sacrifice was offered to Hercules, because the skyphos held by one of the women in the procession (fig. 2) is the shape used for sacrifices in honor of Hercules, according to Servius.[19] Such a skyphos appears, for example, on a round altar of A.D. 81, dedicated to Hercules Victor, in the Capitoline Museum in Rome.[20] Might not the supernaturally large figure with his head in a pithos or well head represent Hercules in a local legend unknown to us? The huge figure of Hercules has an antecedent in Etruscan art of the late sixth century B.C. in the Caeretan hydria showing a giant Heracles slaying Busiris's men. On the Corsini chair, an onlooker holds his hand up to his mouth. Is he registering awe at the *prodigium* taking place before him?[21]

The identification of this strange figure would, in this case, be closely associated with the purpose for which the throne or chair was made. I earlier suggested that the Corsini Throne might have been commissioned by a noble family, for use not in a funeral, as has sometimes been assumed,[22] but in connection with a cult for which the members of the family were responsible, as the Potitii and Pinarii were responsible for the cult of Hercules at the Ara Maxima.[23] In such a context, a representation of Hercules in a pose obscure to us,[24] but clear to its owners, might have carried the same connotations of rebirth, heroization, rejuvenation, or immortality present in other myths. The puzzling figure of this "dunker" would help us to understand the purpose of this throne, in which exotic figures and phrases of situla art have been transformed and translated into something very Roman and juxtaposed with Hellenistic images to form, not an eclectic meaningless potpourri, but a representation of a specific Roman ritual.[25] The identification of the man in the pot as Hercules, whose feats in Rome were soon to be celebrated in Livy's reworking of early Roman history and myth and whose cults had long been important in Roman religion, would provide evidence of Roman awareness of local traditions and of attempts of the artists of this period to find new ways to represent old myths.[26]

The narrative of the Corsini Throne brought together the most diverse elements: archaic and exotic Etruscan and "Gallic" words   109 and phrases[27] mixed in with the Greek and Roman ritual language of altar and sacrifice. Was it written as a prayer to Heracles, that Italic god so incompletely covered by his Greek name?

NOTES

1. An earlier draft of this paper was presented at the meeting of the Archaeological Institute of America, 30 December 1978, in Vancouver, B.C. The monument has been in Palazzo Corsini in Rome ever since its discovery under the Lateran in 1732. See G. de Luca, *I monumenti antichi del Palazzo Corsini a Roma* (Rome 1976) 93-100, pls. 81-85; L. Bonfante, "The Corsini Throne," *Essays in Honor of Dorothy Kent Hill. The Journal of the Walters Art Gallery* 36 (1977) 111-22; B. M. Felletti Maj, *La tradizione italica nell' arte romana* (Rome 1977) 174, 192-94; S. Steingräber, *Etruskische Möbel* (Rome 1979) 22-24 and cat. no. 27, pl. 3,2.
2. F. Prayon, *Frühetruskische Grab- und Hausarchitektur* (Heidelberg 1975) pl. 59.1; Steingräber (n. 1 above) 313-52, cat. nos. 581-791. For the relief decoration, see the embossed bronze Etruscan "Barberini Throne" from Praeneste, W. Helbig, *Führer durch die öffentlichen Sammlungen klassischer Altertümer in Rom*, 4th ed., ed. H. Speier iii (Rome 1969) 2857; G. M. A. Richter, *The Furniture of the Greeks, Etruscans, and Romans* (London 1966) 86, fig. 427; Steingräber cat. no. 28, pl. 3.1. The type was not limited to a funerary use.
3. M. Zuffa, *Studi in onore di Luisa Banti* (Rome 1965) 351-55; L. Vlad Borelli, *StEtr* 41 (1973) 211-12; Bonfante (n. 1 above) 114; Steingräber (n. 1 above) 23, cat. nos. 501-5, etc.; pls. 28-29.
4. W. Lucke, O.-H. Frey, *Die Entstehung der Situlenkunst* (Berlin 1969); Steingräber (n. 1 above) 63, cat. nos. 427-38, pls. 18,19; L. Bonfante, "I popoli delle situle," *DialAr* n.s. 2 (1975) 73-94.
5. Comparisons between situla art and the Corsini Throne have been discussed by P. Ducati, *MonAnt* 24 (1917) cols. 401-58; de Luca (n. 1 above) 93-100; see also Bonfante (n. 1 above) 114-16.
6. Bonfante (n. 1 above) 11-14. For neo-Attic decorations, see W. Fuchs, *Die Vorbilder der Neoattischen Reliefs* (Berlin 1959) pls. 6a,b, 9b, 20a,b. For the use of Pentelic marble, John Ward-Perkins, Amanda Claridge, Demitri Michaelides, quoted by me in "Corsini Throne" (n. 1 above) 111, n. 7.
7. "The strange figure . . . bent over turns out to be a pair of naked wrestlers," I wrote in "Corsini Throne" (n. 1 above) 166-17, citing Ducati, *MonAnt* 24 (1916) 443-44 and I. S. Ryberg, "Rites of the State Religion in Roman Art," *MAAR* 22 (1955) 9. Cyrus Gordon, a specialist on ancient wrestling ("Belt-Wrestling in the Bible World," *Hebrew Union College Annual* 23 [1950-51] 131-36), denied the existence of table-wrestling as a sport. I also thank Gerhard Koeppel, Guenter Kopcke, Ernst Badian, and Mark Davies for useful criticism.
8. I owe the term and most of the following examples to Mark Davies, to whom I am most grateful.
9. 1. A red-figure cup at the Princeton Institute for Advanced Study, *M and M Auction Sale XVI*, 30 June 1956, 33, no. 119, pl. 28. 2. A lekythos in Karlsruhe: *ARV²* 677, no. 13; *CVA*, Karlsruhe, B1814, pl. 26.4. 3. Another cup in Geneva, *Collection Musée d'art et d'histoire*, no. 16908. On the Karlsruhe vase and the Geneva cup the figure is a satyr with a tail; the figure in Princeton is tailless. I am grateful to Dietrich von Bothmer for references and to Homer Thompson for the photograph of the Princeton cup.
10. Metopes from the temple of Zeus at Olympia: E. Curtius and F. Adler, *Olympia* (Berlin 1890-97) *Tafelband* iii pls. 39.7, 45.7 Cf. the metope of the "Theseum" at

Athens. F. Brommer, *Denkmälerlisten zur griechischen Heldensage* (Marburg 1971³) i 40-44.

11. The basic survey is still that of S. B. Luce, "Studies of the Exploits of Heracles on Vases," *AJA* 28 (1924) 296-318. For list of examples, see F. Brommer, *Herakles* (Münster-Cologne 1953) 18-19, 83-85; J. Henle, *Greek Myths: A Vase Painter's Notebook* (Bloomington 1973) 61, 180. This exploit is immediately preceded by Heracles's "battle of the pithos" against thirsty centaurs: Henle 61, 180; K. Schefold, *Götter- und Heldensage der Griechen in der spätarchaische Kunst* (Munich 1978) 124-28.

12. J. M. Hemelrijk, *De Caeretaanse Hydriae* (Rotterdam 1956) no. 5; Helbig (n. 2 above) 2714.

13. A. von Gerkan, F. Messerschmidt, "Das Grab der Volumnier bei Perugia," *RömMitt* 57 (1942) 204-8; G. Hafner, "Porsenna," *Rivista di Archeologia* (dir. G. Traversari) 1 (1977) 36-43, figs. 6-7; R. Bloch, *Les prodiges dans l'antiquité classique (Grèce, Etrurie et Rome)* (Paris 1963) 58; A. Pfiffig, *Religio Etrusca* (Graz 1975) 313-15.

14. Pfiffig (n. 13 above) 313.

15. Rome, Villa Giulia Museum. G. Hermansen, *Studien über den italischen und den römischen Mars* (Copenhagen 1940) 5ff.; Pfiffig (n. 13 above) 348, fig. 137; E. Simon, "Il dio Marte nell'arte dell'Italia centrale," *St Etr* 46 (1978) 138ff., with rich bibliography on the pithos. The Italic representation of a miracle which Simon sees here is close to the scene of the Corsini Throne, as is her interpretation of the volute crater represented on two Etruscan mirrors as containing a magic potion. Cf. G. Bordenache Battaglia, *Le ciste prenestine* I (Rome 1979) 54, 61.

16. J. Gricourt, "Sur une plaque du chaudron de Gundestrop," *Latomus* 13 (1954) 376-83; cf. M. Renard, "Du chaudron de Gundestrop aux mythes classiques," ibid. 384-89. I owe the reference and quotation to Mark Davies.

17. On Cuchulain plunged into three successive vats in order to cool his ardor, see R. M. Ogilvie, *A Commentary to Livy: Books 1-5* (Oxford 1965) 109, on Livy 1.24-25. G. Dumézil, *The Destiny of the Warrior* (Chicago 1970) 134.

18. Ryberg, *Rites of the State Religion* 10; de Luca (n. 1 above) 93-94; Bonfante (n. 1 above) 114.

19. Servius *ad Aen.* 8, 278. Erika Simon, personal letter 11 November 1978.

20. E. Simon, *JdI* 75 (1960) 143, fig. 6; E. Simon, in Helbig (n. 2 above), vol. 2 (1966) 1425.

21. For Caeretan hydriae see nn. 11-12 above; de Luca (n. 1 above 94) quotes Gori's interpretation of the relief decoration as scenes of sacrifices and games in honor of Mithras and the figure of the giant as Mithras-Sol rising out of a base or well: *vir ille magnae staturae, qui nudus corpore brevibus brachiis ingente capite, in aram ita incumbit, ut in ea non se abscondere, sed potius . . . ex ea adsurgere paullatim videatur* (A. F. Gori, *Mus. Etruscum* ii [1737-45] 379ff.). The youth with raised hand could be witnessing an epiphany or *prodigiùm*.

22. De Luca (n. 1 above) 99. Ducati was certain the throne had a funerary purpose; for a contrary view, see Giglioli, *StEtr* 3 (1929) 146.

23. Potitii and Pinarii: Livy 1.7.12 and Ogilvie (n. 17 above) 60-61.

24. There are parallels for obscure myths connected with Hercules in Etruscan—or, rather, Italic—art; for example, for the entrance of Hercules into Olympus, represented as the nursing and adoption of Hercules by Hera or Juno (Uni), on an Etruscan mirror from Volterra, see O. J. Brendel, *Etruscan Art* (Harmondsworth 1978) 368, fig. 285; for other references, see L. Bonfante, *Etruscan Dress* (Baltimore 1975) 204, fig. 143. For other "translations" of Greek myth into Etruscan form, see Brendel 264-65, 269-70; on Caeretan hydriae, see nn. 11,12, 21 above. I thank Paula Sage for useful references.

25. For ancient thrones, see F.-W. von Hase, *Marburger Winckelmann-Programm* (1974) 5-7; T. Klauser, *Die Cathedra im Totenkult der heidnischen und christlichen Antike* (Münster 1927); P. Kranz, *AthMitt* 87 (1972) 1-55; Richter, *Furniture*

111

(n. 2 above) 86, etc.; de Luca (n. 1 above) 99-100. For the Elgin Throne and other Greek chairs, see J. Frel, *AthMitt* 91 (1976) 185-89, and H. Thompson, *Getty Mus. Journal* (forthcoming).

26. Felletti Maj, *La tradizione italica* 139, on the new iconography in the last century of the Roman Republic, designed for the customs and cults of state religion and private life. On the renewed interest in and interpretation of local Italic myths in Rome and Etruria in the late Republic, see Hafner, "Porsenna" (n. 13 above) 40-41, 43, n. 59, with bibliography.

27. Etruscan and Gallic art and language were considered to be exotic in Rome in the late Republic and early empire. The Gallic and Etruscan languages sounded strange and ridiculous in the mid-second century A.D. Aulus Gellius (*NA* 11.7.3f.) tells of a lawyer who used archaic words, which made his hearers laugh as though he had been speaking Etruscan or Gallic (S. Mazzarino, *Historia* 6[1957] 98; A. Pfiffig, *Etruskische Sprache* [Graz 1969] 9). In the late Republic the artist who made the archaizing Corsini Throne used Etruscan models for its shape and "Gallic" models—for so the situla art brought back from the Gallic campaign must have seemed—for its decoration.

12

THE LOCATION OF ADULIS
(*PERIPLUS MARIS ERYTHRAEI* 4)

LIONEL CASSON

The port of Adulis was the most important on the western shore of the Red Sea. Through it passed the major part of Ethiopia's trade,[1] and as Ethiopia's Axumite kingdom grew politically and economically, particularly from the fourth through the sixth century A.D., so did Adulis.[2] From it were exported such native products as ivory, rhinoceros horn, and tortoise shell; into it came a variety of imports from near and far, from Egypt, Arabia and India—even, some argue, from China.[3] Adulis must have been, in consequence, a large and bustling entrepôt. Yet precisely where its harbor lay, where the ships put in to load and unload their cargoes, is a puzzle. In this paper I offer a solution; I hope it will be as convincing as the solutions to numismatic puzzles which we owe to the distinguished scholar to whom this volume is dedicated.

We are fortunate in having an eyewitness description provided by the author of the *Periplus Maris Erythraei*, who wrote sometime in the second half of the first century A.D.[4] At that time Adulis was

> an officially recognized trading post located on a deep bay, extending due south, in front of which is an island called Oreinê ["Rocky"] lying about two hundred stades from the innermost point of the bay towards the open sea, and with both its shores parallel to the mainland. . . . Formerly they used to anchor at this outermost[5] point of the bay on what is called Didorus Island right by the mainland. But there is a ford to it that is able to be crossed by foot, and by means of this the natives dwelling in the area used to raid the island. Adulis, a village of moderate size, stands on the mainland opposite Oreinê, twenty stades inland. From it to Coloe,[6] a city in the hinterland that is the chief trading post for ivory, is a journey of three days, and from there to the metropolis itself, called Axum, another five . . . In front of the trading post in the open sea to the right lie numerous other small sandy islands called Alalaiou which furnish the tortoise shell brought to the post by the Fish-Eaters.

Thus, in seeking to identify the location of Adulis and its harbor, we should look for a site that a) is on or near the mouth of a deep bay extending southwards; b) has in front a rocky island (Oreinê), usable as an anchorage, which is toward the open sea, is 200 stades (about 20 miles) from the innermost point of the bay, and is so oriented that its shores are parallel with the mainland; c) has somewhere in the general vicinity another island (Didorus) so near the mainland that one can cross to it by foot; d) has several sandy islets in the open sea to the right of where the village (as against its harbor) lies.

The obvious candidate for the "deep bay extending due south" is Annesley Bay—or the Gulf of Zula, as it is also called—which lies between 15°3′ and 15°32′ north latitude (fig. 1). It is deep, is oriented north-south, and is in the area where, according to the line of travel and distances given in the *Periplus*, Adulis should be: the strip of coast that has served and still serves as starting point for the routes which mount to the uplands where Axum lies.

This part of the world was for long almost *terra incognita*. Annesley Bay was not properly located and charted until the beginning of the nineteenth century.[7] The first European to visit its shores and render an account of what he saw was Henry Salt, whose *Voyage to Abyssinia* appeared in 1814. In it he reported the discovery of ancient ruins about halfway down the western shore of the bay. They were by the bank of a river some three-quarters of a mile northwest of the modern village of Zula and some four miles in from the coast. The natives called them "Azoole," and, indeed, it was a reasonable conjecture that the name Zula itself was ultimately derived from the same source.[8] Salt concluded that this was the site of Adulis, a conclusion that has never been called into question.[9]

Archaeological investigation of the site did not come until well-nigh a century later, when R. Sundström in 1907 carried out a brief investigation.[10] He was able to trace the ground plan of an important building that had been constructed of ashlar blocks of a black porous stone; rectangular in shape, it measured no less than 38 by 22.5 meters, rose to a height of two stories, was approached by a monumental staircase, and included columns and marble veneering in its decoration. The following year R. Paribeni published the results of a more extended exploration.[11] This brought to light both the scanty but unmistakable remains of a native village that long predated Classical times and the abundant and impressive remains, many of them Christian, of a flourishing town of the fourth to sixth century A.D., the age to which Sundström's discovery belonged.[12] Paribeni unearthed quite a few coins, of which forty-two were of gold; these ranged chronologically from the beginning of the fourth century, or a bit earlier, up to the ninth and tenth.[13] Despite the late date of some of the coins, the excavation revealed clearly that, at the time when the power of Islam spread over this part of the world, the town suffered first destruction and then decay.[14]

The excavation seemed to put the identification beyond any doubt. Here were the ruins of buildings; here was evidence of activity and

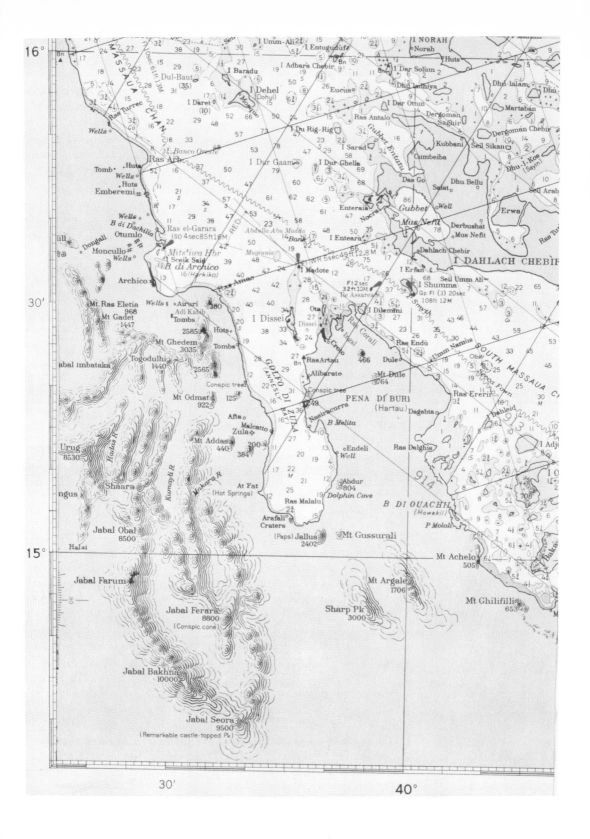

Fig. 1. Annesley Bay, Massawa Harbor, and vicinity. Detail of U.S. Hydrographic Center Chart no. 62008.

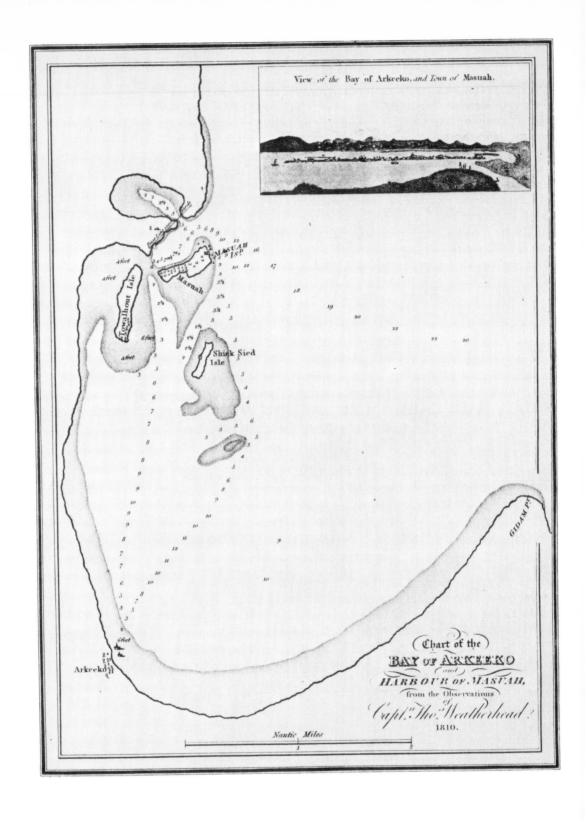

Fig. 2. Massawa Harbor. Reproduced from H. Salt, *Voyage to Abyssinia* (London 1814).

civilization consonant with what we knew about Adulis in its heyday, the fourth through the sixth century A.D. What is more, the location agreed nicely not only with the words of the author of the *Periplus*, but also with those of Procopius and Cosmas Indicopleustes, for all three state that Adulis was a short distance inland. Yet there is one insuperable difficulty that almost every one of those who so confidently made the identification simply glossed over: the site of these ruins, aside from being inland, does not in any way fit the indications given in the *Periplus*. [15]

There is no harbor proper anywhere near the ruins, but just a stretch of beach that descends into the water at so gentle an angle that one must go out hundreds of yards to find sufficient depth to float a seagoing vessel. [16] To be sure, as we shall see later, this does not preclude use as an anchorage. What is decisive is the fact that there are no islands whatsoever along this shore, nothing to answer to the Didorus Island which, the *Periplus* informs us, stood close to the mainland and for long served as Adulis's harbor.

It so happens that on the coast just twenty-five or so miles north [17] of where the ruins lie, there is just such an island. Moreover, it forms part of a superb natural harbor, the only one in the region—Massawa. Massawa in fact fits so very well with what we read in the *Periplus* that knowledgeable commentators who wrote before Salt's discovery did not hesitate to identify it as the site of Adulis. [18] Didorus Island would be what is today called Taulud; the modern causeway bearing water pipes and telephone lines that connects it with the mainland runs over shallows that could well have been the ford used by the raiders referred to in the *Periplus* (fig. 2). And the harbor, just as now, would have been the deep and well-protected inlet bounded on the south by Taulud and Massawa islands and on the north by the peninsula that juts out from the mainland.

If Taulud was Didorus Island, then surely Oreinê, which became the anchorage when marauding made the Taulud-Massawa harbor too dangerous, must be Dissei Island. It faces the open sea at the mouth of Annesley Bay; it is just about twenty miles from the innermost point of the bay; it is so oriented that both its shores lie parallel to the mainland; and it can aptly be called "Rocky," being "volcanic with a series of conical peaks, the summit of which is Monte Dissei, 335 feet high." [19] In fact, it is the sole island in the area that merits such a name. Off its southeastern shore, as it happens, there is a good anchorage. Finally, the sandy islets that were a source of tortoise shell, "in front of the trading post in the open sea to the right," would certainly include Sheik Said, which on older maps is actually called "Isle de la Tortue," and perhaps the islets between it and Dahlac Chebir. Some commentators see a connection between the ancient name Alalaiou and the modern Dahlac. [20]

Massawa then suits nicely the description in the *Periplus* of Adulis's original anchorage. The *Periplus* locates the village and

117

trading post *(kômê; emporion),* as against its harbor, twenty stades—some two miles—inland opposite Oreinê. Inasmuch as Oreinê is said to be "toward the open sea" and the sandy islets to be "in front of the trading post *(emporion)* in the open sea," it follows that Adulis more or less faced open water. And from this it follows that we cannot possibly place the Adulis of the *Periplus* on the ruins found by Salt, since these do not face open water but are halfway down the bay from its mouth.

From about A.D. 750, when Islam began its hegemony over the Red Sea, to the present day, Massawa has been the port par excellence for the area.[21] But Massawa has one serious drawback: it lacks drinking water.[22] As a consequence, it long served only as a harbor, while the town proper grew up on a shore point five or so miles to the south, at Arkiko. Here were the residences, business offices, and warehouses; here goods arriving from the harbor on small boats were transferred to porters or camels for the rugged climb upland, and goods arriving from there were transferred to small boats to be ferried to the harbor for loading aboard seagoing craft.[23]

Arkiko itself cannot be identified with the Adulis of the *Periplus,* for that, we are told, was two miles from the coast. It might well have been inland from Arkiko; if it were so located, Sheik Said would lie to the right toward the open sea, and Dissei would be roughly opposite. No ancient remains have been found there, but that can be explained. The *Periplus* describes Adulis as a "village of moderate size" *(kômê symmetros);* in other words, it was merely a large native settlement, no doubt built of adobe or wood. A settlement of this kind could easily disappear without trace.

But the Adulis of later centuries, of the fourth to the sixth, the Adulis that served as *the* port for Ethiopia's flourishing Axumite kingdom, could not so disappear. From remarks dropped by Cosmas Indicopleustes (2.103), who paid it a visit in A.D. 525 and saw there a monument erected by Ptolemy III, a handsome marble chair with a Greek inscription, we gain the distinct impression of a full-fledged city. And the only ruins to have come to light in the whole region— ruins, moreover, which would well fit such a city—are those that Salt discovered and Paribeni excavated. However, as we have just pointed out, they are nowhere near the open sea opposite Dissei Island, but halfway down the side of Annesley Bay.

One possible solution to the dilemma is to assume that the site of Adulis was shifted some time after the *Periplus* was written. A reason is not far to seek: the need for water. The rise of the Axumite kingdom increased the amount of traffic coming to the port, and the local population serving it must have grown accordingly. At some point the decision could well have been taken to found a new Adulis on the nearest place where water was available, the banks of a river some twenty miles to the southeast.

We have established that, in the days before the *Periplus,* the harbor of Adulis, the place where ships anchored and unloaded, had been the fine natural basin at Taulud-Massawa. In the days of the *Periplus,* raiders had forced a transfer to Dissei Island. Where was the harbor after the site of Adulis had been shifted, when it was handling the far-flung and active commerce of the Axumites in their flourishing period? Procopius states *(Bell. Pers.* 1.19.22): "The city of Adulis is a distance of twenty stades from the harbor *(limen)*—by that much alone does it miss being on the sea." Cosmas, who, it must be remembered, was there in person, says the same (2.103A): "The city of the Ethiopians called Adulis is near the coast, two miles distant, and is the harbor *(limen)* of the Axumites." A harbor named Gabaza is several times mentioned in connection with Adulis, and commentators have concluded that it was the name given to the *limen* referred to by Procopius and Cosmas.[24]

So, following what seemed to be the clear evidence of two reliable ancient sources, scholars have universally assumed that the harbor of Adulis was on the coast due east of the city, presumably just north of the modern village of Malcatto (actually the distance from this point to the ruins is four rather than two miles, but that is not serious). The coast here is, as mentioned earlier, but a very gently shelving beach, no more; the *Periplus* would be fully justified in calling Adulis, as it does other coastal points, *alimenos.*[25] To be sure, the beach here *can* be made into an anchorage; in 1867, when the British were searching for a place to land the expeditionary force that was to march inland and seize the fortress of Magdala, rejecting Massawa because of its lack of water, they chose precisely this beach. However, they had to build a stone jetty 300 yards long and later add an artificial island at the end to make it serviceable.[26] No doubt the Adulitans could have done the same, but if they did, whatever structures they put up have disappeared without trace. It seems strange that a facility of the magnitude of Adulis's harbor in the fourth to sixth century, a facility that must have boasted warehouses ashore as well as piers running far out into the water, could have vanished so totally. Possibly the structures were of wood, but surely some parts, the foundations for example, would have been of stone. Yet no such remains have ever been reported.

From the eight century A.D. on, as we remarked earlier, the port of the region was Massawa. This was where the earliest Muslim craft put in, where the first Portuguese missions to Ethiopia landed at the beginning of the sixteenth century, where Charles Jacques Poncet boarded a boat for Arabia in 1700, and where James Bruce disembarked in 1769.[27] It had also been the harbor, as we have seen, before the days of the *Periplus,* abandoned only because of marauding natives. Thus, if we follow all the commentators in placing the harbor of Adulis during its heyday deep in Annesley Bay, its history would have to go as follows: the first known harbor of the region was where we would expect, at Massawa with its deep, well-protected basin; sometime before the second half of the first century A.D., the date of the *Periplus*, it was moved to Dissei Island, since Massawa was too open to raids from the mainland; then it was moved to the beach in Annesley Bay, to remain there all during the thriving centuries of the Axumite kingdom; when that decayed, it was moved back to its original location, and there it stayed for the next twelve centuries.

I would like to suggest a different development, one that will yield a far more consistent historical picture as well as explain why no ruins were ever found along the coast where Adulis's harbor presumably existed. Its presence there rests squarely on the statement by Procopius and Cosmas that Adulis lay two miles inland from its *limen*. I submit that what both mean by this word is not the main harbor, but merely the small-boat harbor, the nearby point on the coast where the small craft which plied between the main harbor and Adulis put in. The main harbor would have been at Massawa. This was the facility where all seagoing vessels anchored; this was the harbor that had its own name of Gabaza.[28] The abandonment referred to in the *Periplus* surely was of short duration. Once the Axumite rulers had established themselves, they must have policed carefully this part of the coast, since all their rich international trade passed through it. And, with the threat of raids removed, there was no reason not to take advantage of the one good harbor of the region, at Massawa. Thus, when the Muslim conquerors took over, they simply continued to use, as was their way, what had been established by their predecessors. In other words, the harbor at Ethiopia, save for the brief moment recorded in the *Periplus*, was from earliest times to today at Massawa.

NOTES

1. Cf. Pliny 6.172, who refers to Adulis as the *maximum emporium trogodytarum, etiam Aethiopum.*

2. On the Axumite kingdom, see E. Littmann in *RE* Suppl. 7.77-80 (1940), and, on Adulis's importance at this time, G. Hourani, *Arab Seafaring* (Princeton 1951) 42.

3. The *Periplus* devotes a long section (6) to the imports and exports that passed through it. On possible trade with China, see A. Hermann in *Zeitschrift der Gesellschaft für Erdkunde* (1913) 553-55 (but cf. J. Duyvendak, *China's Discovery of Africa* [London 1949] 10-11).

4. The date of the *Periplus*, after a recent flurry of heated argument to lower it to the third century A.D., is back to its previous favored place, the second half of the first century A.D. For a judicious review of the problem, see W. Raunig, "Die Versuche einer Datierung des Periplus maris Erythraei," *Mitteilungen der anthropologischen Gesellschaft in Wien* 100 (1970) 231-42, esp. 240, and, for a listing of the bulky bibliography on the question, M. Raschke in *ANRW* ii.9.2 (Berlin 1978) 979-80, nn. 1342-43.

5. Cf. L. Casson in *CQ* 30 (1980) 495-96.

6. Coloe = Kohaito, where J. Theodore Bent (*The Sacred City of the Ethiopians* [London 1896] 217-25) discovered ruins.

7. See W. Vincent, *The Commerce and Navigation of the Ancients in the Indian Ocean* ii *The Periplus of the Erythrean Sea* (London 1807) 117, where he mentions receiving accurate information about the bay only when his book was already in press.

8. Henry Salt, *Voyage to Abyssinia* (1814) 451-53; for the distance inland, see C. Markham in *Journal of the Royal Geographical Society* 38 (1868) 13.

9. Cf. C. Müller's note in his edition of the *Periplus* in *Geographi Graeci Minores* i (Paris 1855) 257-305; W. Schoff, *The Periplus of the Erythraean Sea* (New York 1912) 60; the original entry in *RE* s.v. *Adule* (1894) and the updated one in Suppl. 7 (1940); A. Anfray in *Journal of African History* 9 (1968) 356; L. Kirwan in *Geographical Journal* 138 (1972) 166-69.

10. *Zeitschrift für Assyriologie* 20 (1907) 171-82.

11. "Ricerche nel luogo dell' antica Adulis," *Monumenti Antichi* 18 (1907) 438-572. Recently excavation has been renewed; see H. Sergew, *Ancient and Medieval Ethiopian History to 1270* (Addis Ababa 1972) 74-75 (photograph of ivory tusk found in 1961).

12. Cf. Paribeni's summary, 565-72. There are no Ptolemaic remains; cf. Kirwan (n. 9 above) 171-72. The large corded amphorae of Egyptian type which Paribeni found (549-50) are to be dated closer to the third to fourth centuries A.D. than earlier.

13. A. Anzani, "Numismatica Axumita," *Rivista italiana di numismatica e scienze affini* 33 (1926) 5-96. The earliest is of an unknown ruler Endybis (51), the latest of Hataz II (92, 94).

14. Paribeni 570-71; Littmann, *RE* Suppl. 7.2. Cf. A. Jones and E. Monroe, *A History of Ethiopia* (Oxford 1935) 45-46.

15. Müller (n. 9 above) 260, offers the desperate suggestion that in the course of time the island disappeared, becoming yoked to the mainland. R. Mauny in *Journal de la Société des Africanistes* 38 (1968) 23, says, "Adulis se trouve près du port actuel de Massawa, au village actuel de Zula," which makes nonsense of the geography.

16. F. Myatt, *The March to Magdala: The Abyssinian War of 1868* (London 1970) 70.

17. Cf. Kirwan (n. 9 above) 166.

18. Vincent (n. 7 above) 93. James Bruce, who was there in 1769, describes the harbor as follows (*Travels to Discover the Source of the Nile* [Edinburgh 1804[2]] iv 201-2): "Masuah . . . is a small island . . . having an excellent harbor, and water deep enough for ships of any size to the very edge of the island. Here they may ride in the utmost security, from whatever point, or with whatever degree of strength, the wind blows." For details of the harbor, see *Sailing Directions for the Red Sea and Gulf of Eden* (Defense Mapping Agency, Hydrographic Center, Pub. 61, 1965[5], rev. ed. 1976) 164.

19. *Sailing Directions* (n. 18 above) 166. Most commentators agree that Oreinê = Dissei Island (or Valentia Island, as it was called earlier): Salt (n. 8 above) 451; Müller (n. 9 above) 259; Mauny (n. 15 above) 23, who, mistranslating the Greek of the *Periplus,* puts it "environ 200 stades de l'entrée de la baie."

20. Most commentators agree that the islets are to be connected with islets in the Dahlac group: Vincent (n. 7 above) 105; Müller (n. 9 above) 260; Schoff (n. 9 above) 66; Littmann, *RE* Suppl. 7.1.

21. C. Conti Rossini, *Storia d'Etiopia,* "Africa Italiana" Collezione di monografie a cura del Ministero delle Colonie iii (Milan 1928) 273.

22. Cf. Myatt (n. 16 above) 70; the British in 1867-68 could not use Massawa as a base for their expeditionary force because of the lack of water.

23. When the Portuguese arrived at the beginning of the sixteenth century, Arkiko was the chief Christian center of the area; see S. Pankhurst, *Ethiopia; A Cultural History* (Woodford Green, Essex 1955) 312-13.

24. An illustration in the Vatican manuscript of Cosmas includes the words *telônion Gabazas;* E. Winstedt, *The Christian Topography of Cosmas Indicopleustes*

121

(Cambridge 1909) 337-38. "The Martyrdom of Arethas," *Acta Sanctorum* lvi *October* x (Paris and Rome 1869) 747 recounts how Caleb, the king of Axum, when preparing to launch an attack on Himyar in South Arabia in 525, "in a certain harbor *(hormos)* called Gabaza, within the district of the city of Adulis, the coastal city (ὑπὸ τὴν ἐνορίαν ὄντι Ἀδουλὶς τῆς πόλεως, τῆς παραθαλασσίας), ordered [60 vessels] to be drawn up on the shore." The editors of this passage take Gabaza (p. 752) to be near the ruins of Adulis, as does Winstedt. Cf. Conti Rossini (n. 21 above) 170, 174.

25. The trading post *(emporion)* of Ptolemais of the Hunts (3) and of Mouza (24).
26. Myatt (n. 16 above) 70-71.
27. Conti Rossini (n. 21 above) 273; C. Rey, *The Romance of the Portuguese in Abyssinia* (New York 1969 [1929]) 38; C. Poncet, *Cairo-Abyssinia and Back,* Hakluyt Society, 2d ser. 100 (London 1949) 154-56; James Bruce (n. 18 above) 201.
28. The sole text to locate Gabaza uses a curious locution, "within the district of Adulis" (see n. 24 above), which argues in favor of putting it further from Adulis than the nearest strip of shore.

13

A FOOTNOTE ON HEROIC REPRESENTATIONS: HELEN'S WEB

ELSBETH B. DUSENBERY

The question of whether heroic and mythological representations were ever intended on pictures on ceramics in the eighth century B.C.—specifically, of course, those made in Athens—has been vexed for a long time.[1] Some scholars point to the lack of attributes, the lack of labels, and the lack of positively unmistakable situations and see only reflections of the life of the Geometric period. Their view is that depictions of mythological and heroic actions probably do not appear in Greek art before the end of the eighth or the beginning of the seventh century.[2] Those who believe that heroic illustration starts earlier in the eighth century point, for example, to outmoded methods of fighting and to equipment like the Dipylon shield[3] as the means by which the painters had indicated that the scenes were to be regarded as heroic. Thus, a battle of duels by warriors on and around a beached ship should be the landing at Troy or the battle for the ships in the *Iliad;* a shipwreck with the one surviving man perched on the keel may well portray the shipwreck of Odysseus; a boy held off the ground by a warrior in front of a seemingly distressed man and woman should be Astyanax about to die.[4]

This note proposes that evidence given by the *Iliad* itself for the existence of some form of mythological representation at the time of Homer has not been granted enough attention. In an apparently unchallenged passage, the poet tells us that when Helen was summoned to the walls of Troy by Iris in the guise of one of her sisters-in-law, she was at work weaving a textile in which she was depicting the struggles of the Trojans and Achaeans suffered because of her. Iris "came on Helen in the chamber; she was weaving a great web, a red folding robe, and working into it the numerous struggles of Trojans, breakers of horses, and bronze-armoured Achaians, struggles that they endured for her sake at the hands of the war god."[5] This passage has been cited in discussions of textile techniques and of clothing.[6] No one, however, seems to have been struck forcibly by

123

this suggestion of the existence of a figural art of Homer's time in which specific heroic actions could be depicted. If Homer did not invent such art in this very passage, it must have been known in some medium, at least in Ionia.

It should be asked whether this figured web could be a reflection from the Bronze Age, as many objects and actions in the *Iliad* have proved to be. A number of scholars think that most of the everyday crafts which are mentioned in the poems, like animal husbandry, shipbuilding, and woolworking, reflect practices of Homer's own day.[7] The kind of weaving establishment we would expect in connection with a Bronze Age palace in Greece or Crete would be, as the Linear B tablets suggest, a workshop with a number of workers, particularly women and children, but also some men, many possibly foreigners.[8] Like the raising of sheep, the making of weapons and chariots, and the production of most other goods and products, spinning and weaving apparently were under the tight control of a bureaucratic administration, rather than simply under the direction of the mistress of the house. We know that Helen had women to assist her,[9] but they are not mentioned in the passage containing the figured web, and at that time she may have been working alone.

There seems no doubt that, after the collapse of Bronze Age palace life, spinning and weaving continued without pause so that clothing and covers could be supplied. The craft must have become entirely a domestic matter; there is no evidence of wealth or social organization sufficient to support a luxury textile production between the end of the Mycenaean period and the eighth century. Given the increasing wealth and stability in the later Geometric period, it seems likely that some households would include handmaidens who could assist with domestic production. This is a different world of work from the highly organized workshops of the Bronze Age palaces, and it is the kind of household which our text reflects.

The figures doing deeds which Helen was weaving do not seem to be part of the textile tradition of Greek lands and are unlikely to reflect fabled Bronze Age weavings. Textiles with colored patterns can be seen in the clothing represented in Mycenaean and Aegean paintings and figurines, but none of these, so far as I know, shows human figures. Patterned weavings, more or less complicated, probably persisted throughout the Dark Ages, and some scholars believe that textiles supplied motives for Geometric pottery decoration and may have been an important element in the formation of the Geometric style.[10] Others have even seen simple Bronze Age motifs in Geometric art and think that these were transmitted from age to age largely through the patterns on textiles.[11]

Helen's web was surely not the product of such a conservative tradition. It was roughly contemporary with, and as astonishing as, the great Attic Geometric vases of the middle years of the eighth century, with their groups of human figures in action. The increasing

124

contact with the Orient and its influence on Greek arts and crafts during the eighth century have often been discussed,[12] and what springs to mind as an influence on Helen's work is the long, unbroken tradition of Near Eastern tapestries and embroideries, which were often decorated with scenes including animals, both real and fabulous, humans, and divinities.[13] As with all other borrowings from the East, figured textiles must quickly have been transformed by Greek needs and artistic style.

We are not likely to see a figured textile like Helen's web, but knowing about it suggests two important things. One is the central role of imported textiles (which have vanished), together with metalwork, ivories, and other durable objects (happily, some are preserved for us), in influencing the character of late Geometric art and bringing to it the new ideas which led to the "orientalizing" art of the seventh century. Even more important is its evidence that, at about the time of the *Iliad,* specific heroic actions could be, and surely were, depicted in art. Was Helen thought of as simply a reporter of contemporary life, as has been suggested for the painters of battle scenes on late Geometric pottery? Strictly speaking, the struggles of Trojans and Achaeans were contemporary for her. They were, however, in the heroic past for Homer's auditors, and if heroic representations did not already exist, they can have been but a short step away. It would be surprising in a period in which human actions were depicted, in which there were no divine or absolute rulers to monopolize the power of images, and in which at least the nobles were involved with poetry and cults harking back to the heroic past,[14] if figural art would not attempt to reflect that past and the relationship of the current generation to it. Helen's web shows that heroic representations existed well before the end of the eighth century, and that the problems of recognizing them are probably more ours than those of Homer's original audience.

NOTES

1. No friends or colleagues were implicated in this trespass into a neighboring vineyard. In place of the usual thanks, I would like to salute Bluma Trell: a teacher for all ages and a friend for all seasons.
2. The following discussions do not admit heroic representations before the end of the eighth century or until the seventh century B.C.: J. Carter, "Narrative Art in the Geometric Period," *BSA* 67 (1972) 25-58; M. E. Caskey, "Notes on Relief Pithoi of the Tenian-Boiotian Group," *AJA* 80 (1976) 26; J. M. Cook, "The Cult of Agamemnon at Mycenae," *Geras A. Keramopoullou* (Athens 1953) 117; R. M. Cook, *Greek Art* (New York 1972) 35-36; K. Friis Johansen, *The "Iliad" in Early Greek Art* (Copenhagen 1967) 17-26; G. S. Kirk, "Ships on Geometric Vases," *BSA* 44 (1949) 144-53.
3. The controversy is over whether the Dipylon shield is a reflection of the Mycenaean body shield, thus indicating heroic subject matter, or was a real shield

type in use at least in the early Geometric period. Pro heroic: T. B. L. Webster, *From Mycenae to Homer* (London 1958) 169-70; pro a real shield: Johansen (n. 2 above) 19-20; Carter (n. 2 above) 55-57. Cf. A. M. Snodgrass, *Arms and Armor of the Greeks* (London 1967) 44-45.

4. These representations are discussed by the authors below, who generally believe in heroic representations, as well as by those who hold the opposite view (n. 2 above). R. Hampe, *Frühe griechische Sagenbilder* (Athens 1936) and *Die Gleichnisse Homers und die Bildkunst seiner Zeit* (Tübingen 1952); K. Schefold, *Myth and Legend in Early Greek Art* (New York n.d.) 21-28; T. B. L. Webster, "Homer and Attic Geometric Art," *BSA* 50 (1955) 38-50. For balanced discussions of the nature of the possible epic scenes: J. Coldstream, *Geometric Greece* (New York 1977) 352-56; G. M. A. Hanfmann, "Narration in Greek Art," *AJA* 61 (1957) 71-72; A. M. Snodgrass, *The Dark Age of Greece* (Edinburgh 1971) 431-32.

5. *Iliad* 3.125-28, trans. Lattimore.

6. A. J. B. Wace, "Weaving or Embroidery?" *AJA* 52 (1948) 51-55; H. L. Lorimer, *Homer and the Monuments* (London 1950) 397; A. B. J. Wace and F. H. Stubbings, *A Companion to Homer* (London 1963) 531.

7. Snodgrass (n. 4 above) 388-90, 435 (with references).

8. For analysis of the palace workshops: L. R. Palmer, *Mycenaeans and Minoans* (London 1965) 111, 115-20; J. Chadwick, *The Mycenaean World* (Cambridge 1976) 80. F. H. Stubbings (n. 6 above) 531, says that "spinning and weaving in Homer . . . were household crafts," but he does not remark what seems the more formal, almost industrial, character of the palace workshops indicated by the tablets.

9. *Iliad* 6.323-24.

10. E.g. B. Schweitzer, *Greek Geometric Art* (New York 1971) 30.

11. J. Benson, *Horse, Bird, and Man* (Amherst 1970) 68-69, 111-12.

12. Snodgrass (n. 4 above) 271, 331, 334-35, 343-45, 350, 417 (with references). For textiles: Lorimer (n. 6 above) 397.

13. For a surviving Near Eastern textile embroidered with animals, sphinxes, and floral motives, from the tomb of Tutankhamun, and for discussion of the influence of foreign textiles on Egyptian weaving during the New Kingdom: E. Riefstahl, *Patterned Textiles in Pharaonic Egypt* (Brooklyn 1944) 28-33. For figured Assyrian textiles of the ninth century B.C.: S. M. Paley, "The Texts, the Palace and the Reliefs of Ashurnasirpal II," *AJA* 81 (1977) 539. For comment on the probable influence of Assyrian textiles of the period of Sargon II (721-705 B.C.) on Greek iconography: Hanfmann (n. 4 above) 73, n. 11.

14. J. N. Cook, "Mycenae 1939-1952: The Agamemnoneion," *BSA* 48 (1953) 33; V. R. d'A. Desborough, *The Greek Dark Ages* (London 1972) 283; Snodgrass (n. 4 above) 192-93, 195, 196, 429.

THOUGHTS ON THE SIGNIFICANCE OF THE LATIN COMPONENT IN THE WELSH LANGUAGE

ROBERT A. FOWKES

Blodeuo Blwma am byth
Floreat Bluma sempiternum

A simplified view of the history of the island of Britain, but one often dimly held despite its simplicity, is that that island, once largely a Celtic land, became a part of the Roman Empire sometime around the middle of the first century and that the Romans departed early in the fifth, after which departure Germanic tribes, conventionally called Angles, Saxons, and Jutes (or, less legitimately, Anglo-Saxons) invaded and occupied the land. The traditional date of their arrival persists in our popular belief: A.D. 449.[1] The oversimplification deepens when *post hoc, ergo propter hoc* assumptions connect the two events. There is, furthermore, need for clarity in considering what is meant by the "departure" of the Romans, for, although the Roman army of occupation may have left, together with colonial administrators, officials, and sundry hangers-on, there was a substantial and mostly inextricable ethnic Roman element that remained in the British population, an ingredient that presumably endures even now.[2] We are prone to regard Britons, Romans, and "Anglo-Saxons" as separate, identifiable blocks moved by the forces of history, picked up and put down in some sort of game, accepted or evicted—a view that utterly ignores the fluidity of biological-ethnic processes. Even on arrival the "Romans" were certainly of mixed ethnic constituency, as were the Britons they encountered, as were the various waves of invaders preceding them, as were the Angles and Saxons (plus a Jute or two) that followed them. The skeletal remains of the first four centuries (or during the portion of that time when inhumation was practiced) show, we are told,[3] further results of mixture, with assimilation of certain "Roman" types to the general "British" physical type. Roman soldiers married British women, or at least had offspring with them.[4] If, after four centuries of Roman Britain, some dictatorial decree had ordered all persons "of Roman blood" to leave and all those "of British blood" to remain, a great part of the population would have been faced with an insoluble paradox.

Neither the Romans nor the Angles and Saxons swept before them, with some irresistible broom, the peoples they encountered, clearing the whole south and east of the island and driving paltry remnants into the western fastnesses of Wales and Cornwall. Had the Romans done this, the Angles and Saxons would have encountered no Britons in what became England, merely those Romans who had missed the channel boats in that fifth-century evacuation—unless we assume, with no obvious justification, that the Celtic population had gradually trickled back into the eastern and southern regions. For it was Celts with whom the Angles and Saxons fought, albeit Celts with an admixture of those ethnic strains imparted during the Roman occupation. Roman soldiers were recruited from Gaul (thus cousins of the Britons were brought to occupy them), from Spain, from Roman Danube provinces (all of these in the first century), and subsequent reinforcements came mostly from Germania.[5] Any notion that the first "Germans" to reach Britain came with the Anglo-Saxon invasion is thus emphatically demolished. So-called Anglo-Saxons thus unwittingly later met people to whom they were partly related—not that the recognition of that kinship would necessarily have moved them to greater mansuetude in their treatment of the conquered.

Moreover, the merchants and tradespeople came mostly from Italy, Northern Gaul, and Greece,[6] and even if their stay was transient, a certain number may have settled, or at least have remained long enough to add further ethnic elements. Traders, peddlers, and the like must have been bilingual or polylingual in order to deal with all strata of the population. In major commercial activities, the language used in Roman Britain was doubtless Latin. But in small-scale retail dealings the traders and merchants would have to use British. This would also apply to shopkeepers, who would have to speak the Celtic language(s) to many of their customers.

The official language of the army was surely Latin; yet the numerous units of non-Roman nationality would certainly use their own languages in everyday personal communication. One is reminded of the army of the Austro-Hungarian empire, where the soliders spoke over a dozen different languages, although German was the chief official one. Moreover, the soldiers of the Roman army had various religions and worshiped their own gods.[7] Inscriptional evidence shows this to some extent. Native gods imply native ritual and native prayers, even though the inscriptions use Latin.

We are given the impression that well-to-do Britons saw to it that their children enjoyed a Roman education. There are even references to the skill of the British in learning Latin.[8] No archaeological findings, however, seem to unearth schools as such. Some aristocratic Britons may conceivably have sent their sons (hardly daughters) to Rome. But education in Roman Britain itself may well have been a matter of private tutoring or of small classes conducted in a room or two of a building which had some other primary function. The unearthed towns of Roman Britain reveal such architectural features as a forum, baths, amphitheater, town hall *(basilica),* and temple (later church; Calleva Atrebatum [Silchester] had a Christian church as well as four or five temples); but no school is shown in such town plans, whether unearthed or reconstructed.[9] One wonders what the situation was in other parts of the empire and also what provisions were made for libraries. It seems, at any rate, that no building was designated as a school but that a Latin education was available to some Britons.[10]

But, regardless of how Romanized the aristocratic Britons may have become, they must have retained their native idiom too. Communication with the "humble" members of the family and household would demand this. In legal cases there must have also been considerable use of the British language, probably with rather extensive use of interpreters.

Polylingualism prevailed in quarters sometimes overlooked by students of the period of Roman Britain (not, however, by Celticists). In parts of what is now Wales, a persistent Irish occupation occurred at a time overlapping that of the late portion of the Roman occupation and extending perhaps a century beyond. The area of Dyfed *(Demetia)* in southwest Wales (not so large as what is now called "Dyfed" in the recent renaming of the divisions of Wales, but somewhat more extensive than what used to be called Pembrokeshire) was mainly bilingual (Goidelic and British) and some of the Irish rulers were evidently trilingual (Irish, British, Latin). It is in this part of Wales that ogam inscriptions are most numerous.[11] These characteristically Irish (Goidelic) inscriptions are found typically on commemorative stones of royal or aristocratic Irishmen. In Wales, some are bilingual, the ogam itself being in archaic Irish, with a Latin "subtitle" (various epigraphic arguments favor Irish as the original). The conclusion to be drawn from these bilingual monuments is not eminently obvious. The Irish rulers would presumably read and understand the Irish portion of the inscription. Many of them would understand, but not need, the Latin version. For whom was it intended? Possibly for literate Britons, who would know Latin (but did not write their own British language). They would not be able to read Ogam Irish (unless one or two took the pains to learn it). It seems reasonable to conclude that the Latin portion was intended for literate British (pre-Welsh) subjects of the Irish. If one is disturbed to note that an ogam inscription on the Isle of Man also has a Latin translation, let it be borne in mind that it has also been suggested that there were British speakers there too for a while. It is also possible, of course, that Latin was intended to carry the fame of the commemorated into future ages via the universal language. Maybe the Irish carvers of those words were unaware that the Imperium was falling apart. (They also confused Romans with Britons somewhat.)

129

The ogam system of writing seems also to have been the source of Pictic writing.[12] But we know very little about that language. It was, however, one still spoken in Britain during the Roman occupation and may have figured in polyglottal combinations (a conceivable, though rare one, would be Pictish/Irish/Welsh/Latin). It was also another native language that had achieved a certain literacy.

The usual claim that British was never written needs partial modification on the basis of numismatic evidence, for British coins antedating the arrival of the Romans often contain the names of Celtic British kings in letters probably taken from Gaulish.[13] Hence writing, however minimal it might be, arrived without waiting for the Romans. It is well known that Britons and Gauls were in communication with each other. In fact, Caesar complained (*De bello Gall.* 4.21) that a fleet of Britons had sailed to Gaul bringing aid to their "cousins" in their fight against Caesar and even joining the Venetic league, thus giving Caesar a cogent excuse for invading Britain. Caesar's well-known reference (1.29) to the records of the Helvetians found in their camp (written "in Greek letters") gives evidence that the native use of writing was by no means confined to religious purposes. Further support in this direction is seen in the La Graufesenque graffiti, which show employment of Gaulish writing in the pottery industry.[14] The Coligny Calendar offers similar evidence.[15] The exciting discovery in the present decade of the "Celtiberian" inscription of Botorrita, Spain, adds further dimensions to the question of the antiquity of Celtic literacy.[16]

One of the lasting results of bilingualism in Roman Britain was the acquisition of an important Latin component in the vocabulary of the language(s) of the Britons. It is still present in Welsh and Breton (with complications) and was also in Cornish until that language's demise. An amazing confusion is often encountered, even on the part of scholars, as to where such influence should be sought. Consider the following statement: "Though the Romans, during four centuries, left abundant traces of their occupation of Britain, yet the traces of their language left in the island are very meager." The author proceeds to discuss such words as *castra, strata,* and their reflexes in English.[17] This before English had yet come to Britain!

Kenneth Jackson in his comprehensive and authoritative work goes so far as to say that this part of the British vocabulary ("Brittonic" is preferred by Jackson) "may be said to form a fragment of a Romance language."[18] Few are likely to accept that specific designation, and it is fairly certain that Jackson is speaking figuratively. Nevertheless, his assertion holds that Romance scholars have almost entirely ignored this element in Brythonic, for it does give testimony on the kinds of alteration undergone by Latin itself during the closing years of the empire. It even provides clues to many points of phonology and lexicon of Latin of a period earlier than that of British Latin (whereas, as might be expected, syntactic and morphological evi-

130

dence is minute). Numerous scholars in the realm of Celtic have looked at this vocabulary.[19]

The reasons for taking ("borrowing," as the common term so inadequately puts it)[20] elements of vocabulary by one language from another are not always as obvious as one might assume. They are fairly clear in such a case as importing an object or practice hitherto unknown in the culture of the "borrowing" language. Then it is reasonable to expect that the name of the new acquisition may also be adopted—with whatever modifications the phonic and morphological system of the recipient language may necessitate. A word like *papyrus* might be an example of such an element (although old coins show papyrus in pre-Roman Britain—or, at least, the knowledge of it).[21] The introduction of hitherto unknown plants, fruits, flowers, and so on might also result in the simultaneous introduction of new words to designate them; it is not impossible, however, for new terms to be coined from elements of the language already extant.

But words for arms and legs were also borrowed by British from Latin, which does not give us the right to assume that those members were unknown in Britain before the Romans arrived (Welsh *braich* 'arm' < *bracchium; coes* 'leg' < *cōxa* 'hip, etc.'), any more than the English word *uncle* implies the absence of those relatives previous to contact with the French-speaking Normans. Words may be taken without obvious need from one language to another. It is possible to surmise that the reasons include factors of prestige, snobbishness, fads, and the like, but in the specific instance the explanation is often a mere guess.

Intriguingly enough, the spoken Latin of Britain which developed for some four centuries in that colony shows a far greater resistance to phonological change than occurred in the Romance languages. Kenneth Jackson is certainly right when he (p. 80) gently rebukes Celticists for treating the sources of Latin loanwords as if they were the classical language of Caesar's day. Well, a few actually were. But even in the centuries following Caesar, British Latin seems to have been quite conservative. Some of the striking features of the sound system of Classical Latin have, in fact, persisted down into modern Welsh of the present day. This article will now look at a few of those features and show how twentieth-century Welsh offers evidence of even Classical Latin pronunciation.

LATIN *C*

The consonant written as *c* in Latin underwent a variety of developments in the Romance languages, depending in part upon its phonetic environment. Even in the pronunciation of Latin itself similar disagreement occurred in different parts of the empire, and

131

present-day attempts to pronounce it and other sounds (in school, church—to the extent that Latin is still used—the law, etc.) show extreme diversity; witness its pronunciation in Italy, France, Germany, Holland, Britain, the United States, and elsewhere. In classical Latin, *c* represented a *k* sound, regardless of what the immediate phonetic environment was. It could have varied microphonetically, depending on whether it was followed by a front or a back vowel. But it remained a *k* sound. In somewhat antiquated (but not invalidated) terminology, all variants of the sound represented by Latin *c* were members of the phoneme /k/. In Welsh orthography, *c* always indicates a *k* sound also. It is not astounding to find the following correspondences:

WELSH		LATIN
cadair	'chair'	*cathedra*
cadwyn	'chain'	*catēna*
calaf	'reed'	*calamus*
calan	'New Year's Day'	*calendae*
cardod	'charity'	*caritātem*
cawell	'creel, basket'	*cavella*
caws	'cheese'	*cāseus*
colomen	'dove'	*columba*
corff	'body'	*corpus*
cwmwl	'cloud'	*cumulus*
cyllell	'knife'	*cultellus*

It is recognized by the writer that the nominative case cited above is not always the actual source of the specific loanword, and that some oblique case was often more likely to be that source. But the nominative is used as a conventional citation to represent the noun paradigm. For *cardod* 'charity' the accusative *caritātem* has been given, but that means merely that the nominative *caritas* cannot have been the origin; the accusative is a possible one. A more cautious writing would probably be *caritāt-,* which is, however, simply another confession of ignorance.

As has been said, it is not astounding to find Latin *c* represented in the above list by a *k* sound in Welsh, because it precedes a back vowel in each instance. The following correspondences, though, are very significant, for they show a *k* sound as the continuant of Latin *c* in positions in which the Romance languages have abandoned the original *k*.

WELSH		LATIN
cengl	'girth, belly-band'	*cing(u)la*
cell	'cell'	*cella*
cest	'chest, receptacle,' etc.	*cista*
cethr	'nail, pin, spike'	*centrum*

ciwdod	'people, tribe'	*cīv(i)tātem*
ciwed	'mob, rabble'	*civitas*
cwyn	'dinner'	*cēna*

LATIN *G*

Similarly, *g*, the voiced counterpart of Latin *c*, is retained initially.

WELSH		LATIN
gefell	'twin'	*gemellus*
gem	'gem, jewel'	*gemma*

The *m* of Welsh *gem* points to a Latin *-mm-*, whereas a single medial *-m-* became [v], written *f* in Welsh; hence *gefell* reflects *gemell-*. This preservation of the voiced occlusive quality of Latin *g*, which is well established in initial position, is not matched by the history of medial *-g-*. The latter (as in a great number of languages) is highly vulnerable and, by modern times, has often vanished in Welsh. This is true of both "borrowed" and "inherited" words. Note:

WELSH		LATIN
gwain	'sheath, scabbard'	*vāgīna*
pau	'land, region'	*pāgus*
gŵyl	'feast, holiday'	*vigilia*
rheol	'rule'	*rēgula*

That there was an intermediate stage at which Latin medial *g* became a voiced velar fricative is likely in view of the fact that Latin *b* and *d* became in Welsh the corresponding voiced fricatives [v] and [ð] respectively.

LATIN *U/V*

The evidence of Latin loanwords in Welsh also helps to demolish the assaults on the pronunciation of Latin *u/v* as a *w* (roughly like that of English *w*). This emerges most obviously in medial position. The examples *ciwdod* and *ciwed*, cited above in the discussion of *c*, show quite conspicuously that a *w* sound was the source—and is still retained in Welsh. The word for 'wizard, diviner,' Welsh *dewin* (*dīvīnus*) gives further substantiation of the *w* character of Latin *v*. The first vowel of *dewin* is, admittedly, somewhat problematical. 133

Such a form implies *devīnus* as its source. Henry Lewis suggests that the sequence *-ī–ī-* became *-e–ī-* in spoken Latin,[22] which seems to be an ad hoc explanation, whether parallels are found in Romance languages or not. At any rate, the evidence of the *w* quality of the consonant is unimpaired. Welsh *athrywyn* 'intervene' (from Lat. *intervenio*), despite the (mostly regular) alteration of the prefix, shows additional preservation of *w*. The word *paun* 'peacock' (from Latin *pavōn-em*) shows *au*, no longer denoting a *u-* diphthong in Welsh; but a Middle Welsh form *pawin* shows the preservation of Latin *-au-* [-au-] down to the Middle Ages. This makes it valid to regard *Iau* 'Jove, Jupiter' *(Iovem)* and *ffau* 'cave' *(fovea)* as indicating the same origin of *au* and thus indirectly pointing to the *w* nature of Latin *v* in the original words.

Latin initial *v-* underwent alteration to *gw-* in Welsh. This is a familiar process and duplicates what happened to Indo-European initial *u̯* (= *w*) in Brythonic Celtic. It also occurred, as is well known, in Germanic loanwords in Romance, cf., for example, Italian *guancia, guanto, guardia,* and *guerra,* all from Germanic words with initial *w-*. Closer to home (from the point of view of the present article), Welsh also treated a few loanwords from English the same way (*gwermod* from Old English *wermōd,* etc.). It would not be pertinent to discuss relative chronology here; suffice it to say that these are all occurrences of the same phonetic process in which a *w* [u̯] becomes *gw* [gu̯]. Welsh examples of loanwords from Latin with initial *v-* abound.

WELSH		LATIN
gwag	'empty'	*vacuus* or **vacus*
gwain	'sheath'	*vagīna*
gwenwyn	'poison'	*venēnum*
gwiwer	'squirrel'	*viverra* 'ferret'; this example illustrates both initial and intervocalic *w*
gwin	'wine'	*vīnum*
gwydr	'glass'	*vitrum*

It happens that, in certain syntactic combinations, the initial *g-* will be dropped in Welsh and the resultant forms (*wag, wain, wenwyn, wiwer,* and the rest) then look even more similar to the Latin sources. This is in part accidental, but it does, in combination with all the other evidence, point to a *w*-like sound of *v* in British Latin (and not only there, but certainly in Roman Latin too).

LATIN *I/J*

Parallel to the development of Latin consonantal *u/v* (but even more conservative, in the main) is that of *i/j*. Initial *j* has, in most descendant languages of Latin, markedly altered its shape. In Welsh, however, loanwords from British Latin retain what was the "Classical" value of that sound. These words are not so numerous as those with *v*, but they are fully as significant. They include *Iau* 'Jove' (also in *Dydd Iau* 'Thursday'), from Latin *Iov-em; Ionawr* 'January' (*Jānuārius*); *Iago* 'James' (*Jacobus*), etc. In the sequence *ju*, the Welsh development was something like *jü > ji > i*, with apparent vocalization of consonantal *j* (but actually constituting a merger of the reflex of *j* plus the "umlauting" of *u* to *ü* to *i*). Hence we find *isgell* 'broth; pottage' (*juscellum*, diminutive of *jūs* 'broth'); *Iddas* (*Judas*—with a final *s* that should not be retained but probably is for reasons of biblical occurrence, possibly with "learned" restoration. It does not, of course, harm the case for *j*). That some of the Latin words and names are themselves allogenous is of no moment in the present connection (*Ieuan < Johannes*, for example, is from Greek, from Semitic).

LATIN *H*

The above examples of Latin loans in Welsh are evidence of the pronunciation of Latin and are surprisingly conservative retentions of sounds going back, not only to colloquial Latin of the time of Roman Britain, but even to Classical times. (The surprise is not equally shared by all students of language.) But the case of *h-* is somewhat different. It has vanished in the attested loans in Welsh, even orthographically.

WELSH		LATIN
afwyn	'rein'	*habēna*
ystyr	'meaning; import'	*historia*
awr	'hour'	*hōra*
ufylltod	'humility'	*humilitāt-em*
osb (arch.)	'guest'	*hospes*

This loss of initial *h* is a universal fact of Romance phonology. It was beginning to occur even in Classical times. Medial loss clearly ante-

135

dated loss in initial position; witness such alterations and alternations in Classical Latin as *nihil: nil,* or *prehendo: prendo.* And the unetymological writings *hinsidias, honera* point to the phonetic nondistinctiveness of *h* even in Cicero's days. Apparently the *h-* had vanished by the time of the effective Roman occupation of Britain, though possibly not at the time of the first invasions. Sometime during the occupation, British Celtic was acquiring an *h* from another source: from Celtic (or Brythonic) initial *s.* The Welsh name of the river Severn: *Hafren* (from Brythonic *Sabrina*) reflects this development. One or two Latin words with initial *s* were apparently acquired before that process had occurred; hence, when it did take place, such words participated in the change. Latin *sextārius* is the source of Old Welsh *hestaur,* Modern Welsh *hestawr* 'a two-bushel measure', and *sērus* 'late' results in Welsh *hwyr* 'late; evening.' But other words show *s-: saeth* 'arrow' *(sagitta); sarff* 'serpent' *(serpens); sôn* 'sound' *(sonus); sych* 'dry' *(siccus); syml* 'simple' *(simplus).* The variation here clearly reflects no phenomenon in Latin itself but rather in Brythonic in its various periods. It looks as if no Latin words with initial *h* (or any other kind of *h*) were adopted at a time when Welsh (or pre-Welsh) had acquired an *h* sound itself. One may speculate that Britons probably never heard a Latin *h* in any words. (Most elements of Latin vocabulary were probably acquired orally.)

There are numerous other points of phonology that could be discussed, but this article has been confined to a few that are especially significant as evidence of the pronunciation of Latin. For whatever reason, the Latin spoken in Britannia seems to have been very conservative, especially in its phonology. Some would see in that conservatism the result of the remoteness of Britain, situated on the edge of the empire—if not the world. Areal linguistics would account for it on the basis of "isolated area" or "peripheral area." Other explanations might point to the generally conservative nature of idioms translated to colonial areas. (Icelandic, for example, is far closer to Old Norse than is Norwegian; the Welsh spoken in Patagonia is more conservative than that of Wales.)

Whatever the cause of its relative conservatism, we can say that the Latin element in Welsh (and Cornish and Breton) provides valuable evidence of the pronunciation of Latin and even vindicates, to some extent, the pronunciation used (or aimed at) in our American "school Latin" of what Stephen Leacock allegedly called the "wainy-weedy-weaky" variety. There has been partial recognition in various countries that the pronunciation of Cicero, Caesar, Vergil, and their contemporaries was far different from that used in most European countries, although change in actual practice has been notoriously slow.[23] Wales finds no difficulty in pronouncing *Caesar* [kaisar], for that is what the orthography implies in Welsh.

NOTES

1. For a partial corrective, see Myles Dillon and Nora Chadwick, *The Celtic Realms* (New York 1967) 18-42; see also S. E. Winbolt, *Britain under the Romans* (Harmondsworth 1945) 39-43; Christopher and Jacquetta Hawkes, *Prehistoric Britain* (Harmondsworth 1952) 146-65.
2. R. G. Collingwood and J. N. L. Myres, *Roman Britain and the English Settlements,* The Oxford History of England i (Oxford, 1968; reprt. of 2d ed., 1937) 313; Kenneth Jackson, *Language and History in Early Britain* (Edinburgh 1953) 98.
3. Collingwood and Myres (n. 2 above) 425-26; Jackson (n. 2 above) 98.
4. Leonard Cottrell, *A Guide to Roman Britain* (Philadelphia and New York 1966²) 138. Although four centuries of occupation would practically assure that etymological cohabitation would result in the biological homonym, it seems difficult to find well-supported statements on actual marriages of Romans and Britons. In the long run, of course, ceremonies are of slight moment. According to Anthony Birley, *Life in Roman Britain* (London and New York 1964) 154, "intermarriage called for no comment."
5. Collingwood and Myres (n. 2 above) 182; Jackson (n. 2 above) 98; R. H. Barrow, *The Romans* (Harmondsworth 1957) 168.
6. Collingwood and Myres (n. 2 above) 182.
7. Jackson (n. 2 above) 98.
8. Cottrell (n. 4 above) 26; John Wacher, *Roman Britain* (London 1978) 84, 191.
9. Winbolt (n. 1 above) 65-67.
10. Wacher (n. 8 above) 84; Birley (n. 4 above) 114-16; John Morris, *The Age of Arthur: A History of the British Isles from 350 to 650* (London 1973) 409-11, with references to individual teachers (Saint Illtud, Paulenus, Tatheus). See also Tacitus, *Agricola,* chap. 22. Some accounts, like that of Birley, purport to treat the conventional educational program, but no proof is offered that it actually applied to Britain.
11. Dillon and Chadwick (n. 1 above) 38-41, 53, 85; V. E. Nash-Williams, *The Early Christian Monuments of Wales* (Cardiff 1950) 3-8; Morris (n. 10 above) 158; Lloyd Laing, *The Archaeology of Late Celtic Britain and Ireland* (London 1975) 94-95.
12. Dillon and Chadwick (n. 1 above) 72-75.
13. Collingwood and Myres (n. 2 above) 58-59; Hawkes and Hawkes (n. 1 above) 151; Dillon and Chadwick (n. 1 above) 23.
14. L. Weisgerber, "Die Sprache der Festlandkelten," *Berichte der römisch-germanischen Kommission des deutschen archäologischen Instituts* 30 (1930) 147-226; F. Hermet, *La Graufesenque* (Paris 1934).
15. G. Dottin, *La langue gauloise* (Paris 1918) 172-207; Dillon and Chadwick (n. 1 above) 15.
16. Karl Horst Schmidt, "Zur keltiberischen Inschrift von Botorrita," *Bulletin of the Board of Celtic Studies* 26 (1975) 375-94; M. Lejeune, "La grande inscription celtibère de Botorrita (Saragosse)," *Comtes rendus des séances de l'année 1973* (Paris 1974) 624; A. Beltrán, "La inscripción ibérica sobre bronce de Botorrita," *Homenaje a D. Pio Beltrán, Anejos de Archivo Español de Arqueologia* 7 (Madrid 1974) 73-85.
17. A. Grosvenor Hopkins, *Tacitus: The "Agricola" and "Germania"* (Chicago 1930 [1st ed. 1897]) 104. Singling out this work for condemnation is admittedly a random act. The writer read the *Agricola* in this edition years ago. It does, however, represent a point of view (or a blindness) shared by all too many who seem to believe that the English language arrived in Britain centuries before the English themselves. Ignorance of Celtic matters is slow to be dispelled.
18. Jackson (n. 2 above) 76.
19. After the pioneers William Salesbury (1547) and Gruffydd Robert (1567), we can mention a number of scholars who have dealt with the Latin loanwords in the Celtic languages, including Sir John Rhys, articles in *Archaeologia Cambrensis*

137

(1873-74); H. Güterbock, *Die lateinischen Lehnwörter im Irischen* (Leipzig 1882); J. Loth, *Les mots latins dans les langues brittoniques* (Paris 1892); Chr. Sarauw, *Irske Studier* (Copenhagen 1900) 1-20; J. Vendryes, *De Hibernicis uocabulis quae a Latina lingua originem duxerunt* (Paris 1902); H. Pedersen, *Vergleichende Grammatik der keltischen Sprachen* i (Göttingen 1909) 189-242; Josef Baudiš, *Grammar of Early Welsh,* pt. 1, *Phonology* (Oxford 1924) 176-78; Henry Lewis, *Datblygiad yr Iaith Gymraeg* (Cardiff 1931) 61-80; H. Lewis, *Yr Elfen Ladin yn yr Iaith Gymraeg* (Cardiff 1943); Jackson (n. 2 above); Harald Haarmann, *Der lateinische Lehnwortschatz im Kymrischen* (Bonn 1970). Since this article was written the following has been announced: Eric Hamp, "The British End of the Spectrum of Romania," *Contemporary Studies in Romance Linguistics,* ed. Margarita Suñer (Georgetown 1978) *(non vidi).*
20. Such "borrowings" apparently are occasionally repaid in a peculiar sense of the word: e.g., Old High German *faldastōl,* which was taken into pre-French; in its further development it became *fauteuil* and in that shape was "taken back" into German. Such linguistic accidents are scarcely sufficient in force to justify terms like "borrowing" and "loans," however.
21. Wacher (n. 8 above) 191.
22. Lewis (n. 19 above) 9.
23. Cf. the brilliant discussion by Giuliano Bonfante, "La Pronuncia del Latino nelle Scuole," *Maia* 19 (1967) 255-78.

15

MAP PROJECTION AND THE PEUTINGER TABLE

ANNALINA AND MARIO LEVI

In the course of several years it has been our privilege to discuss a wide range of subjects with Bluma Trell. We have always admired her contagious enthusiasm and unfailing interest. To the inspiring scholar and, most of all, to a dear friend, we dedicate this essay with pleasure and gratitude.

The Peutinger Table represents the whole inhabited earth as it was known to the Romans. Only its westernmost section is missing. Confronted with a task of the first magnitude, the designer of the original map certainly worked to the best of his ability,[1] but to the modern eye, the result of his labors looks eminently strange. Continents and seas, coasts and rivers are deformed and compressed into a narrow and long strip. Yet we know that, however far from perfect, geographical knowledge among the Greeks and Romans was not to be surpassed until the Great Age of Discovery. The question is whether we should blame the designer's and the copyist's personal ignorance for the peculiar aspect of the map. In the following pages we shall treat the long-debated problem of the Peutinger Table's "deformation." A careful examination of this map and of other surviving specimens of ancient cartography as well show that there is no single answer to the problem. Factors which contributed to the distortion are: some geographical notions that were widespread in antiquity; the principles of Roman cartography; and the purpose and shape of the Table. We shall suggest that a well-defined cartographical class, the *itineraria picta,* were in many ways similar to the Table.

DEFORMATION AND ANCIENT GEOGRAPHY

The inhabited earth was often supposed to be much longer than wide, having the shape of an ellipse or long rectangle. Surrounded by a continuous ocean, it was thought to be divided into three parts—

Europe, Asia, and Africa—by the Tanais (Don) and Nile rivers and by the Mediterranean Sea. The Table reflects these and other theories. For example, that the Caspian Sea should appear on the map as a gulf of the outer Ocean is no designer's whim. Nearly everybody thought that India could be reached by boat from the Caspian. Ptolemy knew that it is a sheet of water surrounded by land, yet he was not aware of its real shape. At first sight, the Orient looks particularly odd on our map. However, we should remember that most Greeks and Romans had rather confused notions about Asia beyond the Tigris and, for that matter, about most regions beyond the orbit of Greco-Roman civilization. Sometimes geographers of Roman times would even be wrong about things and regions which—as the rivers of Gaul—were more or less around the corner.[2] All this contributed to deformation on maps.

DEFORMATION AND ANCIENT CARTOGRAPHY

In this brilliant technological age, it is still virtually impossible to construct a map covering a respectable portion of the earth without some distortion.[3] As we might expect, distortions on Greek and Roman maps were far more extensive, since the ancients (not even Ptolemy) never developed an adequate projection. Born and raised in the Greek scientific tradition, Ptolemy tried—as had other geographers before him—to construct a map based on consistent mathematical principles. But he did not have the necessary data and had to rest upon empirical and inadequate information provided by merchants and other travelers, as well as on distances found in itineraries—so much so that his maps were not free from distortions, and the distances we read in the Peutinger Table are more often accurate than those given by Ptolemy.[4] The massive bibliography that has grown up around his *Geography* reveals how much this text has been analyzed and argued about by scholars of different times and countries. On the other hand, only scant attention has been paid to the opening paragraphs of the eighth book of the *Geography*. They may or may not be Ptolemy's own work,[5] yet they give a most telling and seemingly reliable description of many world maps of ancient times. The author frequently uses metaphors and his style is admittedly obscure. In our opinion, when dealing with the mistakes of his predecessors, he alludes to world maps which had much in common with the Peutinger Table. He states that they gave the greatest part to Europe in length and width, the least in length to Asia, and the least in width to Africa. Europe got the largest section because many place names have to be inserted there. Less thickly settled areas and less well-known regions do not need as much space. Beset by difficulties, most cartographers had to distort the measurements and shapes of the various regions. We are mainly concerned with deformations in maps. The following sentence seems to be especially relevant to our problem:"Ὅπερ οἱ πλεῖστοι περιϊστάμενοι πολλαχῇ διαστρέφειν ἠναγκάσθησαν τά τε μέτρα καὶ τὰ σχήματα τῶν χωρῶν ὑπὸ τῶν πινάκων αὐτῶν, ὥσπερ καὶ μὴ ὑπὸ τῆς ἱστορίας χειραγωγηθέντες. Literally translated, it reads: "In circumventing which [sc. the difficulties just mentioned] in diverse manners, the *greatest number* [sc. of geographers] were compelled by the maps themselves to *twist about* the measurements and the shapes of the regions, as if they had not also been hand-guided [that is, meticulously guided] by systematic observation."[6]

Ptolemy's *Geography* is concerned with mapping only. The principles or philosophic conceptions underlying the maps of the Romans appear in a much-quoted passage of Strabo (*Geog.* 1.1.16). According to this historian and geographer, geography's primary purpose is to serve the interest of the state. Therefore, it should include the whole inhabited earth and describe the neighboring regions with greater care and detail because they are closest to the interest of the state. From this and later sources as well, it would appear that the Romans were unconcerned with scientific cartography and with problems of projection. For them a map was a practical aid to a practical purpose.

DEFORMATION AND THE PEUTINGER TABLE

The eighth book of Ptolemy's *Geography* reveals that serious distortions "of measurements and shapes" were common on world maps of the Roman imperial period. We cannot expect a constant rate of deformation to appear on all maps of that period. The Orange cadasters, the *Forma Urbis Romae,* and some plans of buildings still extant cover a very limited section of the earth and look far less "weird" than the Peutinger Table. Furthermore, the purpose of a map influences its shape and, therefore, the type of its deformation.

The main purpose of the Peutinger Table was to show the road system of the Roman Empire and the distribution on these roads of the stations of the *cursus publicus,*[7] the state post. A roll was eminently suitable. To the traveler, it exhibited in an easy way the principal lines of a route, the distances between stations, and the kind of accommodation he was likely to find on his next stop. It was only natural that the designer of the map should pay but little attention to some physical features of the earth and to most roadless lands. The actual shape and size of seas and lakes were of no concern to him, and on our map most sheets of water appear as narrow ribbons. Since the distances were added in figures, there was no real need of a uniform scale. Some roads may be shown as being much shorter than they really were, others much longer. We notice something very similar on some present-day practical maps, such as those found in subway cars in New York or Milan. There too, one looks in vain for a uniform scale.

The question is now whether our Table has a basic system. Its designer constructed a map where roads, coasts, mountains, and rivers are laid down, as often as possible, in series of parallel and horizontal lines. This is what we may call the principle of "horizontality," based upon a very simple device: entire regions are "folded" and rotated on an axis for as many degrees as necessary. As a result, the map's orientation is very often difficult to determine. All we can say is that it is flexible: there is a tendency to orient with north at the top, but it is easier to find our way through the segments of the Table by referring to "left" and "right," "above" and "below."

For example, a long horizontal coastal strip starts (segment I,1) at Rusibricari Matidie (now Mers el Hadjedje east of Algiers) and goes on, without interruptions, until it reaches Seleuceia and Antioch on the Orontes (segment IX,4). This is far from using a senseless procedure—the ancient cartographer represented the Roman provinces facing the Mediterranean in Africa and the Near East according to definite principles. Here, as in other parts of the Table, the outer Ocean serves as a symbol for the boundaries of the Roman Empire.[8] In those regions, mountains and deserts were a formidable barrier to Rome's expansion toward the interior; so much so that most of her domains were actually limited to a relatively narrow coastal strip. Using Gaza and Memphis as his main pivots, our cartographer stretched that strip along almost parallel lines. His limits were the Mediterranean above and the outer Ocean below. One additional example of "horizontality" is Italy. With Genoa as a pivot, the peninsula is rotated to right and runs parallel to Africa.[9]

ITINERARIES AND OTHER MAPS

Some indication has already been given of the variety of maps which were produced in antiquity. While some covered a small area, others dealt with the whole world. One would fill an entire wall; another would fit the surface of a coin type. Some, like a famous mosaic in Palestrina, were rather landscape paintings than real maps; others were unadorned diagrams.[10] The Romans also had maps called *itineraria picta* ("painted" or "graphic itineraries"). Simple itineraries were merely lists of place names accompanied by distances between one place and the next. A few, engraved on stone or other materials and covering a limited area, have survived. Others have come down to us in manuscripts and are more comprehensive; they include many roads and give a few notes about things of interest along the way. Compared to *itineraria adnotata* ("written itineraries"), *itineraria picta* would save the traveler time and trouble. Vegetius says that generals should have *itineraria picta* besides written ones, "ut non solum consilio mentis, verum adspectu oculorum viam profecturis eligerent" (*Inst. Mil.* 3.6).

It is generally agreed that the Peutinger Table is a copy of an *itinerarium pictum*. The question is now to determine what our map has in common with other maps of its kind. According to E. H. Bunbury, "It would appear that itineraries of a somewhat similar form were not uncommon among Romans under the Empire."[11] In 1883, the year the second edition of his still indispensable work was published, such similarity could only be surmised. The Madaba mosaic map was not discovered until 1884; the shield map of Dura was unearthed in 1923. Both are of great value in a field where there is a dearth of original Roman maps.

An archer of the Cohors XX Palmyrenorum had the notion to have on his shield a memento of his service. A fragment of the parchment that covered the shield (fig. 1) was found in Dura on the Euphrates, in the so-called Archers' Tower. Occupied by the Romans in A.D. 165, Dura was destroyed by the Sassanids ca. A.D. 257. The shield must have been in use before that year. The fragment, now in the Bibliothèque Nationale in Paris,[12] is 40 cm. wide and 18 cm. high. What we see on it is the archer's own version of an *itinerarium pictum:* a blue sea with the remnants of a lively marine traffic, a white line that stands for the coast of the Black Sea and follows the oval shape of the shield, a few blue rivers, and, to the right, a list of stations and distances. Place names and figures are in Greek but distances are in Roman miles; the original itinerary was probably in Latin. Next to the name of each station is a small house, very similar to the "temple" vignettes of the Peutinger Table, symbolizing the building where the archer found shelter. Part of the text is hardly legible, yet we are able to make out the names of a few stations on the Roman road connecting Byzantium to the Danube delta. The first is at the Panysus, a river that flows into the Black Sea, south of Odessus (now Varna), followed by Bihone, Callatis, Tomis, and Istropolis. There was no well-organized Roman road beyond the Danube; our soldier nevertheless continued on his way to Tyra and Borysthenes (Olbia), whence he probably went by sea to Chersonesus, the principal city of the Crimea. Later he reached Trapezus on the southeastern coast of the Black Sea and Artaxata in Armenia; apparently because of lack of space, his itinerary does not mention any station between the two cities.[13]

If we compare the Peutinger Table and the Dura parchment, we must surely conclude that they are based on a common notion of map drawing. In the shield map, as in the Table, we have a list of stations accompanied by distances and vignettes. Here too the orientation is 143

Fig. 1. Shield from Dura Europus, now in the Bibliothèque Nationale. Reproduced from F. Cumont in *Syria* 6 (1925) pl. 1.

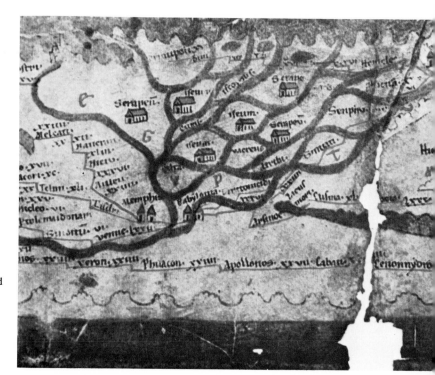

Fig. 3. The Nile delta and Jerusalem, detail of the Peutinger Table. Reproduced from A. and M. Levi, *La Tabula Peutingeriana* (Bologna 1978) seq. 8-9.

Fig. 2. Madaba, mosaic map. Reproduced from M. Avi-Yonah, *The Madaba Mosaic Map* (Jerusalem 1954) pl. A.

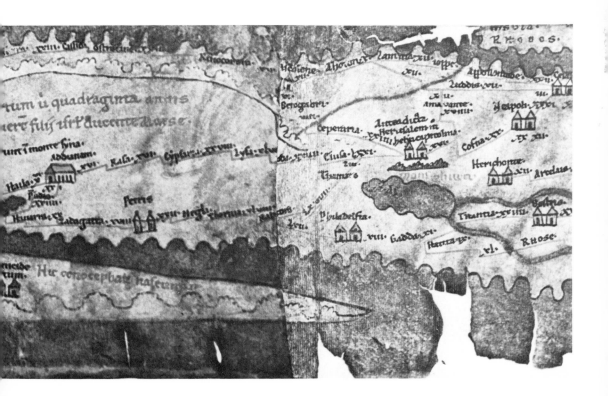

flexible and no need is felt for a uniform scale.[14] The place names are written along a conventional line which stands for the coast of the Black Sea and follows the shape of the map.

There is good reason to believe that another and much later map ultimately derives from an *itinerarium pictum*. Rediscovered in 1884 in Madaba in Jordan, the Madaba mosaic map (fig. 2) was not drawn to the attention of the learned world until 1896. It is part of the pavement of a sixth-century church. Although the work is highly decorative, it is plain that the principal object is to instruct the faithful and to make them aware of the sites hallowed by the Scriptures. Jerusalem was at the center of the map, which included Palestine and a few neighboring areas. The largest fragment now preserved starts with Aenon in the Jordan valley to the north and ends with the Canopic arm of the Nile to the south; it extends from the Mediterranean to the west to Charachmoba (el Kerak) beyond the Jordan to the east. There are mountains and rivers, animals and trees; a few human figures are busy on small boats. Fish are seen swimming in the rivers. We also have a typical resident of the Nile, a crocodile.[15] This colorful picture includes a number of inhabited centers usually represented as clusters of buildings and accompanied by their names in Greek. There are legends like "Ailamon where stood the moon in the time of Joshua the son of Nun one day." The most important landmarks of Jerusalem appear within her city wall. The artist was obviously acquainted with Eusebius's *Onomasticon*. In his *Onomasticon de Locis Hebraicis*, the learned bishop of Caesarea adapted classical geography to the needs of Christian topography and gave a description of the places mentioned in the Holy Scripture, arranged in alphabetical order. Avi-Yonah, however, to whom we owe a careful study of the Madaba mosaic, shows that the selection and distribution of a number of sites are based on an earlier road map.[16] Place names such as *to tetarton* ("the fourth mile") and *to ennaton* ("the ninth mile") indicate the distance to and from Jerusalem and point to such an origin.

Since the purpose of the mosaic was devotional and decorative, the artist did without distances, but he kept the vignettes as symbols for inhabited centers. The shape of the pavement and the space available in the church had some influence, but he seems to have kept the general setup of the original map and followed the principle of "horizontality." Indeed, what is most striking is that both the Peutinger Table and the Madaba map have Jerusalem and the Nile delta arranged in the same row (fig. 3). At first sight, the mosaic map seems to be oriented with east at the top. A more careful examination, however, makes one aware that the orientation is flexible. It is patently clear that the artist pulled the Mediterranean coast out of direction and rotated the Sinai peninsula and Egypt to the east, using Maiumas Neapolis, Gaza's seaport, as a pivot. We can easily recognize two parallel strips: one includes Jerusalem and the delta, the other the Jordan river with the Dead Sea, such places as Praesidium, Thamara, and Moa to the south of the Dead Sea, and a small fragment of a mountain in the desert (Mount Sinai?).[17]

In the Madaba map, as in the Table and the shield of Dura, there is no uniform scale. It would seem, therefore, that scale was a matter of no concern to the designer of an *itinerarium pictum*. In a map of this kind orientation was flexible; place names were arranged along conventional lines which, to a considerable extent, were influenced by the shape of the map. It seems to us that two of the three maps we examined could be taken as evidence for the existence of a kind of rudimentary projection in the more elaborate *itineraria picta*. This projection, based on the principle of "horizontality," may have been ultimately suggested by the oblong shape of papyrus rolls. Nor should we forget that the individual taste and personal interests, not only of authors and compilers but also of copyists and artists, concurred in shaping and reshaping each itinerary map and the various new editions of it. Vignettes as symbols for places seem to be a constant element. Such picturesque representations as boats and people seem to depend on the personal tastes of authors and patrons.

NOTES

1. The Peutinger Table had its origins in the third century A.D. and was revised in the eastern empire in the time of Theodosius II. The existing version, preserved in the National Library in Vienna, is attributable to the thirteenth century. For the date, based on iconographic examination and classification of the vignettes, see A. and M. Levi, *Itineraria picta: Contributo allo studio della Tabula Peutingeriana* (Rome 1967) 169-76; A. and M. Levi, *La Tabula Peutingeriana* (Bologna 1978) 150.
2. J. O. Thomson, *History of Ancient Geography* (New York 1965) 233-34.
3. W. G. Moore, *A Dictionary of Geography* (Harmondsworth 1977) 136, s.v. Map Projection.
4. On Ptolemy's *Geography*, see Levi and Levi, *Itineraria picta* (n. 1 above) 24-25, 35-37 and, more recently, O. Neugebauer. *A History of Ancient Mathematical Astronomy* (New York, Heidelberg, and Berlin 1975) 934-40; Levi and Levi, *Tabula* (n. 1 above) 24. On Ptolemy's errors and distortions, see Thomson (n. 2 above) 345-47; A. L. F. Rivet, "Some Aspects of Ptolemy's Geography of Britain," *Littérature gréco-romaine géographie historique: Mélanges offerts à Roger Dion* (Paris 1974) 55-79.
5. On the problems connected with the eighth book of Ptolemy's *Geography*, see H. Mžick, *Des Klaudios Ptolemaios Einführung in die darstellende Erdkunde* i (Vienna 1938) 8; E. Polaschek, s.v. Ptolemaios als Geograph, *RE* Suppl. 10 (1965) 757-58.
6. Ptolemy, *Geographia* (ed. Nobbe) 8.1.2. The only modern translation we know that covers the eighth book of the *Geography* is the one by E. L. Stevenson. Mžick's German translation does not include it. Stevenson translates our passage: "that which many do without sufficient reason—lest they should appear to depart from traditional accounts—who in their maps consequently are led to make many errors in the measurements and representations of regions" (*Geography of Claudius Ptolemy*, trans. and ed. E. L. Stevenson [New York 1932] 165). His version is based upon Jacopo d'Angelo's Latin *quemadmodum discuriosius*

fecere plurimi qui in tabulis ipsis multo peruertere conati fuere sub mensuris regionum figurisque ne ab historia abscessisse uiderentur (Claudius Ptolemaeus Cosmographia, Bologna 1477, with an introduction by R. A. Skelton. Theatrum orbis terrarum, ser. 1, no. 1 [Amsterdam 1963]). The translation we suggest comes somewhat closer to d'Angelo's version as corrected by Domizio Calderini: *quemadmodum curiosius facere plurimi qui in tabulis ipsis multa peruertere coacti fuere in mensuris regionum figurisque tanquam ab aspectu ipso ueluti manu non ducerentur (Claudius Ptolemaeus Cosmographia, Roma 1478,* with an introduction by R. A. Skelton. Theatrum orbis terrarum, ser. 2, no. 6 [Amsterdam 1966]).

7. On the Peutinger Table as map of the *cursus publicus,* see Levi and Levi, *Itineraria picta* (n. 1 above) 97-123, 133-34, 171-74; L. Casson, *Travel in the Ancient World* (London 1974) 182-90, 301-3; Levi and Levi, *Tabula* (n. 1 above) 97-134.

8. On the symbolic meaning of the ocean in the *Tabula,* see Levi and Levi, *Tabula* (n. 1 above) 13, 16-18, 20, 22, 73.

9. On the distortion of Italy on ancient maps, see also Thomson (n. 2 above) 343.

10. Levi and Levi, *Itineraria picta* (n. 1 above) 17-57; Levi and Levi, *Tabula* (n. 1 above) 25-26; on maps in medieval manuscripts see also A. and M. Levi, "The Medieval Map of Rome in the Ambrosian Library's Manuscript of Solinus (C 246 inf.)," *ProcPhilSoc* 118 (1974) 567-94; O. Neugebauer, "A Greek World Map," *Le monde grec: Pensée, littérature, histoire, documents. Hommage à Claire Préaux* (Brussels 1975) 312-17. Maps appear also on pre-Roman coins: A. E. M. Johnston, "The Earliest Preserved Greek Map, a New Ionian Coin Type," *JHS* 87 (1967) 86-94; on military maps, see R. K. Sherk, "Roman Geographical Exploration and Military Maps," *AuN* 2, no. 1, pp. 534-62; on the Orange cadasters and the *Corpus Agrimensorum,* see O. A. W. Dilke, *The Roman Land Surveyors* (Newton Abbot 1971) 126-32, 159-77; O. A. W. and M. S. Dilke, "Perception of the Roman World," *Progress in Geography* 9 (1976) 41-72.

11. E. H. Bunbury, *A History of Ancient Geography* ii (new ed., New York 1959) 698.

12. Levi and Levi, *Itineraria picta* (n. 1 above) 30-32, 83-84, passim; Levi and Levi, *Tabula* (n. 1 above) 26-28, passim.

13. We follow Cumont's reading of the legends (F. Cumont, *Fouilles de Doura Europos, 1922-1923* [Paris 1926] 323-37; F. Cumont, "Fragment de bouclier portant une liste d'étapes," *Syria* 6 (1925) 1-15. For a somewhat different and less convincing interpretation, see R. Uhden, "Bemerkungen zu dem römischen Kartenfragment von Dura Europos," *Hermes* 67 (1932) 117-25. Incidentally, our soldier was not the first to have a map on his shield. According to Ovid (*Met.* 5.189), *Nileus, qui se genitum septemplice Nilo/Ementitus erat, clipeo quoque flumina septem/Argento partim, partim caelaverat auro.* Of course, Achilles had a larger map: his shield was *vasti caelatus imagine mundi (Met.* 13.110).

14. Levi and Levi, *Itineraria picta* (n. 1 above) 51-53, 82, 93, 143, passim; Levi and Levi, *Tabula* (n. 1 above) 28-30, 114, 121, 147, passim. To the bibliography in Levi and Levi, *Tabula* 28, add H. G. Thümmel, "Zur Deutung der Mosaikkarte von Madeba," *ZDPV* 89 (1973) 66-79. A new edition of the mosaic is now expected: see *Gnomon* 50 (1978) 106.

15. On the fragments of a crocodile, see H. Donner and H. Cüppers, "Die Restauration und Konservierung der Mosaikkarte von Madeba," *ZDPV* 83 (1967) 29.

16. M. Avi-Yonah, *The Madaba Mosaic Map* (Jerusalem 1954) 28-30, fig. 11.

17. On zones on the mosaic map, see also H. Cüppers, "Die Mosaikkarte von Madeba," *AA* 83 (1968) 745.

16

LITERATI IN THE SERVICE OF ROMAN EMPERORS: POLITICS BEFORE CULTURE

NAPHTALI LEWIS

Several years ago I published a papyrus which I regarded as exemplifying the *communis opinio* that "under the Romans men of affairs as well as representatives of the arts and sciences were rewarded with membership in the Alexandrian Museum, with its attendant privileges of ἀτέλεια and σίτησις."[1] But latterly a kind of revisionism has set in, taking the view concerning such "supposed 'non-scholar' members" that "some or even all may have been genuine scholars in their own right."[2] The unwitting catalyst of this revisionism is a certain M. Valerius Titanianus, whose career spanned the end of the second century and the first half of the third.[3] Long since attested in an inscription from Latium as *praefectus vigilum* (an eminence rarely attained by Greco-Egyptians), Titanianus is revealed by the above-mentioned papyrus and by an inscription published in 1965 to have held also the palatine office of *ab epistulis* and to have been a member of the Alexandrian Museum.[4] The new evidence has led to deductions such as "Titanianus in particular had a good claim to be a scholar in his own right, since we know that he once held the post of *ab epistulis Graecis*."[5]

Schematized as a syllogism, the revisionist view holds: 1) Titanianus was appointed to the office of *ab epistulis;* 2) Only literati or scholars were appointed to that office; 3) Therefore Titanianus was a scholar or literary figure. As the conclusion does indeed follow if the two prior propositions are sound, and as proposition 1 is an established fact, it becomes necessary to examine whether proposition 2 is also valid. This can best be done by reviewing the careers of the men known from ancient sources to have held the office of *ab epistulis*.

To this office—"the most influential, though perhaps not the most noticeable"[6] of the palatine secretariats—and to the persons who held it, no fewer than four detailed studies have been devoted in the space of less than twenty years.[7] That by Townend concentrates on the organization of the office, arguing that the division into separate

149

bureaus for Latin and Greek correspondence did not occur before ca. A.D. 166. Millar, Pflaum, and Bowersock, concerned to distinguish the kind of men appointed to head the office, emphasize "the relation of the position of *ab epistulis Graecis* to the rhetoric and culture of the Greek world," see this secretariat directed "par de grands hommes de lettres du monde grec," and find "oriental literati as *ab epistulis* . . . [in] substantial number."[8]

These statements are unexceptionable in reference to certain well-known holders of the office. But does the evidence justify the further, more extreme generalization that "in the second and early third centuries the office of *ab epistulis* for Greek correspondence is found to have been monopolized by eastern Greek sophists and rhetors," or that the office was "toujours confiée à un lettré d'origine grecque"?[9] Was this secretariat really reserved exclusively, or even preferentially, for such men? Were no other backgrounds and qualifications given at least comparable weight by the emperors when appointing to that office?

List I below is a conspectus of the careers of the men who are known, or can reasonably be inferred, to have held the office of *ab epistulis*. Preceding the name of each is the date when he held the office: this is in a few instances given in the sources, but for most it is but loosely approximated. The relevant sources for each individual are given in parentheses at the end of the entry, in most instances by a single reference to Pflaum, where the sources are collected. Problems of chronology, identity, and so on are noted at their respective places.[10]

LIST I

NO.	A.D.	NAME AND CAREER
1	44–54	Narcissus: freedman of the Emperor Claudius, ab epistulis (Dio Cass. 60.34; Suet., *Claud.* 28; *CIL* xv 7500 = *ILS* 1666).
2	ca. 60	Beryllus: paedagogus of Nero, ab epistulis[11] (Josephus, *AJ* 20.183–84.
3	ca. 65[12]	Dionysius of Alexandria: grammaticus, head of the Museum(?),[13] a bibliothecis, ab epistulis et ad legationes et responsa (Pflaum no. 46).
4	69	Secundus: rhetor, ab epistulis (to Otho) (Plutarch, *Otho* 9.3).
5	ca. 85	Abascantus: freedman of Domitian, ab epistulis (Statius, *Silv.* 5.1; *CIL* vi 8598, 8599).
6	ca. 90–105	Cn. Titinius Capito:[14] military offices and decorations, procurator ab epistulis et a patrimonio, iterum ab epistulis, praetoria ornamenta, ab epistulis tertio, praefectus vigilum (Pflaum no. 60).
7	ca. 117	C. Suetonius Tranquillus: writer, named military tribune but resigned in favor of a relative, flamen, local pontifex, a studiis, a bibliothecis, ab epistulis (Pflaum no. 96).

8   ca. 127   C. Avidius Heliodorus: rhetor(?), philosophus, ab epistulis, praefectus Aegypti (Pflaum no. 106; SHA *Hadr.* 16.10).

9   ca. 130   Valerius Eudaemo: procurator ad dioecesin Alexandriae, a bibliothecis Lat. et Gr., ab epistulis, proc. provinciarum, proc. hereditatium, proc. provinciarum (iterum), praefectus Aegypti (Pflaum no. 110; SHA *Hadr.* 15.3).

10   ca. 135   L. Julius Vestinus: sophist, archiereus "of Alexandria and all Egypt" and head of the Museum,[15] a bibliothecis Lat. et Gr., a studiis, ab epistulis (Pflaum no. 105).

11   137   Caninius Celer:[16] writer on rhetoric, ab epistulis (to Hadrian), instructed Marcus (the later emperor) in Greek rhetoric (Philostr. *VS* 1.22; SHA *M.Ant.* 2.4, *Ver.* 2.5; M. Aurelius, *Med.* 8.25; Suidas A528 Adler).

12   137   L. Domitius Rogatus: freedman, quattuor militiae, ab epistulis (to L. Aelius Caesar), procurator monetae, proc. Dalmatiae, pontifex minor (Pflaum no. 140).

13   ca. 150?   [   ]: procurator Achaiae, proc. Baeticae, ab epistulis Latinis (Pflaum no. 214 *bis*).

14   ca. 160–62   Sex. Caecilius Crescens Volusianus: praefectus fabrum, sacerdos curio, advocatus fisci Romae, procurator XX hereditatium, ab epistulis (Pflaum no. 142).

15   ca. 163   T. Varius Clemens: quattuor militiae, procurator provinciarum, ab epistulis (Pflaum no. 156).

16   ca. 165–75   C.(?) [   ]ilius: a commentariis (to the praetorian prefect), procurator Macedoniae, ab epistulis [Gr.? Lat.?], iuridicus Alexandriae, proc. Asiae, proc. summarum rationum, ab epistulis Latinis, senator with praetorian rank (Pflaum no. 178).[17]

17   ca. 166   C. Calvisius Statianus: ab epistulis Latinis, praefectus Aegypti (Pflaum no. 166).

18   ca. 168[18]   Sulpicius(?) Cornelianus: ab epistulis Graecis (Phrynichus, *Ep.* 225, 379, 418 Lobeck = 203, 356, 393 Rutherford; Ael. Aristides 50.57 Keil = 26.335 Dindorf).

19   170   Tarru(n)ten(i)us Paternus:[19] jurist, author *(De re milit.),* ab epistulis Latinis, carried out a diplomatic mission and a military command, praefectus praetorio, ornamenta consularia (Pflaum no. 172).

20   ca. 170   Alexander (the "Clay-Plato"): sophist, ambassador, ab epistulis Graecis (Philostr. *VS* 2.5).

21   172–75[20]   Ti. Claudius Vibianus Tertullus: ab epistulis Graecis, a rationibus, praefectus vigilum (Pflaum no. 252).

22   ca. 175   T. A(h)ius Sanctus:[21] ab epistulis Graecis, procurator rationis privatae, a rationibus, praefectus Aegypti, praef.[22] alimentorum, consul (Pflaum no. 178 *bis,* as revised pp. 1002–7).

23   175   Manilius:[23] ab epistulis Latinis to Avidius Cassius (Dio Cass. 73[72].7.4).

24	ca. 185	Hadrianus (of Tyre):[24] rhetor, sophist, ab epistulis (Philostr. *VS* 2.10; Suidas A528 Adler; Galen xiv, 627 [629]).
25	ca. 187	[Aureliu]s Larichus: ab [epis]tulis [Graecis] (*AEpigr* 1952 no. 6; *Hesperia* 36 [1967] 332).
26	ca. 190	Vitruvius Secundus:[25] ab epistulis(?) (SHA *Comm.* 4.8).
27	2/3d cents.	[ ]: militiae equestres, procurator ad alimenta, proc. ad census accipiendos, proc. ad dioecesin Alexandriae, proc. dioecesis, proc. patrimonii, proc. ab epistulis, a rationibus (Pflaum no. 271).
28	2/3d cents.	Sempronius Aquila:[26] rhetor(?), ab epistulis Graecis (his son-in-law: tribunus plebis, praetor designatus) (*IGRR* iii 188; also(?) Philostr. *VS* 2.11).
29	ca. 200	Aelius Antipater: sophist, tutor of Caracalla and Geta, ab epistulis Graecis, legatus Augusti (in Bithynia) (Pflaum no. 230).
30	ca. 210	Maximus (of Aegae): orator, ab epistulis (Philostr. *ApTy* 1.12.14).
31	214–15	Julia Domna: widow of Septimius Severus, mother of the reigning emperor Caracalla (Dio Cass. 78[77].18.2, cf. 79 [78].4.2-3:see also below, n. 29).
32	ca. 215	Marcius Claudius Agrippa: freedman, advocatus fisci, a cognitionibus, ab epistulis, praeses classis, ornamenta consularia, governor of Pannonia, the three Dacias and Moesia (Pflaum no. 287).[27]
33	ca. 216	M. Valerius Titanianus: ab epistulis Graecis, praefectus vigilum, a Museo Alexandriae (see above, n. 4).
34	217 or 218	[ ]inianus: procurator, a cognitionibus, ab epistulis Latinis (*AEpigr* 1966 no. 431).
35	ca. 220	Aspasius: sophist, ab epistulis Graecis (Philostr. *VS* 2.33).
36[28]	3d cent.	[ ]: advocatus fisci, ab epistulis (Pflaum no. 226 *ter*).

The significant facts—significant for the purposes of this inquiry—that emerge from List I may be summarized as follows. The first holder of the office of *ab epistulis* was the emperor Claudius's freedman Narcissus. At the other social pole from that exslave there is Julia Domna, to whom her son, the emperor Caracalla, for a time entrusted the management of the imperial correspondence.[29] Both of these extremes may be seen as instances of a natural tendency to turn to members of one's own household in times of crisis or emergency, the first in the stresses of bureaucratic innovation, the second under the pressures of a military campaign.[30] Between these extremes the known holders of the office are mostly men pursuing more or less traditional careers of the equestrian order.[31] Omitting the three imperial freedmen of the first century, the remaining thirty-three individuals in the list comprise three categories.

1. By the most generous count, fourteen can be credited with notable literary ability or pretensions, and for at least three of these fourteen the literary interests appear to be avocations from active

careers in imperial government.[32] Julia Domna is a good example of the three. No claimant to literary fame herself, she was the well-informed patroness of a literary salon which "gave the court [its] intellectual or pseudo-intellectual tone."[33]

2. Four others are cited only as holders of the office of *ab epistulis;* nothing more is known of their careers.[34]

3. Cultural attainments figure not at all in the careers of the remaining fifteen, the largest group. They held the office of *ab epistulis* at some stage in an equestrian *cursus* (civil, military, or usually both), which sometimes culminated in senatorial rank.[35]

Pflaum observes at one point (338) that to hold the post of *ab epistulis* "il fallait . . . des facultés stylistiques qui exigeaient une forte culture. Il fallait en outre la confiance entière du prince, ce qui supposait une connaissance longue et intime, nous dirions presque des relations amicales entre l'empereur et son ministre." The priority of these requirements should be reversed. Since the office was held at the emperor's pleasure, his favor was the sine qua non; the qualities of literati were valuable, lending an aura of refinement and cultural patronage to the imperial regime, but those qualities were hardly essential, because stylistic competence for the largely formulaic correspondence could undoubtedly be provided by the more or less permanent undersecretaries and clerks.[36]

It will be useful to review rapidly the evidences of imperial favor and even friendly intimacy discernible in the sources from which our list of *ab epistulis* is compiled. Again omitting the imperial freedmen of the first century (who were obviously trusted servants of the emperor), the following details claim attention. No. 9, who was entrusted as procurator with a larger than normal group of provinces, was probably the Eudaemo who figures in SHA *Hadr.* 15.3 as among the emperor's *amicissimos vel eos quos summis honoribus evexit.* No. 11 was tutor to a future emperor. No. 17 advanced from *ab epistulis* to prefect of Egypt with no, or only a slight, interval. The emperors' relationship to no. 18 is described as λόγῳ μὲν ἐπιστολέα ἀποφήναντες, ἔργῳ δὲ σύνεργον ἑλόμενοι τῆς βασιλείας. No. 19 held all the offices listed within the short span of six years. No. 23 is characterized as τῷ Κασσίῳ συγγενομένου καὶ. . .μέγιστον παρ' αὐτῷ δυνηθέντος. On no. 24 the title of *ab epistulis* was bestowed νοσοῦντι . . .ὅτε δὴ καὶ ἐτελεύτα. No. 25 was referred to by the emperor as ὁ φίλος μου, no. 30 as ὁ φίλος μου καὶ διδάσκαλος.[37] No. 32, born a slave, was advanced through an equestrian career to signal honors of senatorial rank.[38] No. 35 ἦλθε δὲ καὶ ἐπὶ πολλὰ τῆς γῆς μέρη βασιλεῖ τε ξυνών.

All in all, the known *ab epistulis,* after the freedmen of the early years, present us with a very mixed bag of persons and types: an octogenarian on his deathbed, who was obviously dignified with the title of the office *honoris causa;* friends, teachers, and imperial careerists, chosen by the emperors for reasons among which

153

trustworthiness and administrative ability surely loomed large. These men included several whose chief or only prior claim to fame lay in their intellectual activity, but the presence of a Suetonius in the list does not justify the generalization that "pour occuper la direction de ce secrétariat l'empereur faisait appel aux plus grands lettrés de l'époque."[39] The list also contains rhetoricians and sophists who were far from enjoying universal regard as paragons or exemplars of literary style and culture. Avidius Heliodorus (no. 8) is classed among τοὺς μὲν μηδενὸς τοὺς δὲ βραχυτάτου τινὸς ἀξίους ὄντας, and he is reported to have been told to his face that Καῖσαρ χρήματα μέν σοι καὶ τιμὴν δοῦναι δύναται, ῥήτορα δέ σε ποιῆσαι οὐ δύναται.[40] Celer (no. 11) is described as βασιλικῶν μὲν ἐπιστολῶν ἀγαθὸς προστάτης μελέτῃ δὲ οὐκ ἀποχρῶν, which suggests greater administrative than literary ability; and the style of Aspasius (no. 35) is characterized as ἀγωνιστικώτερον and as suffering from ἀσάφεια.[41] It is worth recalling also how many extant imperial letters and promulgations are anything but models of lucidity or style.[42]

Thus, while "literary accomplishments were a well-established basis for obtaining influential patronage and preferment,"[43] the evidence does not support the view that such accomplishments were the only, or even the primary, criterion by which emperors selected their *ab epistulis*. At times certainly, and very likely most of the time, political or military considerations or palace associations were the prime determinants. The case of Julia Domna may serve to epitomize the situation. When Caracalla entrusted her with the management of the imperial correspondence, was it because of her undoubted appreciation of literature and philosophy (manifested most prominently in the salon she patronized at court), or was it because of the influence that this politically powerful woman wielded in the councils of state, first as the wife of Severus and then, more than ever, as the empress mother?[44] Few will doubt that it was the latter.

In sum, the argument that only literati or scholars were appointed to the office of *ab epistulis* simply begs the question. The "revisionist syllogism" posed at the beginning of this paper has been tested and found wanting. Specifically, the presumed universality of proposition 2 collapses under the weight of the accumulated evidence. The office of *ab epistulis* is not by itself sufficient warrant for imputing to its holder any literary or rhetorical or scholarly distinction. We may now turn to examine whether Museum membership by itself justifies such an inference.

Founded early in the third century B.C. by the first or second Ptolemy,[45] the Alexandrian Museum and Library acted as twin magnets to attract the leading minds and talents of the age and make Alexandria the cultural capital of the Hellenistic world. Whether or not they were ever perceived as ivory towers dedicated to pure intellection, the Museum and Library,[46] situated as they were in the city's Royal Quarter, cheek-by-jowl with the palace and the court,[47] were never totally free of the political ambience.[48] The administration of both institutions was tied to the crown, which appointed the Museum's director and the chief librarian. The fact that these appointments were not always based on literary or scholarly or scientific merit alone is strikingly illustrated by our sources. An inscription found at Delos celebrates one Chrysermos son of Herakleitos, a courtier of Ptolemy III or IV, whose offices included that of Museum director.[49] And in the list of chief librarians the famous editor of Homer, Aristarchos, is followed by an otherwise unknown Kydas, who is identified only by a military title appropriate to a courtier intimately associated with the king.[50]

Augustus retained the Ptolemaic pattern of control, appointing the members of the Museum and its head.[51] In this, as in so much of the "statut augustéen de l'Egypte,"[52] subsequent emperors followed in Augustus's footsteps, with "the Museum, now as under the Ptolemies a State institution, supported by a regular subvention and under the direction of an official of equestrian rank appointed by the emperor."[53] Direct contact with the Museum is recorded for Claudius and Hadrian: the former added a Claudian wing to the building and instituted an annual recital of two histories he had written in Greek; the latter, while in Egypt, "in Musio quaestiones professoribus proposuit."[54]

List II below summarizes the careers of the Museum directors and members known from the period of Roman rule in Egypt. The presentation follows the pattern of List I.

NO.	A.D.	NAME AND CAREER (BESIDES MUSEUM MEMBERSHIP)
1[55]	ca. 35	Ti. Claudius Balbillus: superintendent(?) of sanctuaries "in Alexandria and all Egypt," supra museu[m, ab Alexandri]na bibliothece, archiereus, [ad Herm]en Alexandreon, ad legationes et res[ponsa Graeca, trib. le]g(ionis), praef. fabr(um), procurator, decorated in Claudius's British triumph (*PIR*² C813; Pflaum no. 15).
2	38	Didymus (son of Hierax): Alexandrian, nome strategus (*P. Ryl.* 143).
3[56]	ca. 40	Chaeremo: tutor to Nero, prior to that Museum head(?) (Suidas Δ1173 Adler, cf. *RE* 3, 2026).
4[56]	49	Dionysius (of Alexandria): grammaticus, Museum head(?), a bibliothecis, ab epistulis et ad legationes et responsa (Pflaum no. 46).
5	ca. 50	Ti. Claudius Demetrius: banker, Alexandrian, gymnasiarch, Roman citizen (*P. Oxy.* 2471).
6	107 or 126	Valerius Callinicus: archidicastes (*P. Oxy.* 471).

7	ca. 110–38	Polemo (of Laodicea): rhetor, sophist, grammaticus (Philostr. *VS* 1.25.3; Suidas Π 1889 Adler).
8	117–33	Areius: Homeric poet (*CIG* 4748 = *SB* 8355 = *IGLMemnon* 37).
9	117–38	Aelius Dionysius (of Miletus): sophist, promoted to equestrian order, praeses[57] provinciarum (Philostr. *VS* 1.22.3; *BCH* 4 [1880] 405).
10	ca. 120	[ ]: archidicastes, etc.[58] (*BGU* 231).
11	122/3	Servius Sulpicius Serenus: military officer in several campaigns, procurator (Pflaum no. 104 *bis,* where the first inscription now = *SB* 8340 = *IGLMemnon* 20).
12	125	Andronicus: strategus and acting exegetes of Alexandria, archidicastes, etc. (*P. Meyer* 6).
13	128	[ ]apus (son of [M]unatianus, who had been archidicastes): military tribune, strategus of Alexandria, archidicastes, etc. (*P. Mil. Vogl.* 26 = *SB* Beih. 2B4).
14	ca. 130	Pancrates: native of Egypt, poet[59] (Athenaeus 677e).
15	ca. 130	L. Julius Vestinus: sophist, archiereus "of Alexandria and all Egypt" and Museum head, a bibliothecis Lat. et Gr., a studiis, ab epistulis (Pflaum no. 105).
16	135	Claudius Philoxenus: praefectus cohortis, archidicastes (*BGU* 73 and 136 = *M. Chr.* 207 and 86).
17	mid-2d cent.	Tullius Ptolemaeus: strategus of Alexandria, archidicastes, eutheniarch, acting Museum head (*SB* 7027).
18	144	Dionysius (son of M. Antonius Dius, who had been strategus of Alexandria[60]): archidicastes, etc. (*BGU* 729 = *M.Chr.* 167).
19[61]	172	[M. Tillius(?)] Proculus (son of M. Tillius Marcellus, who had been gymnasiarch and hypomnematographus): archidicastes, etc. (*P. Flor.* 68).
20	173	Valerius Diodorus:[62] hypomnematographus (*P. Mert.* 19).
21	ca. 175	Ti. Claudius Eucles Polydeuces Marcellus (son of Ti. Charidemus, who had been archiereus Asiae, military tribune, lifetime gymnasiarch): archiereus, grammateus, benefactor of his city (*IMagn.* 187–90).
22	193–211	Fronto: rhetor, author of many works (Suidas Φ 735 Adler; Keil-Premerstein, *Zweite Reise in Lydien* 210).
23	2/3d cents.	Aelius Demetrius:[63] rhetor (*OGIS* 712 = *IGRR* i 1081).
24	ca. 217[64]	M. Valerius Titanianus: ab epistulis, praefectus vigilum (*BGU* 1617; *AEpigr* 1966 no. 474; *P. Mich.* 620).
25	ca. 217	L. Gellius Maximus: friend and chief physician of the emperor, lifetime priest of Aesculapius, procurator[65] ducenarius (*CQ* 21 [1971] 262).
26	ca. 240	Calpurnius Theo: no details (*P. Oxy.* 3047, 3048).
27	3d cent.	M. Aurelius Asclepiades: prize athlete, bouleutes, prytanis, (*IGURomae* 239–41, 250 = in part *OGIS* 714, *IGRR* i 153, 154, *CPHerm* 7).

28	3d cent.	Fl. Maecius Se[ ] Dionysodorus: bouleutes of Antinoopolis (*SB* 6012).
29	267	Aurelius Plutio: procurator[66] ducenarius (*CPHerm* 53, 59, and 124 + 125 = *W. Chr.* 39, 151, 40).
30	ca. 270	M. Aurelius Hermogenes: vir egregius, tribunus legionis, praefectus alae, procurator a studiis; patron, priest and official at Ostia (Pflaum no. 352).
31	ca. 275[67]	[ ]: no details (*SIG*[3] 900).
32	3d(?) cent.	Balbianus (son of Balbianus, who had been procurator Augusti): praefectus cohortis, archidicastes, etc. (*P. Oxy.* 2978).
33	3d(?) cent.	[ ]us Clodianus: procurator (*AEpigr* 1936 no. 44).

Of the thirty-three individuals in List II, seven—if we include nos. 3 and 4 (see n. 56)—presumably owed their Museum membership to creative or intellectual achievement; it is possible that four more belong to this category, which would bring the total to eleven.[68] Concerning two others we know only that they were Museum members, nothing more.[69] The remaining twenty—nearly two-thirds of the total—had careers in local or imperial government, or in the military, or in both; so also did the four men noted above as possibly belonging to the first group. The possibility exists, surely, that behind one or another of these military or bureaucratic exteriors there lurked an aesthetic gift or scientific mind lost forever to posterity, but it strains credulity beyond the breaking point to suppose that that could be true of all or even of most of them.

A museum in the Greek world was organized as a confraternity devoted to the worship of the Muses; the museum head was the officiating priest of the cult.[70] Museum membership was sometimes indicated by a simple ἀπὸ (or ἐκ) Μουσείου, Latin *a Musio*, but the fuller, presumably official designation was τῶν ἐν τῷ Μουσείῳ σιτουμένων ἀτελῶν.[71] The additional epithet φιλόσοφος, which appears occasionally, must have been for some members more traditional and formulaic than literal: it occurs, for example, in the case of the man whose claim to fame was his widely displayed athletic prowess.[72] In contrast, the exemption from taxation (ἀτέλεια) that membership conferred was very real, a precious privilege enjoyed by relatively few in the Roman provinces.

The other specified benefit,[73] free maintenance (σίτησις) in the Museum, was also a material reality, but it was of no consequence to the many members who did not live in Alexandria. It is altogether possible that nos. 21 and 30, for example, had visited Alexandria at some time in their lives, but they obviously resided at Magnesia and Ostia respectively, and the same is presumably true of the others in our list whose record comes to us from places outside Egypt.[74] Even the members residing in Egypt did not always reside in Alexandria.

Men of means, they had their domiciles where their several pursuits or their individual pleasure dictated. We find no. 2, for example, exercising the office of strategus in the Arsinoite nome and no. 16 presiding at a hearing in Memphis. No. 28 lived at Antinoopolis and no. 20 at Oxyrhynchus, where his purchase of a small riverboat strongly suggests commercial activity.[75] No. 17, who held offices in Alexandria, also had some connection with Tentyra, where his statue was erected. Nos. 27 and 29, who had been all the way to Rome, lived at least some of the time in Hermopolis. In the case of no. 24, two alternatives present themselves: he may have retired to his extensive landholdings in the Arsinoite nome, but the fact that his properties were managed by agents suggests that he may have resided in Alexandria—next best after having to leave Rome?—as an absentee landlord paying occasional visits to his country estates.[76]

To sum up: List II reflects, *mutatis mutandis,* the same picture that was projected by List I. Some two-thirds[77] of the Museum members known from the first three centuries A.D. are identified, not with literature or the learned professions, but with military and political careers. It is readily conceivable that most or even all of these, including the champion pancratiast, were in varying degrees men of education or culture. But that is a far cry from the kind of learning that was rewarded with Museum membership. In other words, the assumption that Museum membership may be taken as prima facie evidence of literary or scholarly distinction is seen to be neither statistically nor logically probable. It does not seem possible to escape the conclusion that Museum membership, with its éclat and its substantial benefits, was an honor awarded by Roman emperors in recognition of notable performance or achievement in any of a wide variety of professional activities: arts and sciences, literature, government service, and even athletics.

Appendix 1: Dionysius of Alexandria— *ab epistulis* to Which Emperor?

According to the Suda (Δ 1173 Adler), Dionysius of Alexandria (no. 3 of List I; no. 4 of List II) ἀπὸ Νέρωνος συνῆν καὶ τοῖς μέχρι Τραιανοῦ. Pflaum (1021) lists him as *ab epistulis Graecis*[78] under Trajan, which may be just an oversight, since he elsewhere (112) observes that "nous aboutissons à l'hypothèse d'une nomination émanant de Vespasien ou de Titus, lesquels ont pu faire la connaissance de Denys pendant cet hiver 69–70 qu'ils ont tous deux passé à Alexandrie." Townend (380) omits Dionysius from his list, thus implying a tenure of office prior to A.D. 95. Millar (87) takes no position in the matter.

It seems to me likeliest, however, that Dionysius held the office of *ab epistulis* under Nero. Several bits of evidence point to that conclusion.

1. In describing Dionysius's highest office, the Suda says, ἐπὶ τῶν ἐπιστολῶν καὶ πρεσβειῶν ἐγένετο καὶ ἀποκριμάτων. In concert with Pflaum (112), I understand this expression as signifying the simultaneous discharge of three functions that usually occur in our sources, certainly by the time of Hadrian, as separate offices: *ab epistulis, ad legationes,* and *ad responsa.* Such a lumping together of responsibilities smacks of an early stage in administrative organization (which was initiated, it will be recalled, by Claudius). And in fact, the only other individual known to have borne a similar title dates from the time of Claudius. Ti. Claudius Balbillus (no. 1 of List II) in the course of his career held the office of *ad legationes et responsa Graeca Caesaris Aug. divi Claudii.*[79]

2. In A.D. 48 or 49, Chaeremo was summoned to Rome to serve as one of Nero's tutors, and Dionysius succeeded him as head of a school in Alexandria and perhaps also as director of the Museum.[80] Dionysius later followed his mentor to Nero's court. The fall of the emperor to whom he owed his preferment, and above all the circumstances of that fall, could have rendered his situation precarious and understandably have impelled him to return to Alexandria.[81]

3. Having served in Rome in the imperial office dealing with embassies, Dionysius might easily have been chosen by the Alexandrians to be a member of the delegation to Trajan that is recorded in *P. Oxy.* x 1242 (= *CPJ* ii 157).[82] Given a name as common as Dionysius, this identification cannot be pressed. But if it should happen to be right, the description ὁ ἐν πολλαῖς ἐ[πιτρο]παῖς γε[ν]όμενος suggests an old man at the end of a long career rather than one currently active.

Appendix 2: Greek Expressions for *ab epistulis*

Documents of the first three centuries A.D. consistently use ἐπὶ τῶν ἐπιστολῶν to refer to the office of *ab epistulis*, which no doubt was the official translation. Alternative designations do occasionally appear, as, for example, ἐπιστολεύς.[83] Rhetorical periphrases are found even in imperial pronouncements, as when Commodus refers to Laricus (no. 25 of List I) as ὁ φίλος μου καὶ τὴν τάξιν τῶ[ν Ἑλληνικῶν ἐπισ]τολῶν πεπιστευμένος, or Caracalla characterizes Antipater (no. 29 of List I) as ὁ φίλος μου καὶ διδάσκαλος κ[αὶ τὴν   ]ν Ἑλλη[νι]κῶν ἐπιστολῶν ἐπιτετραμμένος.[84]

Greek authors of the period, eschewing the pedestrian language of officialdom, designated the office in a variety of ways.[85] Aelius Aristides: τὸν γραμματέα . . . τὸν βασιλικόν (50.57 Keil = 26.335 Dindorf). Dio Cassius: τὸν τὰς ἐπιστολὰς αὐτοῦ διαγάγοντα (69.3.5); τὸν τὰς ἐπιστολὰς αὐτοῦ τὰς Λατίνας διὰ χειρὸς ἔχοντα (72[71].12.3); τὰς ἐπιστολὰς τὰς Λατίνας διοικήσαντος (73[72].7.4); τὴν τῶν ἐπιστολῶν . . . ἑκατέρων διοίκησιν (78[77].18.2). Philostratus: ἠξιώθη . . . βασιλείων ἐπιστολῶν (*Ap Ty* 1.12.14); βασιλικῶν ἐπιστολῶν . . . προστάτης[86] (*VS* 1.22.3); τὸ ἐπιστέλλειν "Ελλησιν (2.5.3 sqq.); ἐψηφίσατο . . . τὰς ἐπιστολὰς ὁ Κόμμοδος (2.10.6); ταῖς βασιλείοις ἐπιστολαῖς ἐπιταχθείς (2.24.1 [sim. 4]); παρελθὼν ἐς βασιλείους ἐπιστολὰς . . . ἐπέστελλε (2.33.3). Phrynichus: (βασιλικὸς) ἐπιστολεύς (225, 379, 418 Lobeck = 203, 356, 393 Rutherford).

NOTES

1. *Mnemosyne* 16 (1963) 257. Müller-Graupa, *RE* 16, 817, had characterized such membership as "blossen Gnadengehalt. . . . Hohe Beamte und ehemalige Offiziere erhielten . . . diese Vergünstigung." See now also V. Nutton, *CQ* 21 (1971) 265-69; F. Millar, *The Emperor in the Roman World* (Ithaca, N.Y. 1977) 505-6.

2. J. C. Shelton, *P. Mich.* xi 620, 2-3n. (p. 84); so too R. A. Coles, *P. Oxy.* xli 75, J. R. Rea, *JEA* 60 (1974) 296, and (less insistently) J. F. Gilliam, *Mélanges . . . W. Seston* (Paris 1974) 219, 222 n. 30, 224. Shelton also cites as support E. G. Turner, *Greek Papyri: An Introduction* (Princeton 1968) 86, but what Turner says is rather different. He does not reject the view that " 'non-scholar members of the Museum' . . . were given this membership as an honor, much in the way academies today give honorary fellowships, or universities honorary degrees"; he merely adds that an individual so rewarded might "also have had some literary pretensions, as a bookish man if not as a writer." This is an apter appraisal. Many a procurator or praefectus then, like many an officer or financier now, might enjoy literature and accumulate a library without fancying himself anything more than an amateur of literature or scholarship; as an example, see Millar's thumbnail sketch (n. 1 above) 89-90 of the public career and literary patronage and dilettantism of Titinius Capito (no. 6 in the list of holders of the office of *ab epistulis* given below). A widespread interest in books, Turner thinks, can help account for the literary finds—remnants, presumably, of private libraries— in remote towns and villages such as Oxyrhynchus or Philadelphia.

3. For the reconstruction of his life span and career, see Gilliam (n. 2 above) 217-25, and my note in *BASP* 13 (1976) 165-66.

4. *Praefectus vigilum: CIL* xiv 4393 = *ILS* 465; *P. Mich.* xi 620. *Ab epistulis: AEpigr* 1966 no. 474. Museum member: *P. Mich.* xi 620. (In *P. Corn.* inv. ii, 25 = *SB* viii 9898, the cognomen was read as Φανιανῷ, which was quickly corrected by Gilliam, *Mnemosyne* 17 (1964) 193-99 to [Τ]ι[τ]ανιανῷ. The document was later discovered to be the first column of *P. Mich.* xi 620, where it is reprinted as corrected.)

5. Rea (n. 2 above). Similarly G. W. Bowersock, *Greek Sophists in the Roman Empire* (Oxford 1969) 53: "There is no warrant to call Vibianus Tertullus a sophist, but his qualifications will undoubtedly have included some kind of rhetorical or literary proficiency."

6. M. P. Charlesworth, *CAH* 10, p. 687.

7. These studies are: G. B. Townend, *Historia* 10 (1961) 375-81; H. G. Pflaum, *Les carrières procuratoriennes* . . . (Paris 1960) 246, 268, 271, 338, 683-84, 1004; Bowersock (n. 5 above) 50-56; Millar (n. 1 above) 87-93, 103-5, 224-27.

8. Millar (n. 1 above) 88; Pflaum (n. 7 above) 268; Bowersock (n. 5 above) 50.

9. Bowersock (n. 5 above); Pflaum (n. 7 above) 1004.

10. The list includes *ab epistulis Latinis* as well as *ab epistulis Graecis* ("men of fairly similar types from both the Greek and Latin worlds," Millar [n. 1 above] 91). It can hardly be objected that a greater degree of literary skill would be demanded for the Greek correspondence (if anything, the reverse might be true); besides, as already noted, the office was initially and for a long time undivided, with a single head in charge of both Greek and Latin correspondence.

11. Josephus's attestation of the title has been impugned by some: see, most recently, G. Boulvert, *Esclaves et affranchis impériaux sous le Haut-Empire romain*, Biblioteca di Labeo iv (1970) 93 n. 9.

12. On this date see Appendix 1.

13. See n. 56. below.

14. He is the first equestrian holder of the office known to us by name, but according to Tacitus, *Hist.* 1.58, *Vitellius ministeria principatus per libertos agi solita in equites Romanos disposuit.*

15. These two offices are generally regarded as having been held in conjunction. The Museum director was a priest, who headed its cult of the Muses. See the discussion below and Pflaum (n. 7 above) 245.

16. On his identity see Bowersock (n. 5 above) 53.

17. He held the office twice, with an interval between. Pflaum (n. 7 above) 1021 assumes that he was *ab ep. Graec.* the first time, and Townend (n. 7 above) 381 joins Pflaum in designating him *ab ep. Lat.* the second time, but the source (*CIL* vi 1564 = *ILS* 1452) has only *ab epist]ulis Latinis . . . ab epistulis[*.

18. He was *ab epistulis* to emperors (plural), i.e., A.D. 161–69 or 176–80. Pflaum 1021 leaves the choice open; Bowersock (n. 5 above) 55 prefers the later period.

19. His name appears in various spellings: see A. Berger, *RE* 4A, 2405; E. Birley, *Bonner. Hist. Aug. Coll.* (1966-67) 44.

20. On the date see Bowersock (n. 5 above) 54, Millar (n. 1 above) 105.

21. Presumably the same man mentioned in SHA *Commodus* 1.6, *orator ei Ateius Sanctus fuit.*

22. The logical emendation by Pflaum (n. 7 above) 1004 for the inscription's *proc.*, which level of office would be out of place at this point in the *cursus*.

23. Thus Townend (n. 7 above) 381. Pflaum without comment lists him as Manilius Pudens, identifying him with the Pudens whose γράμματα Dio Cassius mentions in 72[71].29.1. The identification is possible, but far from certain. An alternative suggestion is that they were two men, one for the Greek and one for the Latin correspondence.

24. Tentatively included by Townend (n. 7 above) 381, but omitted by Pflaum without comment.

25. Listed by Pflaum (n. 7 above) 1021, without comment; by Townend (n. 7 above) with a question mark, for which there is good reason. All that is known about this individual is contained in SHA *Commodus* 4.8: *Vitruvium Secundum, Paterni familiarissimum, qui epistulas imperatorias curarat, interfecit.* The writer's graceless Latin leaves uncertain whether *Secundum* or *Paterni* (no. 19 in our list) is the antecedent of the relative clause. As Paternus was *praefectus praetorio* under Commodus (Dio Cassius 73[72].5.3), the pluperfect *curarat* could refer to his secretaryship under Marcus Aurelius.

26. See n. 31 below.

27. Born a slave, he ended his career in the senatorial class—the most striking degree of advancement in the entire list. He may be the Agrippa mentioned in *P. Oxy.* 3094; cf. the note to line 8 and M. W. Haslam, *AJP* 97 (1976) 189.

28. In addition, Plaum (n. 7 above) 1021 and Millar (n. 1 above) 97 list L. Caecilius Athenaeus as *ab epistulis* (as the *ab studiis* of the inscription is presumably to be emended) *Latinis* under Severus Alexander (A.D. 222–35). But Pflaum also observes (825) that, in view of the low level of this man's other offices, his culminating title of *procurator ab epistulis Latinis* is in all probability to be understood as that of an undersecretary or some such (cf. Pflaum 448 on the distinction between *a rationibus* and *proc. summarum rationum*). In the first few decades of the office and perhaps as late as Hadrian, all members of the staff, from the head of the bureau to the lowliest clerk, were identified simply as *ab epistulis*. The evidence on this phenomenon is assembled and analyzed by P. R. C. Weaver, *Familia Caesaris* (Cambridge 1972) 252-66; for a brief account of secondary ranks (*proximus, adiutor*, etc.), see Boulvert, (n. 11 above) 93-94.

29. For a recently discovered example of Julia Domna engaged in imperial correspondence, see *AEpigr* 1966 no. 430 (where the reference to *REG*, etc. is in error for *RPh* 41 [1967] 44-64). See further n. 44 below.

30. It has been suggested that this was also the case in the appointment of T. Varius Clemens (no. 15): see Pflaum (n. 7 above) 372; Millar (n. 1 above) 104.

31. Precisely when the change from *liberti* to *equites* occurred is uncertain: see n. 14 above and Millar (n. 1 above) 89.

32. Nos. 3, 4, 7, 8, 10, 11, 19, 20, 24, 28-31, 35. Bowersock claims that "between the reigns of Hadrian and Caracalla twelve oriental literati can be distinguished as *ab epistulis*," but by his own admission two of the twelve (nos. 18, 25) are totally unknown except for having held the office and a third (no. 21), though not known to have been a sophist, is simply presumed to have had "some kind of rhetorical or literary proficiency" (Bowersock [n. 5 above] 50, 54). On present evidence, therefore, there is no reason to accord these three a literary or rhetorical background. As for no. 28, "some connection with Philostratus' Aquila from Galatia seems irresistible" (Bowersock 56); perhaps so, but the identification remains uncertain.

33. W. C. Wright, *Philostratus and Eunapius* (Loeb Classical Library 1922) x.

34. Nos. 18, 23, 25, 26.

35. Old beliefs die hard. Of no. 9, for example, Millar (n. 1 above) remarks (102-4), "There is no specific evidence that he was a literary man; but he could well be the Eudaemon whom Marcus Aurelius mentions . . . as brilliant . . . "; and, following Pflaum (n. 7 above) 372, he thinks the career background of no. 15 contrasts strikingly "with that of other *ab epistulis*."

36. On these see n. 28 above. R. Syme's remark in *Historia* 23 (1974) 481 is apt: "With the development of system, habit and bureaucracy, the character and quality of the ruler comes to matter less and less. Be he a boy, a buffoon, or a philosopher . . . the administration goes on unimpaired, being guided by friends and agents of Caesar."

37. Cf. Philostr. *VS* 2.24.2: διδάσκαλος . . . τῶν Σεβήρου παίδων.

38. Truly, in Pflaum's words (n. 7 above) 250, a "favori de l'empereur." See also Pflaum 612.

39. Pflaum (n. 7 above) 246; similarly repeatedly, e.g., 268, 338, 683-84, 1004. See the preceding discussion and n. 40 below.

40. Philostr. *VS* 1.22.3; Dio Cassius 69.3.4-5. However much this last may be discounted for tendentiousness, it surely calls into question Pflaum's characterization (n. 7 above) 268 of Heliodorus as an example of the "grands hommes de lettres du monde grec" in the office of *ab epistulis*.

41. Philostr. *VS* 1.22.3, 2.33.3. Wright (n. 33 above) calls Julia Domna's court "pseudo-intellectual, because when Philostratus speaks of her circle of mathematicians and philosophers, it must be remembered that the former were certainly astrologers . . . and that the latter were nearly all sophists."

42. To cite but one example, see *OGIS* 484, recently restudied by A. D. Macro, *GRBS* 17 (1976) 169-79.

43. Gilliam (n. 2 above) 219. For a recently published example from the fourth century, see *Illinois Class. Stud.* 2 (1977) 184-96.

44. On her imperial role see J. Bidez, *CAH* 12, 613; R. Rémondon, *La crise de l'empire romain* (Paris 1964) 81-82; M. Besnier, *Histoire romaine* 4.1 (Paris 1937) 60: "Uniquement occupé du soin de l'armée et de la défense des frontières, il abandonnait à sa mère, qui l'avait suivi, le gouvernement de l'Empire. Déjà très influente du vivant de Septime-Sévère, Julia Domna fut toute-puissante sous le nouveau règne." This last, like Wright's "virtual regent" (n. 33 above) is perhaps somewhat overstated, but cf. n. 29 above.

45. Whether it was Soter or Philadelphus has long been argued. The prevailing view attributes the foundation to Soter acting on the advice of Demetrius of Phalerum; see, most recently, P. M. Fraser, *Ptolemaic Alexandria* (Oxford 1972) 315.

46. They were certainly not so regarded by the Ptolemaic rulers, who obtained practical services from these institutions as well as the propaganda value of being the leading patrons of the arts and sciences in the Hellenistic world. See M. Rostovtzeff, *Social and Economic History of the Hellenistic World* (Oxford 1941) 1084-86, 1091, 1388 n. 103; see also n. 50 below.

47. Strabo 17.1.8 (C 793): τῶν δὲ βασιλείων μέρος ἐστὶ καὶ τὸ Μουσεῖον.

48. Thus F. E. Peters, *The Harvest of Hellenism* (New York 1971): "The Museum was created, subsidized and controlled by the Ptolemies" (p. 193). "The thinly veiled political allusions in the *Hymns* betray Callimachus in his guise as court poet and propagandist. . . .Callimachus, supported and sustained by the Ptolemies, was in turn giving voice to their policies: the exaltation of the ruling house. . . . The price for the comforts of the Museum, if not onerous, is, however, unmistakable" (pp. 204-5). So too E. A. Barber, *CAH* 7, p. 251: "The Museum is definitely under state-control." Or P. M. Fraser (n. 45 above) 305: "Much of the intellectual production of Alexandria derives directly from Ptolemaic patronage." An amusing anecdote about the stipend (σύνταξις) paid the members is told by Athenaeus 11.493f-494a.

49. *OGIS* 104 = *Insc. de Delos* 1525: Χρύσερμον Ἡρακλείτου Ἀλεξανδρέα τὸν συγγενῆ βασιλέως Πτολεμαίου καὶ ἐξηγητὴν καὶ ἐπὶ τῶν ἰατρῶν καὶ ἐπιστάτην τοῦ Μουσείου.

50. *P. Oxy.* x 1241 ii, 16-17: Κύδας ἐκ τῶν λογχοφόρων. This rarely occurring title (cf. *Prosop. Ptol.* 2, p. 225) has been interpreted as designating a member (honorary?) of the king's bodyguard; so too Barber, *CAH* 7, p. 253. Speaking of the others he observes, "It is a fair conclusion that the Chief Librarian was *ex officio* tutor to the Royal Family." So were some Museum members; Strato of Lampsacus, for example, was a tutor of Ptolemy Philadelphus.

51. Strabo 17.1.8 (C 794): ἔστι δὲ . . . καὶ ἱερεὺς ὁ ἐπὶ τῷ Μουσείῳ, τεταγμένος τότε μὲν ὑπὸ τῶν βασιλέων, νῦν δ' ὑπὸ Καίσαρος.

52. A felicitous expression first used by A. Piganiol at the Seventh International Congress of Papyrology (cf. *Museum Helveticum* 10 [1953] 193) and much repeated since.

53. H. I. Bell, *CAH* 10, p. 297; cf. also Müller-Graupa, *RE* 16, 817.

163

54. Suet. *Claud.* 42.2; Philostr. *ApTy* 1.185; SHA *Hadr.* 20. This recalls the case of Ptolemy Philadelphus, who "once asked Euclid if there was not a shorter road to geometry than through the way of the *Elements,* and Euclid replied that there was no royal road to geometry" (Proclus, *Comm. in Eucl.* 1.4 *ad fin.,* trans. G. R. Morrow, 57). The anecdote is also told of the mathematician Menaechmus and Alexander the Great (Stobaeus 4, p. 205 Meineke, trans. in *CAH* 7, p. 296). For Caracalla and the Museum, see n. 63 below.

55. *SEG* ii 332 is an inscription in which Delphi honors two Pergamene physicians who are $[\tau\hat{\omega}\nu\ \pi\epsilon\rho\grave{\iota}\ \tau\grave{o}\ \mathrm{Mo}]\nu\sigma\epsilon\hat{\iota}o\nu$. The restored formula is conjectural, but it is agreed that the reference is to membership in the Alexandrian Museum; cf. P. Lemerle, *BCH* 59 (1935) 135. But, as the inscription dates from ca. 27 B.C., their appointment to the Museum is likely to have antedated Augustus's annexation of Egypt, and they are accordingly omitted from this list. Attested as "museum members" but also omitted from this list are physicians of Ephesus, as well as Ti. Pomponius Dionysius and Cassianus *alias* Synesius of Athens, because those are among the cities known to have created museums of their own on the Alexandrian model; cf. J. H. Oliver, *Hesperia* 3 (1934) 191-96 and Suppl. 13, 106; P. Lemerle, *loc. cit.;* P. M. Fraser (n. 45 above) 312-16; V. Nutton (n. 1 above) 264. A still further omission from the list is discussed below, n. 61.

56. We are told only that Chaeremo was head of a school at Alexandria, in which position he was succeeded, when he was called to Rome, by his disciple Dionysius. Müller-Graupa (n. 53 above) thought it likely that Chaeremo was director of the Museum ("wohl Vorsteher"); but H. R. Schwyzer, *Chaeremon (Klass.-phil. Studien* 4 1932) 11, had more cautiously concluded that on this evidence it remained an open question ("dahingestellt") whether Chaeremo and Dionysius actually held that office; and Millar (n. 1 above) 505 regards it as "no more than probable that the succession was as head of the Museum." In *P. Lond.* 1912 (= *CPJ* ii 153), which neither Müller-Graupa (n. 1 above) nor Schwyzer took into account, one of the Alexandrian envoys to Claudius is named Chaeremo (l. 17), perhaps the same man as the Chaeremo of our list, who is known to have included an anti-Semitic version of the Exodus in his *History of Egypt* (Josephus, *C. Ap.* 1.288ff.). This identification, should it happen to be correct, might strengthen somewhat the case for his having been head of the Museum; such a personage would lend dignity and intellectual tone to the delegation. The possibility of this identity is thus worth noting, but I know of no evidence that might help prove or disprove it.

57. The Greek word is $\sigma\alpha\tau\rho\acute{\alpha}\pi\eta\varsigma$; for the Latin equivalent see H. J. Mason, *Phoenix* 24 (1970) 157, and *Greek Terms for Roman Institutions,* Amer. Studies in Papyrology 13 (Toronto 1974), s.v.

58. The full title is $\dot{\alpha}\rho\chi\iota\delta\iota\kappa\alpha\sigma\tau\grave{\eta}\varsigma\ \kappa\alpha\grave{\iota}\ \pi\rho\grave{o}\varsigma\ \tau\hat{\eta}\ \dot{\epsilon}\pi\iota\mu\epsilon\lambda\epsilon\acute{\iota}\alpha\ \tau\hat{\omega}\nu\ \chi\rho\eta\mu\alpha\tau\iota\sigma\tau\hat{\omega}\nu\ \kappa\alpha\grave{\iota}\ \tau\hat{\omega}\nu\ \ddot{\alpha}\lambda\lambda\omega\nu\ \kappa\rho\iota\tau\eta\rho\acute{\iota}\omega\nu$.

59. He was appointed by Hadrian as a reward for a bit of flattery, according to Athenaeus 16.677e, who quotes four hexameter lines from one of his poems. Forty more lines are preserved, in whole or in part, in *P. Oxy.* viii 1085.

60. On the father see *P. Oxy.* i 100.

61. It may be—though I think it unlikely—that we should insert at this point in the list Ammonius son of Archias, who in *SB* iii 6674, an inscription of ca. A.D. 170, is characterized as a former *basilikos grammateus* of the Antaeopolite nome $\tau\acute{\alpha}\xi\iota\nu\ \ddot{\epsilon}\chi o\nu\tau o\varsigma\ \dot{\epsilon}\nu\ \tau\hat{\omega}\ \mathrm{Mov}\sigma\epsilon\acute{\iota}\omega$. Weighing against understanding this to designate Museum membership (as the editor assumed without comment: *BSRAA* 19 [1923] 134) are the following considerations: 1) neither this expression nor anything like it occurs in reference to any of the known members; 2) an inscription such as this, which boasts of the public offices (exegetes, gymnasiarch, agoranomos) of the dedicator and of other members of his family for several generations back, would scarcely resort to this pallid periphrasis in place of the well-attested, grand-sounding formula of membership discussed below. In this light Ammonius's *taxis* in the

Museum seems likelier to have been a post in its administration than a place in its membership.

62. E. G. Turner, *JEA* 38 (1952) 92, identifies him as the author of a work on the orators, mentioned by the Suda and (probably) Photius. The identification may be right, but it is not, I think, "clinched" (Turner's word) by the evidence adducible. A particular obstacle is the description of the writer Diodorus, together with his father, as γεγονὼς ἐπὶ τοῦ Καίσαρος Ἀδριανοῦ (Suidas Δ1150, Π2166 Adler); the Diodorus of our list could, therefore, be the writer's grandson *aut sim.*, or even totally unrelated.

63. The case for his being a Museum member is his characterization as συσσίτου in the inscription, which comes from Alexandria; so Dittenberger ad loc., and recently reaffirmed by C. P. Jones, *CQ* 17 (1967) 311-12. Strabo 17.1.8 (C 794) mentions an οἶκον μέγαν ἐν ᾧ τὸ συσσίτιον τῶν μετεχόντων τοῦ Μουσείου φιλολόγων ἀνδρῶν, and according to Dio Cassius 78[77].7.3 Caracalla wanted to burn the books of the Aristotelian philosophers and τὰ συσσίτια ἃ ἐν τῇ Ἀλεξανδρείᾳ εἶχον τάς τε λοιπὰς ὠφελείας ὅσας ἐκαρποῦντο ἀφείλετο. In *VS* 1.22 Philostratus explains to his readers, τὸ δὲ Μουσεῖον τράπεζα Αἰγυπτία ξυγκαλοῦσα τοὺς ἐν πάσῃ τῇ γῇ ἐλλογίμους. On the privilege of *sitēsis,* see the discussion below.

64. For the date, see *BASP* 13 (1976) 166.

65. Cf. Nutton (n. 1 above) 267.

66. Ibid., following *W. Chr.* 39 and 40 intros.

67. The inscription dates from A.D. 305-313, but the designation ἀπὸ Μουσείου appears to belong to the father (name lost), rather than to M. Aurelius Diophantes.

68. Nos. 3, 4, 7, 8, 14, 22, 23 and perhaps 9, 15, 20 (cf. n. 62 above) 25.

69. Nos. 26, 31.

70. A priestly title of one kind or another, including νεωκόρος τοῦ μεγάλου Σαράπιδος, is attested for nearly half the men in List II: nos. 1, 3, 5, 10-13, 15, 17-19, 21, 25, 27, 32.

71. No. 9 omits ἀτελῶν. No. 26, deceased, is styled τῶν . . . σειτηθέντων. No. 30 is characterized as *immunitate Musii fultus.* Hadrian is said to have appointed no. 7 τῷ τοῦ Μουσείου κύκλῳ ἐς τὴν Αἰγυπτίαν σίτησιν (Philostr. *VS* 1.25.3), and to no. 14 he granted τὴν ἐν τῷ Μουσείῳ . . . σίτησιν ἔχειν (Athenaeus 677d-e).

72. No. 27; the epithet is found also with nos. 2, 6, 9, 22, 28, 31. Turner's reminder (n. 2 above) that in this connection " 'philosopher' . . . has a technical sense, 'belonging to the philosophy section of the Museum' " does not alter the fact that some of these men were so assigned out of courtesy or administrative convenience rather than for their professional attainments. One can easily imagine the same kind of considerations at play as those which today determine that an honorary degree is to be L.H.D. rather than LL.D.

73. Under the Ptolemies the members also received a cash stipend (σύνταξις): see n. 48 above. Sources of Roman date do not mention such a stipend, unless it is implied among the "other benefits" that Caracalla is said to have canceled (n. 63 above). Caracalla's action—if actual, and not merely invented by a hostile tradition—presumably was rescinded by one of his successors. At all events, Museum membership, as List II shows, continued to be a valued honor.

74. Nos. 7, 9, 22, 25, 31, 33.

75. The characteristics of such boats, called πάκτωνες, are detailed by L. Casson, *Ships and Seamanship in the Ancient World* (Princeton 1971) 342.

76. So too Gilliam (n. 2 above) 222: "He may well have divided his time between the countryside and Alexandria, as many others did." Another such absentee landlord—though not a Museum member—who has recently come to light is Ti. Julius Theo, whose estate, when he died early in the second century, consisted of lands in several places and perhaps as many as a hundred slaves: cf. *P. Oxy.* xliv p. 170.

77. The number of these men, which now stands at twenty, would be increased almost fivefold if all archidicastae (92 are listed for the Roman period by A. Calabi,

Aegyptus 32 [1952] 410-18) were ipso facto Museum heads. But this view—put forward many years ago by W. Otto, *Priest. u. Tempel im hell. Ägypten* 1 (Leipzig 1905-8) pp. 166-68, 197-99; 2, pp. 388-89, questioned by O. Hirschfeld, *Kais. Verwaltungsb.* (Berlin 1905²) 362 n. 3, and in effect left open by U. Wilcken, *Grundz.* p. 118 n. 1—is rejected by Calabi, ibid. 407-9.

78. *Sic,* but *Graecis* is not in the Suda. The Greek and Latin sections of the office did not originally have separate heads; see above, p. 150.

79. Cf. the career of C. Stertinius Xenophon (Pflaum no. 16). Like Balbillus, he was decorated in Claudius's British triumph and held the office of ἐπὶ τῶν Ἑλληνικῶν ἀποκριμάτων = *ad responsa Graeca,* an office which apparently was discontinued by Hadrian (Pflaum, *Les procurateurs equestres* [Paris 1950] 60). He is further described as φιλονέρωνα, and is identified as ἀρχιατρὸν τῶν θεῶν Σεβαστῶν (i.e., Claudius and Nero).

80. Cf. n. 56 above.

81. Cf. the case of Titanianus (n. 3 above). But Titinius Capito (no. 6 of List I) served as *ab epistulis* under Domitian, Nerva, and Trajan. (Pliny the Younger is, of course, our most familiar example of one whose subsequent career was not impaired by his having held office under Domitian.) If it therefore be asked why Dionysius could not similarly have stayed on after Nero's fall, a sufficient answer, I think, is found in the contrast between the bloody violence of "the four emperors" and the liberal benignity introduced by Nerva and Trajan.

82. The suggestion is made by W. Weber, *Hermes* 50 (1915) 49-50.

83. *OGIS* 679 = *IGRR* i 136.

84. *AEpigr* 1952 no. 6, and *Forsch. Ephesos* ii 26. Mason (n. 57 above) 141, gives the missing word as τάξιν, without, however, indicating that it is a restoration; Millar (n. 1 above) 226 n. 98 favors ?σύνταξι]ν.

85. Some of these expressions, mostly without citation of source, are given by Mason (n. 57 above) 141-42. Some may be translations of corresponding Latin expressions; see n. 86 below. Mason's *exegesin* is an error.

86. Cf. SHA *Hadr.* 11.3, where Suetonius is called the emperor's *epistularum magister.*

17
THE CLYSMA-PHARA-HAILA ROAD ON THE PEUTINGER TABLE

PHILIP MAYERSON

During the past twenty-five years there has been a revival of interest by historical geographers and archaeologists in tracing the ancient road systems leading from Aila to the north and northwest toward the Mediterranean.[1] Where literary and epigraphic sources provided the names of sites, investigations were centered on the identification of way stations which were not as securely known as such places as Oboda, Elusa, or Beersheba. One stretch that was intensively investigated and surveyed produced twelve milestones or markers and evidence of the road having been cleared of stones and bordered with curbstones;[2] another survey revealed the construction of steps where the gradient of the slope was over 20 percent and the erection of 3 m. high walls to protect the edges of the road against erosion.[3]

As in all surveys of this kind, the Peutinger Table—the map said to reflect the main lines of communication in the Roman road system of the fourth and first half of the fifth centuries A.D.—figured largely because it gives the names of sites and the distances between them in Roman miles, as, for example, between Aila and Lysa (fig. 1): *Haila xvi Ad Dianam xvi Rasa xvi Gypsaria xxviii Lysa*. Strangely enough, however, when one turns to a neighboring road system pictured on the Peutinger Table, that which leads from Aila (modern Aqaba) to Clysma (Suez), one finds virtually no discussion of it since the publication of Miller's study of the Table in 1916;[4] and even Miller has little to say about the road other than to identify the sites between Aila and Clysma, Phara and Medeia. The distances, recorded in Roman miles, are as follows: from Clysma to Medeia (*-deia* or *-ocia*) 40 (*xl*), from Medeia to Phara 80 (*lxxx*), from Phara to Haila 50 (*l*). The site of Phara is located under a representation of Mount Sinai (*Mons Syna*), and above the symbol for the mountain are the words *Hic legem acceperunt i(n) monte syna*. Above this inscription, in bolder letters and covering a much larger space, are these words: *Desertum u(bi) quadraginta annis erraver(un)t filii isr(ae)l ducente Moyse.*

167

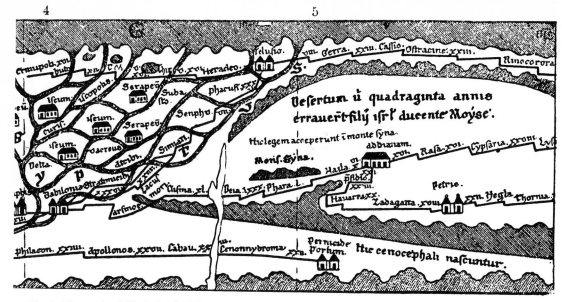

Fig. 1. The roads of Sinai, detail of the Peutinger Table.

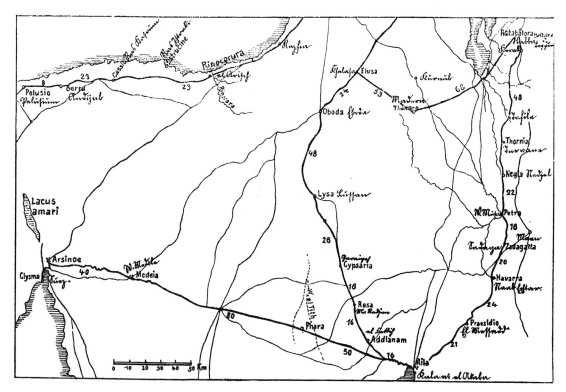

Fig. 2. Sketch map of the Clysma-Aila road. Reproduced from K. Miller,
Itineraria Romana (Stuttgart 1916) cols. 813-14.

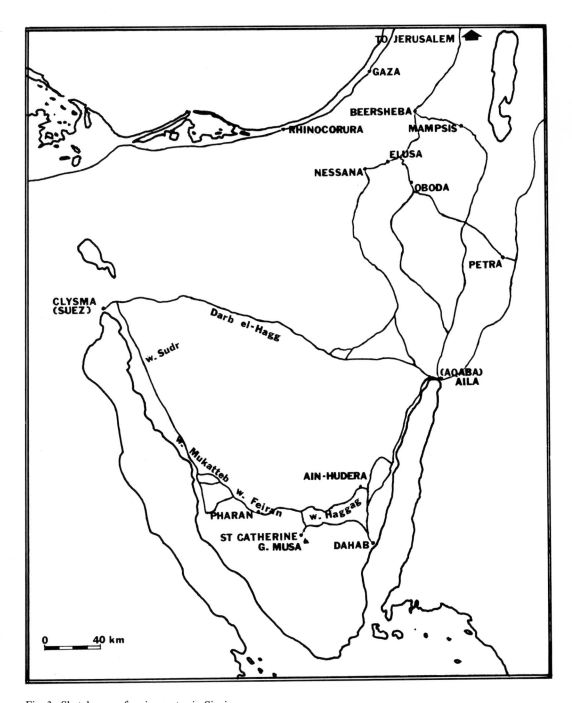

Fig. 3. Sketch map of major routes in Sinai.

According to Miller's sketch map (fig. 2)—apparently influenced by or adapted from J. L. Burckhardt's map in his *Travels in Syria and the Holy Land* (1822)—the road leads in almost a straight line from Clysma to Aila, as if it were identical with the Darb el-Hagg which Moslem pilgrims en route to Mecca once traveled from Suez to Aqaba. Miller identifies Medeia with remains in Wadi Medila and locates Phara just west of Wadi et-Tih.[5] No citation is given in support of these two identifications. Aharoni appears to agree with Miller's interpretation, placing Phara in northern Sinai at eth-Themed, a way station on the Darb el-Hagg, and states: "On the Roman *Tabula Peutingeriana* eth-Themed is called Phara (i.e., Paran). It is probable that this name is given here with the addition of the name of the desert in which it was located, like El(ath)-Paran and that on the Roman map only the second part of the name is preserved."[6]

The interpretations of Miller and Aharoni face a serious obstacle, and that is the identification of Phara, or Pharan, as it is more commonly known. Of all the sites in Sinai, one, and only one, has an enduring history. That is the Pharan cited by the second-century geographer Ptolemy as a *komê* situated deep in the Sinai peninsula (fig. 3),[7] and in the third century called by Eusebius a *polis* "situated to the south beyond (the boundaries of) Arabia."[8] Pharan is the site at which the peripatetic nun Egeria, in the late fourth or early fifth century, stopped on her way to and from Mount Sinai.[9] Pharan is also cited by other pilgrims or monks who traveled to or lived near the "Mountain of God."[10] It is now known by its Arabic name as Feiran, and the remains of a considerable community can still be seen on a high bank overlooking the Wadi Feiran. Ceramic remains from the site provide evidence that it was inhabited as early as the eighth or seventh century B.C.,[11] and probably earlier since the locale has the richest supply of perennial water in all of Sinai. Unquestionably, it was its water supply that made Pharan a center for human habitation over so many centuries.

Why, then, should Pharan be placed far to the northeast in one of the most barren places of the Sinai peninsula? The scholarly dilemma seems to have arisen from attempting to rationalize the figures given on the Peutinger Table for the distances cited for the two sites between Clysma and Aila. One thing is certain: the Pharan that is so well known is no fifty Roman miles from Aila. Medeia, whose identification could help in pointing out the general direction of the route from Clysma, is simply unknown from any source. Its identification by Miller with a wadi with a vaguely similar name is hardly secure evidence for locating the site.[12] One must come to the conclusion that there is something wrong with the figures given on the Peutinger Table.

If the Clysma-Aila road on the Table is examined closely and compared with those leading north of Aila, it will be noted for the latter that the distances between sites are given in very precise numbers, whereas the distances for the Clysma-Aila road are given in round numbers. Take, for example, the road from Aila to Elusa (see fig. 1). There are six stations between the two points, with distances of 16, 16, 16, 28, 47, and 24 Roman miles (220 km.).[13] The Clysma-Aila road, on the other hand, covers 170 Roman miles (250 km.) with only two intervening stations between the termini.

It is clearly evident that the Clysma-Aila route was not a major line of communication during the fourth century, and it is most likely that the cartographer of the Table either had no detailed information regarding this route, or that he only wished to give a schematic notion of it in terms of distances and intervening stations. He did, however, know what he was about in drawing the line of the road as he did. At the very least, his intention is quite clear.

The most prominent feature on the Table for the area under discussion—its only vignette, so to speak—is Mount Sinai, together with the inscriptions bearing on the biblical associations with the mountain and with the Exodus. It would be asking too much of the cartographer to expect, as does Aharoni,[14] that he was locating a general biblical expanse known as the desert of Paran. The map itself is quite explicit in designating Phara (or Pharan) as a geographical place no different from Clysma or Aila. And placing Pharan just under the representation of Mount Sinai must surely indicate that the cartographer associated one with the other. In short, we must accept Phara of the Peutinger Table to be Pharan, an established community in southern Sinai and in close proximity to the mountain which, at the time the map was drawn, was believed to have been the place where Moses received the Law. As to the distance between Clysma and Pharan, 120 Roman miles, I believe it is possible to show that it is reasonably accurate. The 50 Roman miles between Pharan and Aila is another matter and cannot be rationalized.

If, then, Phara of the Peutinger Table is to be identified with Pharan deep in the Sinai peninsula and some thirty-five Roman miles from Mount Sinai, the route from Clysma must head south-southeast (see fig. 3) and not east-southeast, as shown by Burckhardt and Miller. This southern route was the one generally taken by pilgrims on their way from Egypt to the "Mountain of God," and until the fortified monastery at Mount Sinai was constructed in the sixth century on orders from Emperor Justinian, Pharan was the point at which pilgrims could find shelter and refreshment on their way to and from the mountain, where facilities must surely have been limited.

The *itinerarium* of Egeria, dated to the late fourth or early fifth century, is instructive on this point. Although the text of the account is broken and opens with Egeria's approach to Mount Sinai, we hear

171

that she had arrived there from Pharan;[15] after receiving a guided tour of the holy places at Mount Sinai, she returned to Pharan, "which is thirty-five miles from Sinai, and we had to stop there for two days in order to rest."[16] She then describes the return journey to Clysma without mentioning specific stages along the route. At one point she remarks that "there is no road there at all, only sands of the desert all around," and goes on to comment on the skills of the Pharanites in traveling through the roadless desert.[17] Finally, she states, "we arrived at Clysma by the same route and by the same stages by which we had come."[18]

Some twenty-five years after the construction of the fortified monastery at Mount Sinai, now known as the Monastery of Saint Catherine, an *itinerarium* (ca. 570) attributed to Antoninus of Piacenza records yet another route to the Holy Mountain.[19] Antoninus traveled from Gaza to Elusa and then to Nessana, whence he set out on a six-day trek through the waterless "inner desert" on a direct route to Mount Sinai, thereby bypassing Clysma, Aila, and Pharan.[20] At Mount Sinai he learned that the moratorium on raiding by Bedouins had come to an end and that no travelers should remain in the desert through which they had come. Hence, "some returned to the Holy City through Egypt and some through Arabia. From Mount Sinai to the city of Arabia, which is called A(b)ila, is eight stages."[21] Antoninus and his companions decided to return to Jerusalem via Egypt. They traveled to Pharan, which Antoninus describes as a city fortified with walls made of brick and having a police force which patrolled the desert in order to protect monasteries and hermits against Bedouin attacks.[22] En route to Clysma from Pharan, they stopped at Surandela (Arandara)—to Antoninus the site of biblical Elim—where they found a small fortified monastery *(castellum)* containing a church, its priest, and two hospices *(xenodochia)* for the use of travelers.[23] They rested there for two days to recover from the exhaustion of desert travel. Further along the way to Clysma, at a place "where the Children of Israel marked out their camp after passing the Red Sea," Antoninus and his companions came upon another *castellum* with a hospice.[24]

The Antoninus *itinerarium* outlines the two main, and relatively secure, routes from Mount Sinai as drawn on the Peutinger Table. In the fourth century there was no fortified monastery at the Holy Mountain, and Pharan—one day's distance from Mount Sinai and itself considered to be the biblical site where the Israelites battled with the Amalekites—was the center of activity for pilgrims and a "Saracen" community. As we learn from the Antoninus itinerary, travelers from Palestine could go directly either to Mount Sinai and Pharan without making their way to Clysma or Aila; but although the route was much shorter, the risk was greater. The Clysma-Pharan route, on the other hand, offered pilgrims the opportunity of touring Israelite sites both in Egypt and Sinai. Egeria's record of her journey

172

shows that she wanted to be shown the physical sites of biblical events, especially those associated with the Exodus, and she wanted to do so in safety. She traveled the long route from Pharan to Clysma and Egypt; she was escorted by Roman troops "as long as we were traveling through unsafe places"; and after touring Egypt, she returned to Pelusium and reached Palestine "by the same stages of Egypt by which we had come."[25]

If the evidence is secure that Phara of the Peutinger Table is Pharan in southern Sinai and a short distance from Mount Sinai, how accurate is the distance given on the Table (40 Roman miles to Medeia and another 80 to Phara, for a total of 120 Roman miles) between Clysma and Phara? As was stated above, the site of Medeia cannot be located with any certainty. If the conventional route is taken from Clysma to Pharan, Medeia should perhaps be located at a point near Wadi Sudr where there is water and evidence of habitation. We are on a surer footing with the 120 Roman miles between Clysma and Pharan. If we were to use the mileage provided by the *Guide Bleu* for the trip from Suez to the oasis of Feiran via Wadi Maghara (i.e., Wadi Sidri)—there being no one road, since a number of tracks may be taken after leaving the proximity of the coast of the Gulf of Suez—the distance is given as 196 km.[26] At a conversion rate of 1.482 km. to a Roman mile, the distance between Suez and Feiran—or Clysma and Pharan—is 132 Roman miles. This figure, I believe, is close enough to the round number 120 provided by the Peutinger Table. Further, not only is the accuracy of the Table confirmed for this leg of the route, but the correlation of the two mileages also confirms the direction of the route from Clysma: south-southeast.

There remains the final leg of the route as given on the Peutinger Table: Phara to Haila, 50 Roman miles. As was stated above, 50 Roman miles for this stretch of the road cannot be rationalized if the initial section went south-southeast from Clysma to Pharan. If we were to assume that the cartographer omitted a roman numeral, say a *c* before the *l*, it could be possible to rationalize a distance of 150 Roman miles or 222 km. between Pharan and Aila. However plausible it may be to assume this or some other error in text tradition, an emendation would neither prove anything nor be anything other than a hypothetical correction. What can be stated with assurance is that a well-traveled route (hardly a road) did exist between Aila and Pharan-Mount Sinai. The Antoninus *itinerarium* has already been cited to indicate that Aila was an eight-day journey from Mount Sinai.[27] The itinerary of Theodosius (ca. 530), slightly earlier than that of Antoninus, also calls for eight stages betwen Aila and Mount Sinai, "if you are willing to travel through the desert, but if you go through Egypt, it is 25 stages."[28] No other ancient itinerary at hand records a trip along this route, although Eusebius says that "Aila is a three-day trip in an easterly direction" from Pharan.[29] This is an extraordinarily short amount of time to travel a distance of about 250 km. over very

173

difficult terrain. It is interesting to note, however, that the 1895 edition of Baedeker's *Egypt* agrees more with the itineraries of Theodosius and Antoninus in estimating a journey of approximately nine days between Mount Sinai and Aqaba.[30]

In spite of the lack of extant itineraries on the route from Pharan, or Mount Sinai, to Aila, we possess a clear epigraphic record from pilgrims and other travelers en route either from Mount Sinai or Aila. The Wadi Haggag (The Wadi of the Pilgrims), situated a short distance from the spring of Ain Hudera and on the Aila-Mount Sinai route (see fig. 3), holds over 400 Nabataean, Greek, Latin, Coptic, Armenian, and Hebrew-Aramaic inscriptions, the greater number of them being Christian and in Greek. Some of the Christian inscriptions have been dated as early as the fourth century.[31]

It is clear, then, that the weight of the evidence favors identifying the Clysma-Phara-Haila road on the Peutinger Table with the route taken by pilgrims from either entrance, Clysma or Aila, to the "Desert where the Children of Israel wandered for forty years under the leadership of Moses." To identify the road as identical with, or paralleling, the Darb el-Hagg of Moslem pilgrims lacks any support in terms of purpose, of archaeological or epigraphical evidence, or of its representation on the Peutinger Table. Further, the Table gives only a schematic representation of the road, which in no way could serve as a useful guide for travelers to the Holy Mountain. In point of fact, there was no "road" between the points given on the Table; at best it should be called a route or track. The distances cited on the Table are similarly general and of no practical use.

But what is exceptionally graphic on the Peutinger Table is that the route from Pharan-Mount Sinai proceeds to Aila and then to Elusa, and from that point, without any further stages indicated, directly to Jerusalem. Undoubtedly it is one of the two routes which were recommended to Antoninus of Piacenza for his return to Jerusalem.[32] More than any other, it is the itinerary of Theodosius which provides us with a verbal description of the route pictured on the Table. "Near Mount Sinai is Pharan where holy Moses fought with Amalek. From Jerusalem to Elusa there are three stages; from Elusa to Aila, seven stages. . . . From Aila to Mount Sinai, eight stages."[33]

NOTES

1. Y. Aharoni, "The Roman Road to Aila (Elath)," *Israel Exploration Journal* 4.1 (1954) 9-16; M. Harel, "The Roman Road at Ma'aleh 'Aqrabbim ('Scorpions' Ascent')," ibid. 9.3 (1959) 175-79; A. Negev, "The Date of the Petra-Gaza Road," *Palestine Exploration Quarterly* 98 (1966) 89-98; Z. Meshel, "The Roads of the Negev According to the Geography of Ptolemy and the Tabula Peutingeriana," *Excavations and Studies in Honour of S. Yeivin,* ed. Y. Aharoni (Tel Aviv 1973) 205-9 (in Hebrew); Z. Meshel and Y. Tsafrir, "The Nabataean Road from 'Avdat to

Sha'ar-Ramon," *Palestine Exploration Quarterly* 106 (1974) 103-18; ibid. 107 (1975) 3-21, with bibliography earlier than 1954.

2. Meshel and Tsafrir (n. 1 above) 106-18.

3. Harel (n. 1 above) 177.

4. K. Miller, *Itineraria Romana* (Stuttgart 1916).

5. Ibid. col. 820. For the confusion in determining the precise location of Medeia, see R. Weill, *La presqu'île du Sinai* (Bibliothèque de l'École des Hautes Études Sciences historique et philologique, fasc. 171 [Paris 1908]) 115, n. 2.

6. Y. Aharoni, *The Land of the Bible: A Historical Geography* (London 1968) 52, n. 30. For the same identification based on the similar distance between Aqaba and eth-Themed, see J. Ball, *Egypt in the Classical Geographers* (Cairo 1942), p. 157.

7. *Geograph.* 5.16.

8. *Onomasticon,* ed. Klosterman (Leipzig 1904) 166.

9. *Itinerarium Egeriae (Peregrinatio Aetheriae),* ed. O. Prinz (Heidelberg 1960) 2.3, 5.11.

10. See P. Mayerson, "The Desert of Southern Palestine According to Byzantine Sources," *ProcPhilAs* 107.2 (1963) 160-72; "The First Muslim Attacks on Southern Palestine (A.D. 633-634)," *TAPA* 95 (1964) 155-99.

11. Aharoni (n. 6 above) 183: "remains from Iron Age (ca. seventh century B.C.) up to the Arab period without any noticeable gap." Cf. B. Rothenberg and Y. Aharoni, *God's Wilderness* (London 1961) 166: "at the very least, from the Iron Age, *c.* 9th-8th centuries B.C., through the Persian-Hellenistic and Roman-Byzantine periods up to the early Arab period."

12. Miller (n. 4 above) col. 820.

13. See Aharoni (n. 1 above) 15, without his emendations.

14. See n. 6 above.

15. *Itin. Eg.* (n. 9 above) 2.4: *venientes a Faran.*

16. Ibid. 6.1: *Ac sic ergo cum pervenissemus Faram, quod sunt a monte Dei milia triginta et quinque, necesse nos fuit ibi ad resumendum biduo immorari.*

17. Ibid.: *via enim illic penitus non est, sed totum heremi sunt arenosae.*

18. Ibid. 6.4: *nos autem eodem itinere et eisdem mansionibus quibus ieramus, reversi sumus in Clesma.*

19. *Itinera Hierosolymitana Saeculi IIII-VIII (Corpus Scriptorum Ecclesiasticorum Latinorum),* ed. P. Geyer (Vienna 1898) 39. For the sake of simplicity we shall refer to the writer as Antoninus, although the account was written by some unknown person.

20. Ibid. c. 36 (p. 183). Note that Antoninus and his companions arrived at Mount Sinai on the eighth day. The six-day trip undoubtedly was through the waterless stretches of the desert during which water, carried by camels in leather skins, was carefully rationed. For an analysis of the itinerary and of conditions in the region, see Mayerson, "Byz. Sources" (n. 10 above) 169-72.

21. Ibid. c. 39-40 (p. 185): *alii per Aegyptum, alii per Arabiam reverterentur in sanctam civitatem. De monte Sina in Arabia in civitatem, quae vocatur Abila, sunt mansiones octo.*

22. Ibid. c. 40 (p. 186).

23. Ibid. c. 41 (p. 187).

24. Ibid.

25. *Itin. Eg.* (n. 9 above) 9.3, 9.7.

26. M. Baud, *Les Guides bleus: Égypte* (Paris 1950) 694-96.

27. *Itin. Hier.* (n. 19 above) c. 39-40 (p. 185).

28. "De Situ Terrae Sanctae," *Itinera Hierosolymitana* (n. 19 above) c. 27 (p. 148): *De Aila usque in monte Syna mansiones VIII, si compendaria volueris ambulare per heremum, sin autem per Aegyptum, mansiones XXV.*

29. *Onomasticon* (n. 8 above) 166.

30. *Egypt* (Lower Egypt and the Peninsula of Sinai), ed. K. Baedeker (London 1895) 279-80.

175

31. A. Negev, "The Inscriptions of Wadi Haggag, Sinai," *Qedem* 6, (1977) 1-2, 76-77. For a mention of other inscriptions along the northern part of the route to Aila, see Rothenberg-Aharoni (n. 11 above) 83-86. See also B. Rothenberg, "An Archaeological Survey of South Sinai," *PEQ* 102 (1970) 14 (figs. 7-8), 18-19. He traces the route from Aila to Mount Sinai and Pharan, calling it a major Nabataean-Roman road, and, somewhat grandly, "the Aila-Feiran Highroad." In March of 1979, this writer visited the site of Wadi Haggag and, some distance away, Wadi Marrah, and observed the numerous inscriptions carved into brittle mesalike structures. Apart from the inscriptions, I was impressed with the fact that at these sites the terrain is flat enough so that caravans or travelers are not restricted to a "road." It was also apparent that travelers coming up the steep escarpment from Ein Hudera, or before descending to it, must have rested at Haggag, Marrah, or at other sites nearby where they took the opportunity to record their names, unwittingly doing so for posterity and epigraphers.

32. *Itin. Hier.* (n. 19 above) c. 39-40 (p. 185).

33. *Itin. Hier.* (n. 28 above) c. 27 (p. 148): *Iuxta montem Syna in Fara civitate ibi sanctus Moyses cum Amalech pugnavit. De Hierusalem in Elusath mansiones III, de Elusath in Aila mansiones VII. . . . De Aila usque in monte Syna mansiones VIII.*

18

THE TEMPLE OF MESSA
ON LESBOS

HUGH PLOMMER

In later Roman days the most sumptuous temple on Lesbos was perhaps at Eresos. This must have had a facade of more than eight columns (eleven, if we are to believe the fascinating coin in Price and Trell).[1] There seems to be no trace of it today, and I hope that, on Lesbos as elsewhere, their book will renew the search for buildings surely too important to have perished altogether. But for a century and a quarter, ever since its discovery by Boutan in 1856, the Temple of Messa has remained without a rival on the island. It was excavated by R. Koldewey during December 1885 and January 1886 and published in his compendious survey of Lesbos.[2] Its place in Lesbian political and religious history was discussed and determined, so far as present evidence admits, by Louis Robert in a few masterly pages in the *Revue des études anciennes*.[3] He sees it as the ancient shrine of Messon, or Meson, known from texts and inscriptions as the Temple of Zeus, Dionysos, and Aiolis, originally the Aeolian mother goddess, who was not at first either Hera or Demeter, and who was identified in Roman imperial times with the Elder and the Younger Agrippina under the epigraphically attested title θεὰ Αἰολὶς Καρποφόρος Ἀγριππῖνα. From this shrine, he thinks, emanated the numerous electrum coins of Early Classical and Fine style issued by "the Lesbians" (a sufficient number bear the legends ΛΕ and ΛΕΣ), many of them collected in the *BMC* (*Troas,* pls. 31–34). According to the papyrus fragment of Alcaeus, *P.Oxy.* 2165, it was the "great common" *temenos* established by them and his description of it as "prominent in the view" (εὔδειλον) fits it very well. For, though only nine meters (thirty feet) above the sea, it is in the center of a rich plain at the head of the great landlocked Gulf of Kallone, accessible and inviting to all the settlements around. It is also nearly equidistant (twenty to twenty-five miles) between the three principal cities, Mytilene, Methymna, and Eresos, which suits its role as a common shrine and also its name. The question must occur whether the temple on a bronze issue of the Lesbian *Koinon* of the reign of Marcus Aurelius[4] is this shrine of Messa. It resembles Messa in being octostyle, but unhappily seems to be Corinthian, while Messa was Ionic. So I must leave my conundrum with Professor Trell and turn to the building itself.

It was a large temple—larger, for instance, than Athena Polias at Priene. If it was a common shrine, already possessing rights of sanctuary in the days of Alcaeus, its history is important for the general history of Lesbos and even the whole Aeolid. So it would be good to know when it first acquired its status and when it enjoyed the considerable prestige attested even now by the existing remains. As Robert observes, "S'il était possible, par l'examen de l'architecture, il serait très intéressant de préciser la date."[5] He adds, a little teasingly, "Il serait historiquement très important de pouvoir descendre jusqu'à Alexandre." And I suppose it would be pleasant to think that Alexander rewarded Lesbos for the sufferings it endured in his cause in the winter of 334/3.[6] But it would be even pleasanter to identify and enjoy a truly Classical work from the great days of Greece.

Unhappily, this is still one of the most puzzling of all Greek temples. Partly this is due to the site, which is almost permanently waterlogged these days, even though, paradoxically, it is now further from the Gulf. When I visited it in November 1977, after a very dry autumn, there was still water in the foundations. Koldewey described it, after rain had fallen, as resembling an island among the swamps. Its latest excavator, B. Petrakos, found things no better. Koldewey did wonders, considering the brevity of his campaign and the conditions under Ottoman government a century ago. But he never cleared away the apsidal Byzantine church, which remains on top of the cella; and he could not clear the west end or much of the south *pteron*, which were owned by a separate proprietor. He found many blocks of the temple in a Turkish farm to the northwest. This was two hundred yards away, already ruined when he made his map (pl. 18, 1) and not obviously visible to me. The blocks found by Petrakos were mostly near the temple (to its south), and included some stretches of the horizontal sima of a *rinceau* pattern more boldly carved than Koldewey (pl. 21) might have suggested. They seem comparable, indeed, to the bold *rinceaux* of Tegea or fourth-century Ephesus. But he publishes little else that is new, though he apparently found and cleaned the fragment of the all-important architrave block with carved astragals along the middle fascia of the front, Koldewey no. 173. There is a good photograph of this in the French résumé of Petrakos's first campaign.[7] As for the subsidiary buildings, according to Petrakos these had all been swept away by the river. It therefore seems as if little more will now be found, unless someone pumps the temple dry and examines all nine compartments into which the foundation walls divide the *krepis*[8]—especially that below the *cella*. One must praise Koldewey for the clarity of his report and his drawings, only regretting that he did not publish more blocks in their entirety. For, as it is restored, and as I present it in illustrations perforce

178

reproduced from Koldewey, this temple combines features found together, perhaps, nowhere else. Some seem to move it far down into Hellenistic times. There is no doubt, for instance, that it was octostyle and pseudodipteral, and the earliest pseudodipteral temple on the coast of Asia Minor is often supposed to be the work of Hermogenes, whom it is the fashion to date well down in the second century B.C. (Dinsmoor, *Architecture of Ancient Greece* [London 1950³] [= *AGG*] 274). Vitruvius names two pseudodipteral temples, Diana at Magnesia by Hermogenes and Apollo at Alabanda by Menesthes.[9] We know very little of the second architect or even of his temple (*AGG* 276). Even the dates that we give Hermogenes still seem to me less than certain. His customary moldings, for instance, show both a roundness and a sympathy with Classical Greek detailing[10] that have few obvious parallels in the Hellenistic age, late or early, though we may grant that in some ways they anticipate the Augustan "Classical Revival." His architrave crowns at Teos and Magnesia, which they do share with some other Ionic temples (e.g., the Smintheum[11]), are even fuller and heavier than those on the Erechtheum and consist of a crowning fillet, a large cavetto with carved truncated palmettes, alternately normal and "honeysuckle," a very thin fillet, an egg and tongue, and a bead and reel, all totaling more than one quarter of the entire architrave.[12] Vitruvius, of course, does attribute to Hermogenes the invention of the "octostyle pseudodipteral" temple, because it combined economy of columns with sumptuousness of effect.[13] But, as everyone knows, it appears much earlier in Doric—at Temple G, Selinus, for instance. And if, as I hold with Dinsmoor (*AAG* 91), the Olympieum at Athens started out as Doric, it too may well have been designed to be pseudodipteral. If one takes its final ground plan (*AAG* 282) and omits the inner peristyle, the resemblance to several early Sicilian temple plans is striking and seems to show that the great Pisistratid project had a direct influence on its slightly later contemporaries in Sicily (*AAG* 79).

However, Messa is not only octostyle and pseudodipteral, but also has important resemblances to an acknowledged Hellenistic temple, surely "late" even if not precisely dated, the Smintheum at Chryse in the Troad.[14] Both buildings are of eight Ionic columns by fourteen, and both measure along the stylobate 133 by 74 feet. Moreover, Pullan could restore the order of the Smintheum with complete confidence (*AI* iv 46, col. 1); it shared with Messa fairly lofty column bases, dispensing with plinths, and the design of its architrave, with beads and reels separating the fasciae along the front. This became common in Roman times but is hardly known before. Finally, Messa and the Smintheum share with Hermogenean temples the combination of frieze and dentils not found on buildings before the Philippeum and the Monument of Lysicrates, both of the 330s.

Despite all this, I still believe that Messa is older than Athena Polias at Priene, which was dedicated by Alexander in the winter of

Fig. 1. Temple of Messa, restored elevation. Reproduced from R. Koldewey, *Die Antiken Baureste der Insel Lesbos* (Berlin 1890) pl. 20, 1.

Fig. 1. Temple of Messa, restored elevation. Reproduced from R. Koldewey, *Die Antiken Baureste der Insel Lesbos* (Berlin 1890) pl. 20, 1.

334/3[15], and I would unhesitatingly support Koldewey's conclusion of his own discussion (*Lesbos*, p. 58): "Nach allem darf man den Architecten von Messa für einen Vorgänger des in der Mitte des vierten Jahrhunderts v. Chr. thätigen Pytheos halten und den Tempel von Messa unbedenklich der ersten Hälfte desselben Jahrhunderts zuweisen." I must go into the temple in some detail in order effectively to support this statement, and, as things stand, even after the two campaigns of Petrakos, I shall have to base my argument almost exclusively on Koldewey, pls. 20 and 21 (figs. 1, 2). The arguments, too, are largely his, though I shall add a few of my own.

Take first the materials. The cella walls and virtually the whole exterior were of a cream-colored volcanic liparite, quarried, according to Koldewey, from an outcrop near Pyrrha, a few miles south on the Gulf. Only the roof gutters were of white marble and only the frieze—uniquely—of a red conglomerate, the "rothen Stein von breccienartiger schönen Zeichnung" of Koldewey (55). The core of the *krepis* was a trachyte, a similar stone, but darker. The effect must have been beautiful but unusual. Koldewey noted (48) the great labor expended on filling and smoothing the upper surfaces of the stone courses. In later times, buildings of white marble were uncommonly abundant on Lesbos; and it is interesting that Messa should share its building stone with the famous archaic temple of Kolumdado (Koldewey 44-46), a few miles to the north.[16] So the materials, at least, point to a Classical and not a Hellenistic date. Even conglomerate was coming into its own about 400 B.C. It was used, for instance, as a wall facing in the Menelaion of Sparta.

The extremely precise workmanship of Messa also inclines one towards a Classical dating. The stylobate blocks, while having none of the normal stereotyped squareness of Asian Ionic, are worked with beautiful raised *scamilli* of circular plan on their upper surfaces, to

Fig. 2. Temple of Messa, the Order. Reproduced from R. Koldewey, *Die Antiken Baureste der Insel Lesbos* (Berlin 1890) pl. 21.

support the round bases of the columns. Koldewey ingeniously argued that these corrected the downward and outward tilt of the stylobate designed to throw off rainwater, and indeed Wiegand illustrates a similar correction of tilt under the square plinths of the columns at Priene[17]. Koldewey concluded that this is what Vitruvius meant by his *scamilli impares*. In the present state of the temple, one cannot decide the angle of the *scamilli*, as he himself could not. But the work is fine.

Fig. 3. Column drum, anathyrosis.

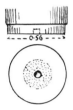

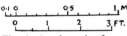

Fig. 4. Anathyrosis of column drum, scale drawing.

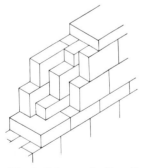

Fig. 5. Scheme of cella wall.

Again, Messa repeats little details of Kolumdado. Its builders, for instance, normally used a "double swallow-tail" clamp with a downward prong protruding from either tail, a type used also at Kolumdado (Koldewey, pl. 16, 9–11). But Hellenistic builders normally used simple pi-clamps resembling miniature goalposts.[18] Just as cogent, to my eyes, is the working of the column drums. Their lengths at Messa, as Petrakos found, were by no means uniform, and, rather unusually for an Ionic temple (at any rate of this size), the bottom of the shaft shared a block with the *torus* of the base.[19] However, I suppose that the drum, of which fig. 3 shows the bearing surface, rested immediately upon one such composite block. Note the great extent of the smooth surface, much bigger than in normal anathyrosis, and the small cylindrical dowel hole in the center. Both features are shared by the archaic columns of Kolumdado (fig. 4; Koldewey, pl. 16, 5).[20]

The *krepis* of Messa is unusually constructed. The foundation walls of all four sides of the cella are prolonged across the *ptera* to meet those of the stylobate, thus dividing the whole interior of the *krepis* into nine compartments, one under the cella and eight around it. This probably served to tie the building together on its marshy terrain. The levels are well preserved, even after all the battering of the superstructure, and the device shows some thought and care. The cella walls, too, display an elaborate and unique technique, established by Koldewey (pl. 22) from the evidence of an anta-block. Each course of flat "throughs" appears to be surmounted by two courses of upright stretchers ("orthostates"). But the wall has a thickness of three, not two orthostates. So, to break joint with the stretchers, a hidden core consists of a course of orthostates between two courses of "half-orthostates" (fig. 5). This unexpected experiment in construction seems to me more like the Delphic treasuries published by Dinsmoor in *BCH* 1912 and 1913 than the slicker, less painstaking work of Hellenistic times.

I turn at last to the architectural style, for most of which I must rely on Koldewey. The *krepis* has three large steps, Doric in proportion and in height equal to the mean diameter of a column shaft. In this it is quite unlike normal Ionian and Hermogenean temples—the Smintheum, for instance, had eleven shallow steps on the front—and resembles only Priene and Kastabos, the latter of which, I argued,[21] was strongly influenced by the older Doric Temple of Asklepios at Epidaurus.

The column bases are unusual in not having plinths. They resemble the Attic temples and the Smintheum in this, but the actual bases could not be more Ionian, with a *torus* surmounting a pair of flattened *scotiae*, or *trochili*. They are closest, perhaps, to Priene and Sardis, and, like these, they still have the bead between the *torus* and the column shaft, retained for centuries in Ionia but dropped in Attica after Athena Nike. The bases of the Smintheum, on the other hand, are of the type very familiar in imperial Rome, of two *trochili* between *tori*, examples of which include the Temple of Castor and the Pantheon. On the coasts of Asia Minor the Smintheum provides "the solitary and rather unsatisfactorily dated example."[22]

The shafts are less usual, with the normal Ionic twenty-four flutes, indeed, forming simple arcs of circles, but with very thin fillets, almost arrises, between them (fig. 6). Each fillet is only one-seventh the chord of the flute (Koldewey 54 and pl. 23, 3), whereas in most temples (such as Priene and the Erechtheum) it is one-quarter or more. The earliest Ionic, of course, had arrises, not fillets, and this intermediate stage, of twenty-four flutes and thin fillets, is represented at Messa and also in the mid-fifth-century Ionic temple at Locri. Messa shares other peculiarities with Locri.[23] While not quite pseudodipteral, Locri has end peristyles two column spaces in width and side peristyles of "Doric" width, half a column wider than in normal Ionic. Thus we almost see at Locri a bridge between Messa and the pseudodipteral or nearly pseudodipteral temples of archaic Magna Graecia and Sicily. Finally, Messa, like Locri, has shafts of twenty-four flutes, but an echinus of only twenty carved eggs. But whereas at Locri the clash between shaft and echinus is obviated by a floral necking band and a plain bead, at Messa the carved bead and reel follows the rhythm of the echinus above it and clashes with the alignments of the flutes directly below. Fig. 5 shows this and corroborates Koldewey's restoration of the echinus, of which I found no fragment in 1977. Deviations from twenty-four eggs are rare in developed Ionic. Ephesus and its reflection, Sardis, used a lofty echinus with sixteen large eggs. On the Erechtheum, the echinus was so reduced that it had thirty-two small eggs. Once again, Messa shows unusual and seemingly early details.

Fig. 6. Uppermost drum of column shaft.

The capitals were of Ionian type, with volutes small and far apart and eyes so far out (an early feature!) that they were not even tangent to the shaft. Each volute performed three revolutions, to the three and one-quarter of Priene. The *pulvinus* on the sides was divided into three compartments, of which only the central was decorated with a column of palmettes in lyre scrolls, though tendrils did escape into neighboring compartments at the top. This seems a more disciplined version of, for instance, the design of Sardis. It seems far removed from the treatment of each *pulvinus* as a "thunderbolt" or "Christmas cracker" so common in Pergamene and Hermogenean buildings. The eyes of the volutes were hollowed to receive separate pieces of red conglomerate, matching the frieze. This is common in good work of the fifth and fourth centuries (e.g., Bassae and Priene). The red color was bold and perhaps garish. It does not have to be late.

Fig. 7. Architrave block, soffit and front, from facade of cella building.

The entablature of Messa, at first sight elaborate, is actually distinguished by the simplicity of each detail. The architrave, as we saw above, has no elaborate "Hermogenean" crown, but rather a simple egg and dart with astragal, almost duplicating the molded frieze crown. Its soffit (fig. 7) has a mere bead and reel around its sunken panel,[24] less elaborate than the moldings of Priene (Wiegand, *Priene* 101) or even the Lesbian leaf of the naiskos at Didyma (*Didyma, Zeichnungen*, pl. 74, 1–8). Again, even the beads and reels along the fasciae differ significantly from those at the Smintheum and most later temples. The two lower rows are the same size. At the Smintheum (*AI* iv, pl. 29) they are very noticeably graded. On the show temples of Rome, there is great variety in shape and size—on the Pantheon Portico for instance, the bottom fascia has a plain bead, the middle a cyma reversa, and the top a crown consisting of an abacus, a larger cyma reversa, and a larger bead.[25] Among Ionian temples, I have found only Zeus Sosipolis at Magnesia with an external architrave (and also an architrave to the main door) where the carved beads are equal as at Messa (*Magnesia* 147–51). The obvious reasons for such repetition could be either idleness or an early date. But the builders of Zeus Sosipolis and Messa were certainly not idle.

Having seen nothing of the frieze or the dentils, I can add little to the remark I made above that they are not known to have been used together on a dated building before the 330s. However, it is clear that Koldewey saw on the tops of the frieze blocks dowel and clamp marks very similar to those on the blocks of liparite; as he urged, a polychrome frieze of this sort, with a background of special colored stone, has its closest parallel in the Erechtheum.

The cornice is as interesting as any part of the building. Its corona has a soffit with a remarkable downward sweep, which serves here to make the front fascia more nearly proportionate to the unusual height of the entablature. In section, this soffit is almost a quadrant. I know of nothing like it outside Lesbos. True, the soffit on the internal Ionic order of Bassae is abbreviated horizontally (G. Roux, *Architecture de l'Argolide* [Paris 1961] pl. 18). But the curve has none of the depth of Messa, where the corona is undercut to nearly half its height. And I believe that at Bassae the whole cornice was reduced for a purely utilitarian reason—to give more light to the frieze from above.[26]

I found no cornice block at Messa. But I found a small block, of white marble and of the very best period, in the garden of the museum at Mytilene. I include a photograph (fig. 8) and a cross section (fig. 9). Here again the Temple of Messa, though a little less pronounced than this miniature example (which perhaps ought, given the scale which is one-third that of Messa, to have crowned an order some fifteen feet high), takes its place with local work of the most exquisite kind. It would be pleasant to have a study, from someone with the knowledge and the leisure, of these Lesbian cornices.

I have now listed the chief peculiarities of Messa as they strike me. Many of them appear to me, as they did to Koldewey, to put it well before Hellenistic times. Indeed, the very fact that it has so many unusual features provides the best argument that it should be a true Greek building, of ca. 400 B.C.[27]

Fig. 8. "Lesbian" cornice block similar to those of Messa; in the Museum Garden, Mitylene.

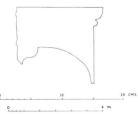

Fig. 9. Cross section of cornice block.

Fig. 10. Unidentified block with carved ovolo.

Possibly more can yet be found of it, if the Byzantine remains are removed from the cella and the nine compartments of the *krepis,* especially the central, are explored to the very bottom. But I pin my hopes for the immediate future on M. Robert, to discover another inscription, or Professor Trell, to turn up a coin.

NOTES

1. *Coins and Their Cities: Architecture on the Ancient Coins of Greece, Rome, and Palestine* (London and Detroit 1977) 202 and fig. 397. They leave it in limbo at the end of their series of octostyle temples, and their reticence seems to me very wise.
2. *Die Antiken Baureste der Insel Lesbos* (Berlin 1890) 47-61 and pls. 16-26 (of which my figs. 1, 2 reproduce his pls. 20.1, 21).
3. *REA* 62 (Paris 1960) esp. 308-15.
4. *BMC, Troas* pl. 35.2.
5. Robert (n. 3 above) 308, n. 7.
6. Arrian, *Anabasis* 2.1. He writes only of operations round Mytilene itself; they do not seem to have extended beyond its environs.
7. *BCH* 1968, *Chronique des Fouilles* (G. Daux) 938, fig. 2.
8. See Koldewey, pls. 19 and 20 (2).
9. Vitruvius 3.70, line 1 (in the *editio maior* of Immanuel Rose).
10. L. T. Shoe, *Profiles of Greek Mouldings* (Harvard 1936), *Text,* passim. See especially pp. 24–25 ("Orolo IV").
11. For Teos and the Smintheum, see still *Antiquities of Ionia* iv (London 1881) [hereafter *AI*]. For the Temples of Artemis and Zeus Sosipolis at Magnesia, see C. Humann, *Magnesia am Maeander* (Berlin 1904) [hereafter *Magnesia*].
12. Compare *AI* (n. 11 above) pl. 25 (Teos) and *Magnesia* (n. 11 above) 51. The architrave crown of the Erechtheum's north porch is even more elaborate—with no crowning fillet, for instance, but a cyma reversa instead. It is far daintier in effect, but it is just under one-quarter of the whole architrave. See Paton and Stevens, *Erechtheum* (Cambridge, Mass. 1927) pl. 22.
13. Vitruvius 3.72, lines 16ff. The passage also credits him with the "eustyle" disposition.
14. Published once in *AI* (n. 11 above) by Pullan, after his exploration of 1866—after which the site was filled in again. Apart from his note in *AAG* 272, Dinsmoor provides no bibliography.
15. The block recording its dedication was drawn for *AI* (n. 11 above) 23, fig. 11. It affords a rare and very welcome "absolute date": cf. Strabo *C* 641.
16. Its "Aeolic" capitals, well published by Koldewey, can be studied in the Museum Garden in Mytilene, and modern reconstructions of their design in a cinema on the waterfront of the South Harbor. It is officially called Klopedi these days.
17. Th. Wiegand and H. Schrader, *Priene* (Berlin 1904) 88 [hereafter *Priene*].
18. A. Orlandos, *Les Materiaux de Construction* (Paris 1966) ii 109ff.
19. It shares this feature with the Temple of Hemithea (J. M. Cook and W. H. Plommer, *Sanctuary of Hemithea at Kastabos,* fig. 14 and pl. 13.6), where the smaller scale makes it more natural. (By a strange coincidence, the length of Kastabos on the stylobate, 74 feet, equals the width of Messa).
20. Here traced as fig. 4. Strangely, Koldewey gives only one drawing of a corresponding face at Messa, no. 5 on pl. 23. This one, at least, had normal anathyrosis and a square empolion hole, and judging by its width (1.05 meters), it must have come from the bottom of the shaft. Culpably, I did not measure my own drum, and can plead only that my time at Messa was limited and the site very prickly.

185

21. Cook and Plommer (n. 19 above) 151-52.
22. D. Strong and J. B. Ward-Perkins, *Papers of the British School at Rome* 30 (1962) 8. In this excellent paper, the authors even broach the possibility of "reverse influences from the capital" upon the Smintheum.
23. Published by E. Peterson in *RM* (1890) 170ff. The thin fillets are best shown on pp. 178 and 192. The plan of the two successive temples appears on pl. 8. Bassae affords another instance of very thin fillets, but it is perhaps too extraordinary to be of much help.
24. This block (fig. 7) was drawn by Koldewey (pl. 25, 14 and 15) and rightly assigned by him to the architrave of a front of the cella building. Its front has two fasciae only (the molded crown of this face directly surmounted the single bead and reel at the top), and its whole thickness from front to back must have been, on the soffit, 90 centimeters (35.4 inches), 3 centimeters less than the 93 centimeters (36.6 inches) of the external architrave. I did check carefully Koldewey's measurements and calculations for this particular block.
25. Other variations with various moldings (always, however, increasing in heaviness as one moves upwards) can be studied most easily in Normand's *Parallel of the Orders*, ed. R. A. Cordingley (London 1928) pls. 28, 42, 43, 44, 46. Only the internal Order of the Pantheon (pl. 45) has two plain beads of equal size above the first and second fascia. The idea of beads along fasciae could have reached Messa from the north door of the Erechtheum (Paton and Stevens [n. 12 above] pl. 25).
26. I believe that, like the Temple of the Athenians on Delos, Bassae dispensed with an internal ceiling over the cella. Its beautifully finished translucent tiles, with the aid of the holes or *opaia* known to have existed in some of them, transmitted considerable light to the frieze and very little rain to the stone floor, while the underside of rafters and tiles would have been tricked out with some colored patterns to give some of the effect of a ceiling. The curious who wish to follow this line of thought could begin with C. R. Cockerell, *Aigina and Bassae* (London 1860)—especially pl. 7 for the roof tiles—and O. Broneer in *Corinth* i, pt. 4 (Princeton 1954) 87, for roofs with *opaia*. F. Courby, in *Delos* xii (Paris 1931) 186ff., reconstructs the cella of the Temple of the Athenians, which had no ceiling; F. Poulsen, in *Mélanges Holleaux* (Paris 1913) 225-32, publishes the roof of an adjacent building, the "Sanctuary of the Bull," which seems to have copied this feature of the temple. A similar roof at Aigion in Achaea was restored on the evidence of a tile with a painted underside on pl. 83; cf. J. Hittorff and L. Zanth, *Recueil des Monuments de Ségeste et de Sélinonte*. This conjecture, though made as long ago as 1870, seems to me to be contradicted at present by no evidence that I can recollect.
27. I found and photographed (fig. 10) one block of this temple, which is not in Koldewey, but I failed to notice its importance and so did not measure it as I should have done. The molding is very unusual, having a carved egg and dart without a bead and reel below it, but instead a plain, flat face. To the best of my memory, the carved molding was about two inches high. An obvious place for such a molding, without astragal, is the abacus of an anta-capital. Molding and wall-face both seem too large for such a member, if general Greek practice is a guide. But the molding, at any rate, would be about equal to the abacus of the column capital—6.5 centimeters (or 2.5 inches), according to Koldewey.

19
OLD TESTAMENT MOTIFS IN THE ICONOGRAPHY OF THE BRITISH MUSEUM'S MAGICAL GEMS
MORTON SMITH

Professor Bluma Trell has contributed so much to our knowledge of the religious iconography of the eastern Mediterranean in Classical times that it seems appropriate to present this preliminary report on a topic from that field in acknowledgment of her work, as pilgrims to ancient Ephesus may have offered to the great goddess little models of her temple.[1]

Ancient Jewish iconography is a topic particularly interesting because strictly forbidden by the ten commandments: "You shall not make yourself a statue or any picture."[2] Consequently, its widespread occurrence is evidence of the rejection, interpretation, and neglect of the biblical text by which Christianity, rabbinic Judaism, and other varieties of the cult of Yahweh ramified, as well as of the influence of biblical material on pagans. This range of possible significance makes the various sorts of evidence difficult to interpret. The most difficult is probably that on the magical gems, since the provenance and date of most gems are unknown and their relation to documented varieties of the cult is commonly uncertain. The Jews were famous and the Christians notorious as magicians; Christians commonly accused the Gnostics of practicing magic; and so on.[3] Rumors and accusations are confirmed by the many Jewish elements in pagan magical papyri and by entire magical texts, a few from Jewish, more from Christian and from Gnostic circles. One turns, therefore, with interest to the magical gems—after the papyri and *defixiones* our largest primary source for ancient magic—to see what their iconography will show of biblical material.

It shows little. This is the more surprising because its vocabulary is rich with biblical names. IAΩ (the Greek equivalent of Yahweh, the name of the Israelite god) is most frequent here, as it is in the magical papyri. *Sabaoth* (a transliteration of an epithet of Yahweh which the Septuagint commonly rendered *pantokrator* and the English versions "of hosts") is very common, whereas *pantokrator* is rare. The names of the archangels, especially Michael, Gabriel, and Raphael, occur   187 often. "Solomon" has somehow become attached to a mounted warrior, commonly shown spearing a prostrate woman. His ungentlemanly behavior was excused by the explanation that the seeming woman was a she-demon who went about by night to kill newborn babies. Infant mortality in the ancient world was about 50 percent, so stones of this type are numerous. Besides these common names there are not a few that occur rarely, and a good many magical formulae that can be explained, with more or less likelihood, as transliterations of Hebrew terms, often biblical. Given this strong biblical element in the vocabulary of the magical gems, we should expect them to picture a good many biblical figures—certainly Moses with his rod (more likely healing plagues or producing water than dividing the sea; the gems were made for practical purposes), Elijah raising the dead or performing cures, the bronze serpent on the pole (to cure snake bite), and so on. To our surprise, none of these particular scenes occurs in the British Museum's collection (the world's largest) of some six hundred gems.

As to the biblical elements that do occur in the iconography, the first question to be asked is whether Hebrew letters are to be considered iconographic elements, and, if so, whether or not they should be thought biblical. On eight stones[4] are inscriptions only or mainly in what seem or pretend to be Hebrew letters—in all cases letters of the square alphabet that became common before Maccabean times and has been used ever since. Four of these stones show only the text, two show only text and *ouroboros*. A few other stones use Hebrew or Aramaic occasionally—the most famous instance being the words *Yeshu M[eshiah]* over the representation of the crucifixion on no. 231 (on which see *Jesus the Magician* 61–62), but here the words should undoubtedly be distinguished from the imagery. No. 515, to be discussed below, has a circle of letters that perhaps were intended to be thought Hebrew, but their resemblance to Hebrew is so remote that the piece cannot be considered in this group. Of the eight stones specified in n. 4, one deserves special attention.

No. 369 (fig. 1; green jasper, much worn, oval, 18 mm. wide x 12 mm. high x 5 mm. thick) is cut as a typical seal of the postexilic period,[5] being engraved on one side only with two parallel lines, close together, running longways across the middle of the field. Above the upper line is engraved (in reverse, so that the seal would be readily legible) *rḥmym* (?); similarly below the lower line, *mhb* (?), followed by a trefoil. (The engraving in reverse distinguishes the piece from most magical gems, which were not intended for use as seals and are engraved direct.) All of these inscribed elements are encircled by a frame line paralleling the edge of the stone. The final letters of both words are uncertain. The terminal *m*, cut as a circle, might be *s*. The lower line of the *b* does not extend, as it should, behind the vertical; were the letter not final, it would be read as *k*, but since the terminal form of *m* was used above, the terminal form of *k* should be expected

here. Therefore, this letter would seem more probably a *b*. If these readings are correct, the seal said "Mercy, Maḥub," Maḥub presumably being the owner's name and divine mercy what he wanted. The trefoil is an abbreviated palm or lulab—the two are commonly identified. However, *Maḥub* is not a usual formation and I have not found it as a personal name. So far as I know, the old seal form, with the parallel lines separating the two lines of inscription, does not appear elsewhere with the square alphabet, let alone with an added palm/lulab, a sign of Hellenistic or later times. The stone may be a fake, but the wear argues for authenticity.

The Hebrew or pseudo-Hebrew letters on the other stones of this group make no sense to me, nor do they make nonsense of the sorts recognizedly magical. Gershom Scholem, who was so kind as to study my photographs of them, could make nothing of them, and remarked that the letter forms of no. 363 were certainly modern; those of several others probably so; and those of others, like no. 495, impossible in Hebrew. I conclude that such lettering on pretendedly magical gems is an iconographic, not a linguistic, element, but that it is only remotely connected with the Hebrew Bible and should not be considered a biblical motif in their iconography. This is not to say that all stones which carry such lettering are medieval or modern. Since Jews in antiquity were famous as magicians, ancient engravers may have used what they thought to be Hebrew letters to give their stones a pretense to magical powers. However, for most of these pieces, later dates seem more likely.

Another pair of stones should be mentioned here and then excluded. These are nos. 25 and 360, both of the same type, of the Renaissance or later.[6] Although intended to portray God and the angels, they do not clearly refer to any specific biblical passage. Since the deity is shown standing, Ps. 99:1, "Yahweh reigns, let the peoples tremble! He *sits* on the cherubim, let the earth be moved!" would seem inappropriate.

No. 44 (fig. 2), however, shows that the title "He who sits upon the cherubim" was not always taken literally. A yellow jasper (oval, 17 mm. wide x 13 mm. high x 3 mm. thick), it shows, on its larger face, Sachmet with a lioness's head and nude human body, standing to the left, holding in her extended right hand a gorgon's head, in her left hand, bent to her breast, a rod, and in the crook of her left arm a whip. On the margin is *Abrasax*. On the reverse is a figure standing to the left in a chariot drawn to the left by two bearded serpents; over the serpents is IAΩ and over this an eight-pointed star and two *Z*s with crossbars, all three made magical by the addition of a circle at each end of each of the lines that compose them. This figure has a historical explanation. The seraphim of Yahweh's entourage in Isa. 6:2 were later identified with the serpents, also called *seraphim*, in Num. 21:6. Hence their companions, the cherubim, became serpents by contagion. Since Yahweh sat on them, they formed a serpent-throne.

Fig. 2. No. 44, reverse. *Reproduced by permission of the Trustees of the British Museum*

189

Ezekiel had seen Yahweh's throne and described it as wheeled and flying (1:26, etc.); it therefore came to be thought a chariot. Hence the snake-drawn chariot of Triptolemus, which we have here, could be used as a representation of Yahweh "sitting on the cherubim"—though here he has to stand because Triptolemus did, and because the driver of a chariot had better do so. That the gem cutter represented Yahweh is not noteworthy; he thought of him as Iao and any number of anguipedes and other figures were so labeled. The noteworthy thing is that when he wanted to represent a biblical scene (Yahweh sitting on the cherubim), he had no Yahwist model available and therefore pressed into service the chariot of Triptolemus.

No. 133 (fig. 3; green jasper, oval, much pitted, 14.5 mm. high x 12 mm. wide x 2 mm. thick, engraved only on its larger surface) carries a crude representation of an oblong object with facing herms rising from its two ends.[7] The herms are winged and wreathed, and each, with the arm nearer the viewer, holds out a wreath over the oblong. On and below the oblong are the letters TΣTΛ | ORA/E (*sic* = AME) | TON. C. King recognized in this the altar of Rome and Augustus at Lyons, as represented on the coins of the mint of Lyons, used to represent the Ark of the Covenant, which is indicated by the mis-spelled *tetragrammaton*.[8] Bonner in *SMA* followed King, adding the observation that *tetragrammaton* was "applied to" the name YHWH by Philo (*Vita Mosis* 2.115).[9] However, Philo does not write of "the tetragrammaton," but only says that the Name "is of four letters" (*tetragrammaton . . . einai*). Again we find that when the artist wanted to represent a biblical object he had to appropriate a pagan image. If there was a native Jewish image he presumably did not know of it.

This type is also interesting because its approximate date and area of provenance both can be inferred with some assurance and con-tradict the common belief that gems with magical inscriptions began to be made in the eastern Mediterranean regions in the first century A.D. This type was probably formed between 10 B.C. when the altar was dedicated and some time, perhaps a quarter-century, after the last issue of coins representing it. This last issue, a small one, was under Nero.[10] The picture was closely connected with the Julio-Claudian dynasty and was a specialty of the Lugdunum mint; it circulated mainly in Gaul and was imitated on Celtic coinage. These facts give some probability to the notion that the gem type was created in Gaul. The probability is strengthened by the fact that there was a considerable Jewish and later Christian settlement at Lyons, and by the misspelling of *tetragrammaton*, the Latin style ligature A/E,[11] and the Latin G and R in the middle of the word. The present gem is a later copy of the Latin type, made in the Greek east by a gem cutter who, in the first line of the inscription, turned Latin E into Greek Σ, and, in the second, misread G as O. He doubtless copied the

R and ligature of the second line exactly because he thought them of magical significance.

No. 318 (fig. 4; cornelian, oval, 16 mm. high x 12 mm. wide x 4.5 mm. thick, most of the right half broken away) and no. 555 (fig. 5; orange jasper, oval, 18 mm. high x 14 mm. wide x 3 mm. thick, in a gold frame) both show a seven-branched lampstand intended to represent that prescribed for the tabernacle by Exod. 25:31ff. No. 318, uninscribed, has at the left of the lampstand a two-handled vase containing a palm branch. No. 555 has on the reverse a four-line inscription in Hebrew letters: *l'bwm / l'br' / l'gśz / l'zzb'gb.* This is badly cut; the letters with dots under them might be read otherwise; and no reading makes sense. Presumably, however, it is an imitation of the ten commandments, as indicated by the initial *l'* ("Thou shalt not") of each line. The lampstand not only has arms that end in candleholders (!), but has them so arranged that the lower ones stick out at odd angles beneath the upper, instead of rising vertically to the same level. Contrast the designs on ancient sarcophagi, where limitations of space required similar distortions but knowledge of the object preserved the lamps at the ends of the branches and the necessary upright position (Goodenough, *Symbols* iii, nos. 788, 789). In no. 318 the lampstand has the same design as that of the Jerusalem Temple, shown on the arch of Titus, and commonly imitated in the catacombs. As often in the catacombs, long flames (not candles!) rise from the lamps (cp. Goodenough iii, nos. 806, 808, 810, 817). Also, the palm/lulab is commonly found together with the lampstand on ancient funerary inscriptions (Goodenough iii, nos. 710, 711, 715, 717, etc.). Accordingly, it seems likely that no. 318 is ancient and no. 555 of the Renaissance or a later imitation. This is the first Jewish picture we have seen on the gems.

No. 469 (fig. 6; brown limonite, roughly circular, 31.5 mm. wide x 34 mm. high x 6 mm. thick, a projecting ring for suspension has been broken from the top) and no. 515 (fig. 7; black obsidian, oval, 22 mm. high x 19 mm. wide x 3 mm. thick, chipped at the bottom) present another picture derived from biblical story, not Greco-Roman iconography. The story is Abraham's near-sacrifice of Isaac. The theme was of great importance in ancient Jewish piety and accordingly popular on amulets; Bonner, *SMA,* pictures three (nos. 343-45), and Goodenough iii adds a fourth.[12] Significantly, these representations of the same scene differ so greatly that none can be a variant of any other. This fact suggests that in this case there was no center of production, common tradition, or other authority which the Jewish and/or Christian makers of these amulets followed. When they had to picture a scene for which no convenient classical cliché could be used, each went his own way. This is why the subject of the two British Museum stones has not hitherto been recognized, though the inadequacy of the artists helped to keep the significance of their

Fig. 5. No. 555. *Reproduced by permission of the Trustees of the British Museum*

Fig. 6. No. 469. *Reproduced by permission of the Trustees of the British Museum*

Fig. 7. No. 515. *Reproduced by permission of the Trustees of the British Museum*

191

work a secret. Sir E. A. Wallis Budge, in *Amulets and Superstitions,* says that no. 469 was given to the British Museum by Sir Rider Haggard and represents "the Birth of Christ . . . Mary is seated under a tree and she holds [an ankh] . . . in one hand."[13] Actually Isaac is shown on the altar, his arms spread wide, his head towards Abraham, who stands behind the altar and bends over it, raising his knife (Budge's ankh). The angel intervenes from left, raising his hand to stop the blow. Behind the angel is a sapling, substituting for the biblical shrub, with the substitutionary ram tied to it, since he could not be caught in it (as the Bible says he was, Gen. 22:13). Saplings are easier to draw than shrubs, and there was a classical convention to represent them; this artist followed it. The reverse of the stone does show Budge's ankh with, around it, the inscription "One God in heaven."[14] The artist of no. 515 simplified drastically: Abraham stands facing left, his knife raised. The angel, reduced to a wing, a head, and a pair of arms, swoops down from behind and collars him. A tangle of lines in front of Abraham, perhaps intended to represent a crouching Isaac bound to the altar by a rope around his neck, looks like a botch. The scene has been reduced to a circle around which runs a hatched line (possibly a debased *ouroboros*), around which runs a line of letters perhaps intended to be taken for Hebrew—if so, they would prove the artist's ignorance of the language. Around the letters is a plain frame line; the reverse is blank. The arrangement of the figures here is basically similar to that of Goodenough's iii, no. 1038 (right end) and 1041 (reversed), but this might be happenstance. The treatments differ completely. If there was a common original, it must have been either remote or neglected or both.

No. 470 (fig. 8; grey haemitite, a long, oblong oval, 41.5 mm. high x 14 mm. wide x 3.5 mm. thick, a large chip lost from the lower right margin) and no. 497 (fig. 9; same stone, shape, and size as no. 470, 44.5 mm. high x 19.5 mm. wide x 3.5 mm thick) show the second great theme of Jewish piety, Moses with the tablets of the Law. Their subject has not been recognized because they give Moses six wings and he has a cock's head in no. 470, a donkey's or lion's head in no. 497.[15] The identity of Moses is clearest in no. 470, where the tablet he holds aloft with both hands is inscribed IAΩ and two of the dancing Israelites of Exod. 32:6 and 32:19 are capering around his knees. (Most of the dancer on the right has been chipped away, but the head remains.) On the reverse of the stone is engraved *Abrasax* and Δ" (*deka logoi?*). In no. 497, only IA is visible on the tablet of the Law (Bonner saw only the A but the I is clear), and the Israelites have been replaced by palm fronds recalling Elim (Exod. 15:27). There are ten stars in the field. The reverse reads "Stomach, digest!"; a similar De Clercq gem cited by Bonner has *Stomachou;* it is good to know that the revelation of the Law was not wholly useless. Here, as against the preceding case, it is clear that the engravers followed one highly peculiar tradition, which dictated not only the subject and its treat-

Fig. 8. No. 470. *Reproduced by permission of the Trustees of the British Museum*

Fig. 9. No. 497. *Reproduced by permission of the Trustees of the British Museum*

192

ment, but even the kind of stone and its shape and size. Nevertheless, their works show important differences: no. 470 equates Moses with the anguipede, cock-headed god, commonly labeled *Abrasax* and IAΩ, who seems to have been a general practitioner. No. 497 equates Moses with Set (if donkey-headed) or with Helios (if lion-headed), but in either event proposes to use him especially for stomach trouble. The relation between great spiritual powers and trivial physical purposes is one of the perpetual paradoxes of magic; one explanation of it may be that stomach trouble does not seem trivial to those who suffer from it.

Finally, no. 584 may show biblical scenes, possibly from the story of Noah or from that of Jonah, but the work is so sketchy and the content so uncertain that, although it must be mentioned, it had better not be discussed.

From the preceding list it appears that one of the most remarkable traits of the magical gems is the rarity with which they show biblical scenes or objects, by contrast with the frequency of their use of the names of biblical beings and of other Hebrew or Aramaic words. Also surprising is the centrality of the things shown to "orthodox" Jewish piety. The interpretation of these facts must wait for further study, but the facts are clear and clearly need to be explained.

NOTES

1. Acts 19:24 and the commentaries of Bruce and Conzelmann. Examples for the popular practice were the representations of naophorous rulers, discussed in Bluma Trell, "A Link between the Medieval West and the Pre-Greek East," *Congresso Internazionale di Numismatica, Roma, 1961,* ii *Atti* (Rome 1965) 541ff. For a magnificent *naïskos* in gold, see P. Amandry, *Collection Hélène Stathatos: Les Bijoux Antiques* (Strasbourg 1953) no. 232.
2. Exod. 20:4, cf. Deut. 5:8, the minority reading and versions.
3. On the Christians and Gnostics, see M. Smith, *Jesus the Magician* (San Francisco 1978) 46-64, 94f., etc.; on Jews, 69f., 79, etc., with the relevant notes at the back of the volume.
4. Nos. 99, 103, 363, 366, 369, 386, 495, 555. (These, and the other numbers used in this article, are those the gems will carry in the catalogue I am now preparing. Several systems of numeration have been used in the past and many gems still carry the earlier numbers, some of which will appear in the photographs.)
5. See, for instance, the collection recently published by N. Avigad, *Bullae and Seals from a Post-Exilic Judean Archive* (Jerusalem 1976); *Qedem* 4. This seal form appeared already in the late monarchic period, but became prevalent after the Exile.
6. See C. Bonner, "Amulets Chiefly in the British Museum," *Hesperia* 20 (1951) 305-6, and A. A. Barb, "Diva Matrix," *Journal of the Warburg and Courtauld Institutes* 16 (1953) 218.
7. Goodenough's notion that these herms represent Erotes (*Jewish Symbols in the Greco-Roman Period* ii, Bollingen Series 37 [New York 1953] 241 and n. 224) is refuted by comparing them with the examples of Erotes that he cites. He printed a photograph of the stone (ibid. iii, no. 1069; see below). This seems to be the gem

described, not quite accurately, by C. de Murr, *Description du Cabinet de M. Paul de Praun* (Nuremburg, 1797) 350, no. 1603 (a reference I owe, as I do much else in this article, to A. A. Barb).

8. C. King, *The Gnostics and Their Remains* (London 1887²) 441-42 and pl. H, no. 2, with the lettering inaccurate and reversed.

9. C. Bonner, *Studies in Magical Amulets,* University of Michigan Humanistic Series 49 (Ann Arbor 1950) 29 and n. 32.

10. The last reference in H. Mattingly, *Coins of the Roman Empire in the British Museum,* i (London 1965) is on p. 279, n. *: ''The famous 'Altar' rev. of Lugdunum is revived on rare semisses of Nero, semi-barbarous in style.''

11. Cp. RE = RNE, given as a typical example in I. Limentani, *Epigrafia Latina,* 3d ed. (Milan, n.d.) 148.

12. No. 1038, from R. Garrucci, *Arte Cristiana* vi. (Prato 1880) pl. 492, no. 11. *Non vidi.*

13. Reprinted as *Amulets and Talismans* (New York 1961) 129f.

14. For this formula, see E. Peterson, *Heis Theos* (Göttingen 1926) 261-62.

15. Bonner (n. 6 above) described no. 470 (with minor inaccuracies) on p. 328, with a picture on pl. 97, no. 30. He noted the similarity to no. 497 and to a stone from the De Clercq collection (no. 3456) on which the figure is unquestionably lion-headed. In the same article he also described no. 497, as no. 44 (picture on pl. 98); he had mentioned it previously in *SMA,* p. 53 and no. 12.

20
LABYRINTH: ANATOLIAN AXE OR EGYPTIAN EDIFICE?

ROBERT R. STIEGLITZ

Contributing to a festschrift for Professor Bluma L. Trell is more than an honor—it is also sheer pleasure for me. The honor stems from having known Bluma as scholar, teacher, and colleague. The pleasure is derived from knowing her as friend and collaborator. Since Bluma has contributed so much to our understanding of ancient architecture, it seemed only appropriate to select for this study one of the greatest, but hardly best-known, edifices of the ancient world.

Over a century ago, H. K. Brugsch proposed to regard the Greek term *labyrinthos* as a loanword from Old Egyptian *lapi-ro-hunt* 'Temple on the Mouth of the Sea', the famous Egyptian shrine at Lake Moeris (modern Birket Qarun).[1] Today, however, it is commonly accepted that Greek *labyrinthos* is "to be connected with the Lydian word *labrys,* which signifies a double-edged axe, a common sacred symbol among the ancient Cretans and their neighbors in Asia Minor."[2] The aim of this study is to argue in favor of the former proposal, and, indeed, that the Greek word *labyrinthos* is not derived from the Lydian word for the "double-axe."

The difficulties in connecting the Lydian and Greek terms were already recognized by M. P. Nilsson, but he nevertheless did accept the *labrys* proposal as the actual etymology of the Greek term, and so did many others.[3] The originator of the connection between *labrys* and *labyrinthos,* M. Mayer (1892),[4] evidently had in mind *Labrandea,* the Carian epithet of Zeus, so called, according to Plutarch (*Moralia: The Greek Questions,* 45 [302a]), because the god's statue was depicted holding an axe rather than the usual thunderbolt.[5] It was therefore assumed that Greek *labyrinthos* is to be analyzed as *labyrinth-os,* a pre-Hellenic toponym with the *-nth-* suffix which originally meant something like 'Place of the Double-Axe'—in spite of the fact that the primary meaning of the Classical Greek word was 'a winding architectural complex, a maze'. The idea of connecting the Minoan maze with the Anatolian axe seemed even more attractive when double-axes were discovered to be an important Minoan religious symbol, extensively utilized at Knossos and other Minoan sites.

The modern notion of connecting the Greek word with a Lydian or Carian term was, however, not shared by the ancient historians. They connected the Cretan labyrinth with the Egyptian structure of the same name. Indeed, there were four temples in the ancient world which qualified for the appellation "labyrinth," and these were discussed in detail by Pliny (*Natural History* 36.19.84-93). First and foremost among these structures was the Egyptian labyrinth near Hawara, southeast of Lake Moeris in the Fayum. Pliny says that this building was doubtless the historical model used by Daedalus for the construction of the labyrinth at Knossos, the latter being a mere one-hundredth part of the Egyptian structure: *hinc utique sumpsisse Daedalum exemplar eius labyrinthi quem fecit in Creta non est dubium, sed centensimam tantum portionem eius imitatum* (*N.H.* 36.19.85).[6] The other three labyrinths of fame were those of Knossos, at Lemnos, and the tomb of the Etruscan king Porsena near Clusium.

It is Herodotus (2.148), however, who has left us the most ancient description of the original Egyptian complex and its amazing subterranean structures. According to him, it had twelve courts and three thousand rooms, half of which were underground.

> I have seen this building, and it is beyond my power to describe; it must have cost more in labour and money than all the walls and public works of the Greeks put together—though no one would deny that the temples at Ephesus and Samos are remarkable buildings. The pyramids too, are astonishing structures, each one of them equal to many of the most ambitious works of Greece, but the labyrinth surpasses them.[7]

Herodotus thus thought that the Egyptian labyrinth surpassed at least two of the later "Wonders of the World": the Pyramids at Giza and the Temple of Artemis at Ephesus. According to Strabo (17.1.3,37), each nome of Egypt had its own palace and halls within this complex, which was constructed entirely of stone, with monolithic blocks covering every ceiling of its many rooms. Diodorus Siculus (1.66.3-6) described this labyrinth as an enormous royal tomb for the "Twelve Kings," which contained numerous reliefs. According to him, it was in the form of a square whose side was a stade in length. Strabo (17.1.37) ascribed similar dimensions to the complex.

This Egyptian labyrinth may indeed have been a great religious and national administrative center, but its purpose remains conjectural. The structure is associated with Pharaoh Amenemhet III of the Twelfth Dynasty,[8] but it is not certain if he was the builder of the original complex at the site.[9] We may, however, regard the reign of Amenemhet III (ca. 1842-1797 B.C.) as the *terminus post quem* for the date of the Egyptian labyrinth.

The Egyptian name for this complex was *R-pr-r-hnt* 'Shrine at the Mouth of the Lake'.[10] It was pronounced something like *Rapir(i)hint(i)* or *Lapir(i)hint(i)*, which, I believe, was transmitted into Greek in the form *Labyrinthos*. Accordingly, we may analyze the Greek term as follows. The Greeks rendered Egyptian *R-pr* 'Shrine, Temple' as *Laby-*, although it was probably pronounced *Rapi* or *Lapi*.[11] Biblical Hebrew, for example, rendered Egyptian *Pr* in toponyms as *Pī*, thus: *Pitōm* < *Pr-Itm* (or *Pr-Tm*) 'House of Atum' (Exod. 1:11); and *Pî-Beset* < *Pr-B3stt* 'House of Bastet' (Ezek. 30:17). But Classical Greek consistently rendered *Pr* names as *Bū-*,[12] e.g.: *Boubastis* < *Pr-B3stt; Bousiris* < *Pr-Wsir* 'House of Osiris'; *Bouto* < *Pr-W3dt* 'House of Edjo'. The second element of the name, Egyptian *-r-* 'mouth', in an oblique case, probably vocalized as *ri*, was rendered precisely by Greek *-r(i)-*. The last element, Egyptian *ḥnt* 'lake' came into Greek as *-inth-*.[13] Greek often omitted the laryngeal /ḥ/, and when final /t/ was pronounced in Egyptian, it was often rendered by Greek *theta: Nēith* < *Nt* (or *Nit*);[14] *Hathōr* or *Athyr* < *Ht-Ḥr* 'House of Horus'; *Nephthys* < *Nbt-Ḥwt* 'Lady of the House'.

It is likely that the Greek word *labyrinthos* was adopted by Mycenaean Greeks, from Minoan[15] or directly from Egyptian sources, in much the same way as the Mycenaeans at Knossos adopted the personal name *Ai-ku-pi-ti-yo* 'the Egyptian',[16] a name which later appears in Homer (*Odyssey* 2.15) as *Aigyptios*. This name, from which is also derived the term for "Egypt," is itself derived from the name of another famous temple in Egypt: *Ht-k3-Ptḥ* (pronounced *Hikuptaḥ*) 'House of the *Ka* of Ptah' at Memphis, which was located less than fifty miles northeast of the *R-pr-r-ḥnt* 'Temple at the Mouth of the Lake', the "Labyrinth."

NOTES

1. Cf. "Das altägyptisches 'Seeland'," *ZAeS* 10 (1872) 89-91; and H. K. Brugsch, *Dictionnaire géographique de l'ancienne Égypte* (Leipzig 1879; reprt. Hildesheim and New York 1974) 501.
2. H. J. Rose, *A Handbook of Greek Mythology* (New York 1959) 184.
3. *The Minoan-Mycenaean Religion and its Survival in Greek Religion* (Lund 1968²) 233ff.
4. Ibid.
5. On the Carian site of Labranda, see *Herodotus* 5.119.
6. Diodorus Siculus (1.61.3-4) relates a similar version of Daedalus in Egypt.
7. Translation by A. de Sélincourt, *Herodotus: The Histories* (Baltimore 1954) 188.
8. Cf. J. H. Breasted, *A History of Egypt* (New York 1905) 194.
9. Strabo (17.1.37) wrote that the Egyptian labyrinth was built by King Imandēs (called Ismandēs, or Memnon in Egyptian, in 17.1.42). According to Diodorus Siculus (1.61.1), King Mendes, or Marrus, built the labyrinth; but in 1.66.3 he ascribes its foundation to the "Twelve Kings" who ruled Egypt for fifteen years before the reign of Psammetichus of Sais (who was one of these twelve). Pliny (*N.H.* 36.19.84) relates that the Egyptian labyrinth was, by tradition, first built 3,600 years before his time by King Petesuchis or Tithoes, and was rebuilt by King Nemesis. The latter may be a corruption of *Nemerēs* (< *N(y)-m3't-R'*), the

prenomen of Amenemhet III. On the Greek versions of this name, see A. H. Gardiner, *JEA* 29 (1943) 42.

10. Cf. E. A. Wallis Budge, *The Mummy* (London 1894²; reprt. New York 1974) 22.

11. Coptic preserved the pronounciation of Egyptian *R-pr* as *r̄pe* or *rpeie;* cf. W. E. Crum, *A Coptic Dictionary* (Oxford 1939) s.v. In the Fayumic dialect of Coptic, *la* or *le* are often found instead of *ra*.

12. Greek also voiced Egyptian /k/ to /g/ in *Aigyptos* < *Ht-k3-pth;* see below.

13. Gardiner (n. 9 above) 37ff., argued at length that Egyptian *ḥnt* was pronounced *ḥōne,* like its Coptic descendent *hōne.* If his argument is correct, the Mycenaeans or Minoans may have borrowed this term when the final /t/ was still pronounced in Egyptian (probably because of a following vowel). When final Egyptian /t/ was not pronounced, it was not preserved in Greek transliterations, but when it was, it was often rendered by the Greek *theta,* as in the examples cited below. The Egyptian toponym *R-ḥnt* 'Mouth of the Lake' came into Coptic as Lehōne (Arabic *Illāhūn*). But this is a very late formation, when final /t/ was certainly no longer pronounced. Note, however, the r/l interchange.

14. On the possible reading of the original Egyptian name as *Nỉt* or *Nrt,* see A. H. Gardiner, *Egyptian Grammar* (London 1966³) 503 (R24).

15. The term *da-pu₂?-ri-ti-yo* on a Linear B tablet from Knossos (KN Gg 702.2) is interpreted by some authors as a reference to the labyrinth at Knossos (reading *Dabyrinthoio* for *Labyrinthoio*), see T. B. L. Webster, *From Mycenae to Homer* (New York 1958) 49ff. M. Ventris and J. Chadwick, *Documents in Mycenaean Greek* (Cambridge 1959) 310, were skeptical about this interpretation. If it is, nevertheless, correct, it would certainly prove that *labyrinthos* entered Greek before 1250 B.C.

16. On this name, known from Linear B tablet KN Db 1105 + 1446, see R. R. Stieglitz, *Kadmos* 15 (1976) 85.

INDEX

A

Abraham, 191-92
Abrasax, 189, 192
Abydos, 20-21, 72-73
Achaeans, 123, 125
Adulis, 113-22
Aegae, 87, 92, 94, 98-99
Aegis, 21
Aeneas Silvius, 89
Aenus, 20
Agrippa, 70
Agrippina, 98, 177
Aharoni, Y., 170-71
Aigion, 186
Aila, 167, 170-74
Aiolis, 177
Alabanda, 179
Alcaeus, 177
Alexander mosaic, 21
Alexander of Pherae, 43-44
Alexander IV, 20
Alexander the Great, 17, 20-22, 24-25,
    178-79; mints, 20, 25; portrait, 21, 23;
    type of Lysimachus, 23-26; type of
    Ptolemy, 17, 22, 25-26; type of
    Seleucus, 22-25
Alexandria, 25-26, 40-41; library,
    154-55; museum, 149-52, 154-58
Alexandria Troas, 20-21
Alkamenes, 90, 95
Allath, temple of, 39
Amenemhet III, 196
Amphipolis, 20-21
Andromeda, 71
Anguipede, 193
Annesley Bay, 113-22
Antigonia, 20
Antigonus, 20
Antioch (Pisidia), 81
Antioch (Syria), 40-41, 53, 82
Antefixes, 60, 64-65
Antinous, 96
Antoninus of Piacenza, 172-74
Antoninus Pius, 97
Apollo, 179
Apollonis, 87, 89, 93-94, 98
Aqaba. *See* Aila

Arabia, 113
Ara Maxima, 109
Arch of Titus, 93
Architecture, 47-49, 51-53, 60-64, 73,
    77-79, 177-85
Arsinoe, 20
Artemis, 179
Asia (province), 80-82
Asia Minor, 20-21, 23-24, 179, 183
Asklepios, 182
Astyanax, 123
Athena, 17, 20, 53-54, 72
Athena Nike, 182
Athena of Allath, 39
Athena Polias, 178-79
Athens, 24, 26, 69, 179, 182-83
Auge, 74
Augustus, 31, 79, 81
Aurelius, 52, 54
Avi-Yonah, M., 145
Axum, 113-14, 118-20
Azara herm, 23

B

Bassae, 183-84, 186
Bernini, 48-49
Bigae, 60, 64
Bilingualism in Roman Britain, 129-30
Bithynia, 20
Bizya, 78
Boxers, 107
Britain, 82, 129-30
British Museum, 29-30
Bruce, James, 119
Bunbury, E. H., 143
Burchardt, J., 170-71
Bureaucracy. *See* Civil Service
Busiris, 109

C

Caeretan hydriae, 108-9
Caesar, 105, 130-31, 136
Cahn, H., 24-25
Calendae, 132
Candelabra. *See* Menorah

199

Capitol, 73
Capitoline Museum (Rome), 109
Caracalla, 72, 77, 79-80, 95, 97
Cartography. *See* Maps
Cassander, 20
Catena, 132
Cella, 132
Celtiberian, 130
Celtic art, 109
Cena, 133
Central Asia, 35
Centrum, 131
Cerberus, 108
Cerveteri, 105
Chariot, elephant-drawn, 17
Ch'en Pan, 35
Cherubim, 189-90
Chiaroscuro, 22, 26
China, 33-36, 113
Chinese Turkestan, 34-36
Chiusi, 105
Christianity, 187-94
Christians, 40
Cibyra, 87-89, 93. 97-98
Cingula, 131
Cius, 20
Civil service, Roman, 149-50, 153, 155,
157-58
Claudius, 89, 150, 152, 155
Clement XI, 48-49
Clement IX, 47
Clement X, 47
Clement XII, 49
Clysma, 167, 170-74
Coins, 17-47, 51-55, 69-74, 77-83, 130,
177
Coligny Calendar, 130
Colophon, 20
Columba, 132
Commodus, 51-54, 89, 96-97
Constantinople, 40-41
Constantius II, 40-41
Corpus, 132
Corupedium, 20
Cosmas Indicopleustes, 117-20
Cossus Lentulus, 95
Countermark, 44
Crete, 43-44
Cultellus, 132
Cunningham, A., 29, 31-32
Cursus publicus, 141
Cyme, 86, 91, 94, 96
Cyzicus, 40, 70, 89

D

Dacian captives, statues of, 61, 64
Dahlac Chebir Island, 117

Decalogue. *See* Ten Commandments
Decapolis, 51-54
Delos, 186
Delphi, 182
Demetrias, 26
Demetrius Poliorcetes, 20, 25-26
Demosthenes, 24
De Romanis, A., 64
Deultum, 71-72
Diadem, 21
Diadumenianus, 98
Diana, 179
Didyma, 184
Die sharing, 44, 81
Dionysiac scene, 108
Dionysus, 177
Dipylon shield, 123
Dissei Island, 117-20
Divinus, 133-34
Domitian, 82, 88, 93, 98
Dura Europus shield, 143, 146-47

E

Eagle, 17, 22
Ecbatana, 17
Egeria, 170-73
Egypt, 113
Elagabalus, 52-53, 79, 89, 96
Elephant, 17, 21
Elusa, 167, 171-72, 174
Emerita, 79
Ennodia, 43-44
Entablature-attics, 60-61, 64
Ephesus, 20, 23, 87-89, 92, 95, 178, 183
Epidaurus, 182
Equestrian statues, 64
Eras, 52-54
Erechtheum, 179, 183-84, 186
Eresos (Lesbos), 177
Eros, 73-74
Ethiopia, 113, 118-19
Etruscan art, 105, 108-9
Eurystheus, 108
Eusebius, 170, 173
Euxine, 20

F

Fan Ye, 33, 35
Faustina II, 96
Flacilla, 40
Flavius Chrysanthius (painter), 70
Forma Urbis Romae, 141
Forum of Caesar, 88-89, 90-92, 99

G

Gaba, 53-54
Gabaza, 119-20
Galilei, 49
Gallienus, 74, 81
Gatteschi, G., 64
Gauls, 105, 109
Gemellus, 133
Gemma, 133
Geography, ancient, 139-40
Geometric period, 123-24, 125
Germanicopolis-Gangra, 77-83
Gismondi, I., 64
Gordian I, 74
Gordian III, 72, 81, 95, 97
Greek culture in the Roman Empire,
    149-58
Gulf of Kallone, 177
Gulf of Zula, 114
Gundestrop cauldron, 109

H

Hadrian, 96, 99, 151, 153-55
Haila. *See* Aila
Hameran family (engravers), 147-49
Han, 35
Harbors on the Red Sea, 113-22
Hebrew, 188-89, 191-92
Hector, 74
Helen of Troy, 123-24
Helios, 21
Hellespont, 22
Helmet, panther-skin, 17
Helvetians, 130
Hera, 21
Heraclea, 20, 40-41
Heracles, 74, 109-11
Heracles head: type of Alexander the
    Great, 22, 25; of Lysimachus, 22; of
    Perdiccas III, 25
Hercules. *See* Heracles; Heracles head
Hermitage Museum, 35
Hermogenes (architect), 179, 183
Hero, 72-73
Herodes Philippus, 53
Hierocaesareia, 87, 89, 94, 98
Historia, 135
Homer, 21, 123-25
Hou Han Shu, 33-35
House of the Faun, 21
Hoards, 33, 39-41
Hsiu Mo Pa, 35
Hyrcanis, 87, 89, 93, 97

I

Iliad, 123, 125
Ilium, 74
India, 29, 33, 36, 113
Indo-Parthian coins, 32-33
Indo-Scythian coins, 31
Indus Valley, 33-34
Innocent XI, 48
Ionia, 20
Ionian League, 74
Ipsus, 20
Ireland, 129
Isaac, sacrifice of, 192
Islam, 114, 118-20
Itineraries, Roman, 139-48

J

Jackson, K., 130
Januarius, 135
Jihonika, 34
Jordan River, 53
Jovian, 40-41
Judaism, 187-94
Julia Domna, 79, 95
Julia Maesa, 79
Julian II, 40-41
Juscellum, 135

K

Kallone, Gulf of, 177
Kaniska, 34-35
Kashgar, 35
Kastabos, 182
Kharosthi script, 32-33
Khotan, 34-35
Kolumdado (Lesbos), 180, 182
Krahmer, G., 24-25
Kujula Kadphises, 29, 31-35
Kushan, 29, 31-35
Kyrieleis, H., 21

L

L. Marcius Philippus, 53-54
L. Plautius Plancus, 73, 75
Labrandea, 195
Labrys, 195
Lampsacus, 20-24
Laodiceia, 98
Larisa, 43
Latin, 128-36
Leacock, Stephen, 136
Leander, 72-73
Lesbos, 177-84

Library of Alexandria, 154-55
Linear B, 124
Lion protome, 20
Livy, 109
Locri, 183
Lucius Verus, 97-99
Lyons, 81, 190
Lysicrates, monument of, 179
Lysimachan style, 26
Lysimachia, 20-21, 24
Lysimachus, 20-26
Lysippus, 23, 25-26, 96

M

Macedonia, 20-21, 23-24
Macrinus, 98
Madaba map, 143, 146-47
Maderno (architect), 48
Magdala, 119
Magna Graecia, 183
Magnesia, 20, 21, 23-26, 86, 88, 90, 95, 97, 179, 184
Malcatto, 119
Maps, Roman, 139-48
Marcus Aurelius, 82, 96-98, 177
Mars, 108
Marsyas, 72
Massawa, 116-20
Mat, 32
Medals, 47-48
Medea, 109
Medeia, 167, 170, 173
Menelaion, 180
Menesthes (architect), 179
Menorah, 191
Messa (Lesbos), 177-84
Mes(s)on, 177
Methymna, 177
Military careers, Roman, 150-53, 156-58
Miller, K., 167, 170-71
Minerva, 108
Mint practice, 80-81
Mints, 20-26
Mithradates, 97
Mons Syna. *See* Mount Sinai
Moses, 192-93
Mostene, 87, 93-94, 98
Mount Sinai, 167, 170-74
Museum of Alexandria, 149-52, 154-58
Myrina, 87, 89, 92, 94, 96, 98
Mytilene, 20-21, 177, 184

N

Neith, 197
Neo-Attic style, 105
Nero, 99

Nessana, 172
Nicomachus (painter), 69-70, 73
Nicomedia, 40
Nike, 17, 25
Noah, 70-72
Nymphaeum, 51-53

O

Odysseus, 123
Ogam inscriptions, 129-30
Olta, 108
Olympieum, 179
Orange, 141
Otacilia Severa, 97
Overstrikes, 43-44
Ovid, 73

P

Paintings, 69-74
Palazzo Corsini (Rome), 110
Palmyra, 39-40
Pan Ch'ao, 34-35
Pantheon, 48, 183-84
Pantocrator, 187
Paphlagonia, 77, 80-82
Paribeni, R., 114, 118
Parium, 20
Pasitelean art, 90-91, 99
Patroclus, 74
Paul V (pope), 47
Pausanias, 69
Pella (Macedonia), 20-21, 23, 25-26
Pella (Syria), 51-54
Pentelic marble, 105
Perdiccas III, 25
Pergamum, 20-21, 23-24, 97, 183
Perinthus, 20, 97
Periplus Maris Erythraei, 113-21
Persepolis, 17, 26
Perseus, 71
Peutinger Table, 139-48, 167, 170-74
Pfuhl, E., 25
Phaistos, 43-44
Phara(n), 167, 170-74
Pherae, 43-44
Philadelpheia, 86, 91, 96
Philetaerus, 23-24
Philip I, 72
Philip I (Roman emperor), 78, 80-81
Philip II, 20, 70, 97
Philip III, 20
Philippeum, 179
Piazza del Popolo (Rome), 47-48
Piazza della Rotonda (Rome), 48
Pictish, 130
Pithos, 107-8
Pliny the Elder, 53, 70, 73

Polyeuktos, 24
Pompeii, 21, 69, 71
Pompey, 53
Poncet, Charles, 119
Porches, 60-61, 64
Portraits, 17, 25; of Alexander the
    Great, 17, 22; of Demosthenes, 24; of
    Ptolemy I, 17; of Seleucus, 17
Praeneste, 108
Praisos, 43-44
Praxiteles, 91, 99
Priene, 178-79, 181-84
Provincial administration, 80-83
Procopius, 117, 119-20
Prymnessus, 74
Ptolemaic style, 26
Ptolemy (geographer), 140-41, 170
Ptolemy I, 17, 20-26
Ptolemy III, 118
Pyrrha, 180
Pyrrhus, 20
Pytheos, 180

Q

Q. Cornuficius, 89
Quadrigae, 60-61, 64

R

Rainaldi (architect), 48
Ram horn, 20, 23
Red Sea, 113-22
Rejuvenation, ceremony of, 109
Ressauts, 60, 64
Rhetoricians, Greek, 150-52, 154, 156
Rome, 36, 73, 77, 80, 109-11, 182-83

S

Sabina, 89
Sabaoth, 187
Sagitta, 136
St. Peter's (Rome), 48-49
Salt, Henry, 114, 117-18
S. Giovanni dei Fiorentini (Rome), 49
S. Teodoro al Palatino (Rome), 48
S. Maria de' Miracoli (Rome), 47
S. Maria di Monte Santo (Rome), 47
S. Maria Rotonda (Rome), 48
Sardis, 20, 85-86, 88-90, 95, 182-83
Scopas, 22-26
Secretaries of Roman emperors, 149-57
Seleucus I, 17, 20, 22, 25-26
Selinus, 179
Septimius Severus, 79, 81-82, 95
Seraphim, 189

Sestus, 20, 72-73
Set, 193
Severn, 136
Severus Alexander, 72, 97
Sextarius, 136
Shields, 61, 64, 123, 143, 146-47
Siccus, 136
Sicily, 179, 183
Signa, 60-61, 64
Silchester, 127
Sino-Kharosthi, 34
Situla art, 105, 108
Smintheum, 179, 182-83
Smyrna, 21
Solomon, 188
Soter Megas, 29, 32, 35
Sophists in the Roman Empire, 150-52,
    154, 156
Sparta, 180
Statius, 73
Stoa Poikile, 69
Stomach, amulet for, 192-93
Strabo, 141
Strack, P., 64
Synnada, 70
Syracuse, 73
Syria, 51-54
Suez. *See* Clysma
Sundström, R., 114
Surandela, 172
Susa, 17, 25-26

T

T. Julius Ferox, 99
Tabula Peutingeriana. *See* Peutinger
    Table
Taxila, 29, 33-34
Tax exemption, 157
Tegea, 178
Temnus, 87, 89, 91-92
Ten Commandments, 187, 192
Teos, 20, 179
Tetragrammaton, 190
Textiles, 123-25
Thebes, 26
Theodosius, itinerary of, 173-74
Thessalonica, 40-41
Thessaly, 43-44
Thompson, M., 21, 24
Thrace, 20, 24
Thyateira, 89
Tiberius, 36, 85, 88-92, 95, 99
Titus, 79
Tmolus, 86, 91, 96
Trade, Roman with Far East, 113-22

Trajan, 64, 79, 82, 88-89, 96, 99
Trajan, Column of, 57
Trebonianus Gallus, 72
Triptolemus, 190
Triumphal arch, 61
Triumphator, 60-61
Trojans, 123, 125
Troy, 123
Turfan, 35
Tyche, 53

V

Vacuus, 134
Vagina, 133
Valens, 40-41
Valentinian I, 40-41
Valerian, 95-96
Vatican, 47-49
Venenum, 134
Vergina, 70
Vespasian, 96
Vima Kadphises, 29-36
Vinum, 134
Vitruvius, 179, 181

W

Wadi Haggag, 174
Weaving, 124
Wrestlers, 108

Y

Yabgu, 31-33
Yahweh, 187-94

Z

Zeionises, 34
Zeus, 17, 21, 177
Zeus Ammon, 20
Zeus Sosipolis, 184
Zula, 114; Gulf of, 114

Lionel Casson was educated at New York University (A.B., 1934; M.A., 1935; Ph.D., 1939), where he is currently professor of classics and chairman of the Department of Classics. During his distinguished career he has been named a senior fellow by the National Endowment for the Humanities and has been awarded two Guggenheim fellowships, as well as serving as director of the Summer Session in Classical Studies of the American Academy in Rome. He is a member of several professional organizations and of the editorial advisory boards of *Archaeology* and *American Neptune*. Among the many publications of which he is author or editor are *Literary Papyri* (1950), volume 2 of *Excavations at Nessana; The Ancient Mariners* (1959); *Six Plays of Plautus* (1963); *Ships and Seamanship in the Ancient World* (1971); *The Plays of Menander* (1971); *Travel in the Ancient World* (1974); and *Daily Life in Ancient Rome* and *Daily Life in Ancient Egypt* (1975).

Martin Price is deputy keeper of the British Museum. In addition to his regular contributions to *Numismatic Chronicle,* he has published extensively in *Revue Numismatique, Numismatic Circular,* and other professional journals. His major publications include volumes 4 and 6 of *Sylloge Numorum Graecorum; Coins of the Macedonians* (1974); *Coins and the Bible* (1975); *Archaic Greek Coinage: The Asjut Hoard* (with Nancy Waggoner; 1975); and, with Bluma Trell for Wayne State University Press, *Coins and Their Cities: Architecture on the Ancient Coins of Greece, Rome, and Palestine* (1977).

The manuscript was edited for publication by Jacqueline Nash and Sherwyn T. Carr. The book was designed by Mary Primeau.

The typeface for the text is Times Roman, based on a design supervised by Stanley Morison in 1931. The display type is also Times Roman. The text is printed on 80 lb. Mead's Moistrite Matte finish paper and is bound in Holliston Mills' Kingston Natural Finish cloth over binder's boards. Manufactured in the United States of America.